THE WELL

THOMAS HARDY was born in Higher Bockhampton, Dorset, on 2 June 1840; his father was a builder in a small way of business, and he was educated locally and in Dorchester before being articled to an architect. After sixteen years in that profession and the publication of his earliest novel *Desperate Remedies* (1871), he determined to make his career in literature; not, however, before his work as an architect had led to his meeting at St Juliot in Cornwall, Emma Gifford, who became his first wife in 1874.

In the 1860s Hardy had written a substantial amount of unpublished verse, but during the next twenty years almost all his creative effort went into novels and short stories. *Jude the Obscure*, the last written of his novels, came out in 1895, closing a sequence of fiction that includes *Far From the Madding Crowd* (1874), *The Return of the Native* (1878), *Two on a Tower* (1882), *The Mayor of Casterbridge* (1886), and *Tess of the d'Urbervilles* (1891).

Hardy maintained in later life that only in poetry could he truly express his ideas; and the more than nine hundred poems in his collected verse (almost all published after 1898) possess great individuality and power.

In 1910 Hardy was awarded the Order of Merit; in 1912 Emma died and two years later he married Florence Dugdale. Thomas Hardy died in January 1928; the work he left behind—the novels, the poetry, and the epic drama *The Dynasts*—forms one of the supreme achievements in English imaginative literature.

TOM HETHERINGTON is the retired Senior Tutor of Christ Church College, Canterbury, and Principal Lecturer in English. For his Ph.D. he prepared a critical edition of *The Well-Beloved*. He has broadcast his own poetry and short talks on a variety of subjects on BBC Radio 4.

OXFORD WORLD'S CLASSICS

*For almost 100 years Oxford World's Classics have brought
readers closer to the world's great literature. Now with over 700
titles—from the 4,000-year-old myths of Mesopotamia to the
twentieth century's greatest novels—the series makes available
lesser-known as well as celebrated writing.*

*The pocket-sized hardbacks of the early years contained
introductions by Virginia Woolf, T. S. Eliot, Graham Greene,
and other literary figures which enriched the experience of reading.
Today the series is recognized for its fine scholarship and
reliability in texts that span world literature, drama and poetry,
religion, philosophy and politics. Each edition includes perceptive
commentary and essential background information to meet the
changing needs of readers.*

OXFORD WORLD'S CLASSICS

THOMAS HARDY

The Well-Beloved

Edited with an Introduction and Notes by
TOM HETHERINGTON

OXFORD
UNIVERSITY PRESS

OXFORD
UNIVERSITY PRESS

Great Clarendon Street, Oxford OX2 6DP

Oxford University Press is a department of the University of Oxford.
It furthers the University's objective of excellence in research, scholarship,
and education by publishing worldwide in

Oxford New York

Athens Auckland Bangkok Bogotá Buenos Aires Calcutta
Cape Town Chennai Dar es Salaam Delhi Florence Hong Kong Istanbul
Karachi Kuala Lumpur Madrid Melbourne Mexico City Mumbai
Nairobi Paris São Paulo Singapore Taipei Tokyo Toronto Warsaw

with associated companies in Berlin Ibadan

Oxford is a registered trade mark of Oxford University Press
in the UK and in certain other countries

Published in the United States
by Oxford University Press Inc., New York

Text, Introduction, Note on the Text, Select Bibliography,
Explanatory Notes © Tom Hetherington 1986
Chronology © Simon Gatrell 1985

The moral rights of the author have been asserted

Database right Oxford University Press (maker)

First issued as a World's Classics paperback 1986
Reissued as an Oxford World's Classics paperback 1998

British Library Cataloguing in Publication Data

Data available

Library of Congress Cataloging in Publication Data
Hardy, Thomas, 1840–1928.
The well-beloved.
(Oxford world's classics)
Bibliography: p.
I. Hetherington, T. B. (Thomas Baines)   II. Title.
PR4750.W35   1986   823'.8   86–12615
ISBN 0–19–283560–2 (pbk.)

3 5 7 9 10 8 6 4 2

Printed in Great Britain by
Cox & Wyman Ltd.
Reading, Berkshire

CONTENTS

ACKNOWLEDGEMENTS

I SHOULD like to express my gratitude for help received to the staffs of the British Library Department of Manuscripts, the University of London library and the University of Kent at Canterbury library; to Mr R. N. R. Peers and the staff of Dorset County Museum; to James Gibson, Ian Gregor, Samuel Hynes, Michael Millgate and Richard L. Purdy; and most particularly to Simon Gatrell for his advice and to my wife, Marigold, for her support.

GENERAL EDITOR'S PREFACE

THE first concern in The World's Classics editions of Hardy's works has been with the texts. Individual editors have compared every version of the novel or stories that Hardy might have revised, and have noted variant readings in words, punctuation and styling in each of these substantive texts; they have thus been able to exclude much that their experience suggests that Hardy did not intend. In some cases this is the first time that the novel has appeared in a critical edition purged of errors and oversights; where possible Hardy's manuscript punctuation is used, rather than what his compositors thought he should have written.

Some account of the editors' discoveries will be found in the Note on the Text in each volume, while the most interesting revisions their work has revealed are included as an element of the Explanatory Notes. In some cases a Clarendon Press edition of the novel provides a wealth of further material for the reader interested in the way Hardy's writing developed from manuscript to final collected edition.

I should like to thank Shirley Tinkler for her help in drawing the maps that accompany each volume.

SIMON GATRELL

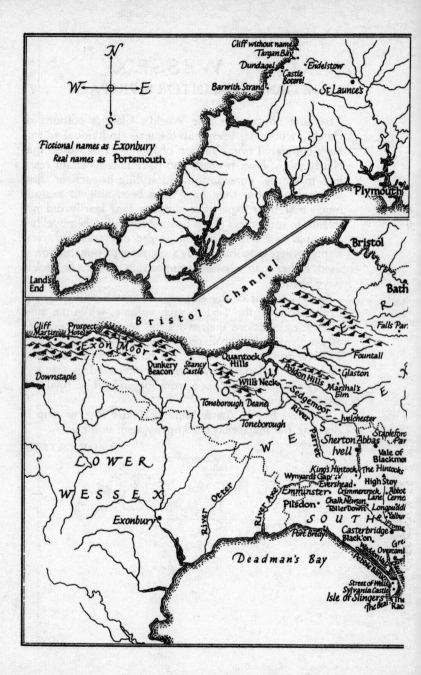

N

W   E

S

Fictional names as Exonbury
Real names as Portsmouth

Cliff without name
Targan Bay
Endelstow
Dundagel
Castle
Boterel
Barwith Strand
St Launce's

Plymouth

Bristol

Bath

Land's
End

Bristol
Channel

Falls Par.

Cliff
Martin
Prospect
Hotel
Exon Moor
Fountall
Dunkery
Beacon
Stancy
Castle
Quantock
Hills
Glaston
Poldon Hills
Will's Neck
Marshal's
Elm
Downstaple
Sedgemoor
Ivelchester
Toneborough Deane
River Parret
Toneborough
Stapleford
Par.
Sherton Abbas
Ivell
Vale of
Blackmor
LOWER
King's Hintock
The Hintocks
Wynyard's Gap
High Stoy
Evershead
WESSEX
Crimmercrock
Lane
Abbot
Cerne
Emminster
Chalk Newton
Toller Down
Pilsdon
Longpuddle
Yalbur
River Otter
SOUTH
Frome
Exonbury
Casterbridge
Black'on
Port Bredy
Weston
Overcomb
Deadman's Bay
Pebble Bank
Street of Wells
Sylvania Castle
Isle of Slingers
The Beal
The
Race
River Aro

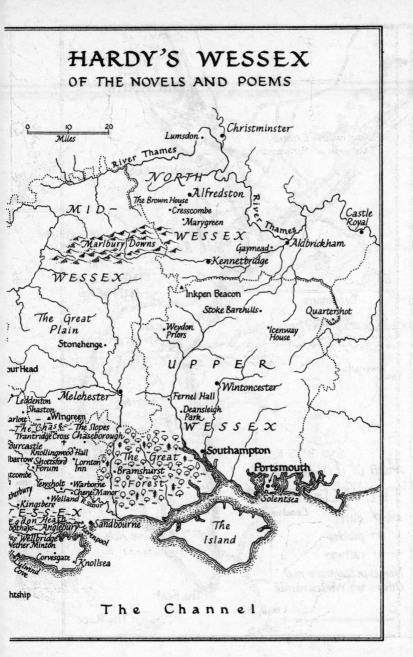

HARDY'S WESSEX
OF THE NOVELS AND POEMS

0   10   20
Miles

River Thames

Lumsdon   Christminster

NORTH

The Brown House   Alfredston

MID-   Cresscombe

Marygreen

WESSEX   River Thames   Castle Royal

Marlbury Downs   Gaymead   Aldbrickham

Kennetbridge

WESSEX

Inkpen Beacon

Stoke Barehills   Quartershot

The Great   Weydon Priors   Icenway House

Plain

Stonehenge

UPPER

ur Head

Wintoncester

Leddenton   Melchester   Fernel Hall

Shaston   Deansleigh Park

arlott   Wingreen   WESSEX

The Chase   The Slopes

Trantridge Cross   Chaseborough

urcastle   Knollingwood Hall   Southampton

ibarrow   Shottsford   Lornton Inn   Portsmouth

tcombe   Forum   The Great

l   Tensholt   Warborne   Bramshurst   Solentsea

therbury   Chene Manor   Forest

Kingsbere   Welland & Stour

ESSEX

Egdon Heath

othays   Anglebury   enpool   The

es   Wellbridge   Island

Nether Minton

Corvesgate

ilwind   Knollsea

Cove

htship

The   Channel

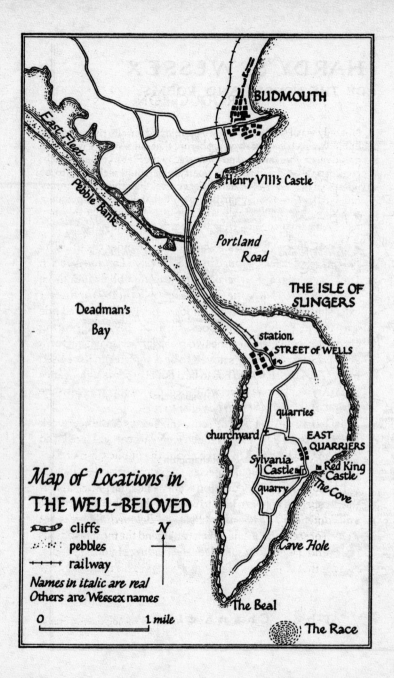

BUDMOUTH

East Fleet

Pebble Bank

Henry VIII's Castle

*Portland
Road*

THE ISLE OF
SLINGERS

Deadman's
Bay

station
STREET of WELLS

quarries

churchyard   EAST
                    QUARRIERS

Sylvania   Red King
Castle   Castle
        quarry   The Cove

Map of Locations in
THE WELL-BELOVED

〰️ cliffs   N
⋰ pebbles
╫ railway
*Names in italic are real
Others are Wessex names*

Cave Hole

0   1 *mile*

The Beal

The Race

INTRODUCTION

Not only was [The Well-Beloved] published serially five years ago but it was sketched many years before that date, when I was comparatively a young man, and interested in the Platonic Idea, which, considering its charm and its poetry, one could well wish to be interested in always . . . There is, of course, underlying the fantasy followed by the visionary artist the truth that all men are pursuing a shadow, the Unattainable, and I venture to hope that this may redeem the tragi-comedy from the charge of frivolity.[1]

THE serial form of this tale was published under the title *The Pursuit of the Well-Beloved* in the *Illustrated London News* in 1892. *Tess of the d'Urbervilles* had been published in three volumes in 1891; *Jude the Obscure* followed in 1895 and, after extensive revision, *The Well-Beloved* with its abbreviated title was finally published in book form in 1897. Appearing chronologically between the two major novels in its first form and as the last of Hardy's novels to be completed in its revised form, *The Well-Beloved* has to be a novel of some significance in Hardy's career as a writer, especially as this was also the period of transition from novelist to poet.

In December 1891, Hardy sent a prospectus of the new work to the *Illustrated London News*. Two years earlier Hardy and Tillotson's had failed to agree about the publication of *Tess* because Tillotson's had objected to certain episodes, including, predictably, the seduction scene. The final paragraph of the prospectus was intended to reassure them about the nature and content of *The Pursuit of the Well-Beloved*: 'There is not a word or scene in the tale which can offend the most fastidious taste; and it is equally suited for the reading of young people, and for that of persons of maturer years.'[2] This makes strange

---

[1] Extract from letter published in *The Academy* on 3 April 1897; quoted in the *Life*, p. 286.
[2] Quoted by R. L. Purdy in *Thomas Hardy: A Bibliographical Study*, p. 95.

reading when one considers that in *The Pursuit of the Well-Beloved* Pearston (the original spelling) falls in love with Marcia while drying her underclothes, lives with her in a London hotel as man and wife while waiting to get married; agrees with her to separate and to remarry if either of them so wished without troubling about legal divorce proceedings; twice becomes involved in bigamous arrangements and twice tries to kill himself. The reader is tempted to assume that there must have been an element of wry Hardyan humour in the assurance he gave to Tillotson's, but his own comments on both the serial and the book suggest that he meant it. His despairing and caustic attitude to the formalities and legalities of marriage, and what he saw as their withering effect on true affection, may have affected his judgement of the results he was producing in his first published version.

The novel which emerged in book form in 1897 from these melodramatic roots is—literally—a very different story. Aspects of the development of the novel in two main stages in 1897 and 1912 will be considered here and later, but what principally emerged in 1897 was a story with two dominant themes: the search for perfection in womanhood, a perfection which exists only subjectively in the mind of the pursuer and is dependent on what constitutes perfection for him; and the effects of the passage of time.

Shelley's influence on Hardy is evident in the story in the Shelleyan interpretation of a pursuit of the Platonic Idea, signalled by the quotation from 'The Revolt of Islam' on the title-page, 'One shape of many names', and by later quotations. In Hardy's own version, the lover is loyal to his vision of the perfect Beloved whom he finds temporarily embodied in any number of feminine forms. His inconstancy to individual women is justified in his own mind by his fidelity to the 'goddess'. The choice of sculptor for Pierston's career gives Hardy the opportunity to portray him in a two-fold pursuit: of a woman who will embody the imagined 'Dea' and of success in his attempts to achieve the same aim in his sculpture; both doomed to failure.

The search for an Ideal at the expense of the real was not a new concept for Hardy. Angel Clare in *Tess of the d'Urbervilles* has some of the same qualities as Pierston. He loves Tess 'dearly, though perhaps rather ideally and fancifully'. At the time of her marriage to Clare, Hardy describes her as 'a sort of celestial person . . . one of those classical divinities Clare was accustomed to talk to her about'. After Tess's fatal confession to Clare, Hardy tells us that 'Clare's love was doubtless ethereal to a fault, imaginative to impracticability. With these natures, corporeal presence is sometimes less appealing than corporeal absence; the latter creating an ideal presence that conveniently drops the defects of the real'.[3] Fitzpiers in *The Woodlanders* is introduced by Hardy as a man who 'much preferred the ideal world to the real' and his name seems to be deliberately recalled to the reader by Pierston's in its revised spelling. Knight, in *A Pair of Blue Eyes*, 'loved philosophically rather than romantically'.[4] All demand a particular kind of perfection from the women of their choice; all are themselves disastrously flawed as lovers; and all eventually become aware of this.

Hardy was to take this kind of relationship a stage further in *Jude the Obscure*. Jude, like Jocelyn, is in pursuit of a Well-Beloved. Unlike Pierston, his is embodied for all time in one person only, his cousin Sue, but there is an identity between the two objects of desire. Sue is 'so uncarnate as to seem at times impossible as a human wife'; she is 'that aerial being', a 'disembodied creature', a 'sweet, tantalizing phantom' who quotes Shelley's 'Epipsychidion' with reference to herself as a 'seraph of Heaven, too gentle to be human' and a 'Being' whom the poet's spirit meets 'on its visioned wanderings far aloft'.[5] When Phillotson's friend Gillingham suggests that the relationship between Sue and Jude is 'Platonic', Phillotson corrects him: 'Well, no. Shelleyan would be nearer to it.' There is a further comment from Phillotson on Sue and Jude: 'They seem to

[3] Op. cit., Chs. XXXII. XXXIII and XXXVI.
[4] *The Woodlanders*, Ch. XVI; *A Pair of Blue Eyes*, Ch. XX.
[5] 'Epipsychidion', 11.21–2, 190–1.

be one person split in two!'⁶ Could this have been the only kind of relationship which might have satisfied Jocelyn? 'Epipsychidion' is quoted in *The Well-Beloved*, its influence is evident, and in it Shelley tells Emilia Viviani, *his* Well-Beloved: 'I am not thine: I am a part of *thee*.'⁷ There is another link with *Tess*, originally entitled *Too Late Beloved*: Shelley addresses 'his' Emily as 'O too late/ Beloved!'⁸ Just as there is some identification in this context among the three beloved women or phantoms in *Tess*, *The Well-Beloved* and *Jude*, so there is among the three lovers: Jocelyn Pierston holds the middle ground in characterization between the largely continent Angel Clare and the more carnally afflicted Jude; none is himself without blemish in moral terms but each prizes highly his own image of woman in her most desirable form. (There is, incidentally, another counterbalance between Tess and Jude, even if expressed in simplistic terms: Tess, the Well-Beloved of Clare, and Jude, the pursuer of a Well-Beloved, Sue, both deviate from a path apparently leading to happiness through the tug of their own fleshly desires at times when they are particularly susceptible.)

The theme of the Shelleyan neo-Platonic Well-Beloved, the ideal woman who is pursued from one transitory abode in the flesh to another, is made more explicit in the revisions for the first book edition of *The Well-Beloved* in 1897. In the original Chapter I of 1892 there is a reference to a former love as being now 'an empty shell which had once contained his ideal for a transient time'. In 1897 this disappears with the rest of the original first chapter, but in the new first chapter Pierston's conception of his 'Well-Beloved' is set out more plainly: 'the migratory, elusive idealization he called his Love who, ever since his boyhood, had flitted from human shell to human shell an indefinite number of times.'

In Part I, Chapter ii of 1897 Hardy introduces the following passage:

⁶ *Jude the Obscure*, III.ix, IV.iii, IV.v and IV.iv.
⁷ Op. cit., 1.51; and see note to p. 107.
⁸ 'Epipsychidion', II.131–2.

Never much considering that she [the Well-Beloved] was a subjective phenomenon vivified by the weird influences of his descent and birthplace, the discovery of her ghostliness, of her independence of physical laws and failings, had occasionally given him a sense of fear. He never knew where she next would be, whither she would lead him.

There are two new elements here which are expanded during the progress of the story: that Pierston's unawareness of the subjective nature of his experiences causes him to be apprehensive of this apparently uncontrollable force; and that his ancestry and origins in the Isle of Slingers will have a powerful influence on his relations with women.

The development of the link with Pierston's 'island' ancestry adds an element not present in 1892. In a conversation with his friend Somers, he acknowledges that this may have some influence on his attitude and behaviour with regard to his Well-Beloved: ' ". . . We are a strange, visionary race down where I come from, and perhaps that accounts for it" ' (1897, p. 50). When he learns of the death of Avice I and realizes his loss, he begins 'to divine the truth': that he could only be constant to a woman of the same 'island' race as himself, with the same 'ground-quality' as the recently dead Avice I. Herein lies a new dilemma: that 'he might never love a woman of the island race, for lack in her of the desired refinement' (1897, p. 116). He reiterates this view later in his acquaintance with Avice II: that only a family from the 'isle' could provide 'the clay' for his ideal partner, but it seems unlikely to him that the Caro family can provide the ideal supplement to his own nature (1897, p. 158).

A story based on the pursuit of such an incorporeal concept as Pierston's has inherent difficulties for the author in the portrayal of the actual human relationships. Even Hardy's skill as a story-teller does not entirely overcome the problems. Pierston's attitude to Avice I is ambiguous: he proposes to her impulsively (as he does to Marcia, Avice II and to Avice III through her mother) while fully aware that his feeling for her was 'rather comradeship than love' (I.ii). Though there is the suggestion of physical passion between Marcia and Jocelyn and clear indications that they live together in a Covent Garden tavern, at no time does Hardy portray any affection in their speech or their behaviour towards each other, either in 1892 or in 1897; only Avice I shows real human warmth. For Pierston the attraction of Avice II and Avice III is their hereditary link with Avice I and his artist's sense of the completion of a design in associating himself with them. Only in old age do Pierston and Marcia achieve a mature muted regard for each other. In their early acquaintance, Marcia's first response to Jocelyn's impetuous proposal of marriage is so cold-blooded and calculating as to be barely credible: 'Will you ever be a Royal Academician?' she asks. Her reasons for accepting his proposal are apparently his satisfactory reply to this query, his further information that it is easy to get a licence to marry, and most of all the opportunity to offer a snub to her father. We are told she is 'excited': it can only be a very basic sexual arousal for nothing in her attitude suggests any kind of romantic fervour or high personal regard for Pierston.

These elements are still present in the final version of the novel, but in other ways Hardy made many changes in 1897, 1903 and 1912 to strengthen the story-line and render the narrative more acceptable. The changes were so fundamental and extensive in 1897 that it is not surprising that it had taken Hardy nearly five years to face up to this task, the longest gap between serial and book publication of any Hardy novel. The major change which brought about the most far-reaching amendments to the story was the removal of the marriages to Marcia Bencomb and Avice III. As indicated above, these marriages had led to narrative devices likely to strain the credulity of the reader, certainly of any nineteenth-century reader of the 1892 serial.

To begin with, Marcia wrote to Pearston after they had separated with a remarkable proposal, even allowing for their plans to reside in different continents: ' ". . . I fail to see why, in making each our own home, we should not make our own matrimonial laws if we choose. This may seem an advanced view, but I am not ashamed of advanced views . . . any new tie we may form can affect nobody but ourselves" ' (1892, p. 481). It would still seem an

advanced view to many people today, but Pearston com-
plied with it to the extent of eventually marrying Avice III
without knowing whether Marcia was still alive, as indeed
she was. The problems which Hardy then faced in trying
to bring his novel to a conclusion are suggested by the
following narrative tangle. When Pearston discovered that
Avice III was distressed that her marriage to him
prevented her from re-establishing her relationship with
her former lover, Leverre, he first of all, in a barely credible excess of magnanimity, made her promise to marry
Leverre when he confirmed to her that she was 'free',
though he was in fact aware that in doing so he might be
causing her to commit bigamy. He then changed his mind
and attempted to commit suicide by drowning. He again
essayed suicide by tearing his head wound open in the last
chapter when he learned from the returned and hideously
old Marcia that his marriage to Avice III had been
annulled.

All these extravagantly coloured events are avoided in
1897 by removing the two marriages and making conse-
quential changes elsewhere in the text. Instead, Pierston
and Marcia part unmarried as a result of a clash of personalities in the tense situation resulting from their living
together in a London tavern while waiting for a special
licence to marry. In the case of Avice III, the growing
realization of the true age of Pierston and the distressing
circumstances of Leverre's falling ill when Avice III meets
him for the last time (as it seems), cause the normally
dutiful girl to elope with him. A change concomitant with
the removal of the two marriages was the elimination of
some of Hardy's more pronounced criticisms of the laws
and social code concerning matrimony.

In spite of the changes he had made, Hardy felt it
necessary in 1903 to remind his readers that narrative
strength and plausibility were not his prime aim in this
particular work, by adding a new penultimate paragraph
to the preface: 'As for the story itself, it may be worth
while to remark that, differing from all or most others
of the series in that the interest aimed at is of an ideal or

subjective nature, and frankly fantastic, verisimilitude in the sequence of events has been subordinated to the said aim' (1903, p. vi).

In 1912 Hardy made a few further changes concerning Pierston's relationship with Marcia and Avice II's with her husband. At two points in Part I, Chapter viii, Hardy made more explicit the nature of Pierston's and Marcia's association in the London hotel by the addition of a phrase:

[Marcia:] '. . . It is not nice, my living on like this!'
(1897, p. 61)

[Marcia:] '. . . It is not nice, my living on with you like this!'
(1912, p. 40)

and later:

. . . Pierston concluded that Marcia had accompanied her parents
(1897, p. 72)

. . . Pierston concluded that Marcia had discovered that nothing was likely to happen as a consequence of their elopement, and that she had accompanied her parents.   (1912, p. 47)

With regard to the episode in which Pierston hears two people quarrelling without at that time realizing that it is Avice and her husband, Hardy changes a few words to make it clear that on each occasion it has been these two whom Pierston has overheard:

Hearing people about—among others a couple quarrelling, for there were rough as well as gentle people here in the island
(1897, p. 173)

Hearing people about—among others the before-mentioned married couple quarrelling, the woman's tones having a kinship to Avice's own   (1912, p. 111)

Although this makes Pierston's later discovery of Avice II's married state more meaningful, it is hardly an improvement as it renders it barely credible that Pierston should not have realized earlier that it was, in fact, Avice's voice that he had heard and that she was, therefore, one of the couple he recognized as being married.

Occasionally the process of building up a sentence continues from 1892 to 1897 to 1903 or 1912, usually defining potential or actual relationships more clearly. In the conjecture about what would have happened if Avice I had met Jocelyn near the ruins of the castle, the three versions run as follows:

the betrothal would have taken place (1892, p. 515)

the primitive betrothal would probably have taken place
(1897, p. 119)

the primitive betrothal, with its natural result, would probably have taken place. (1912, p. 78)

When Pierston asks Avice II why she had married Ike, her answer becomes increasingly explanatory through three versions:

'I was obliged to, according to the custom, after walking wi' en.'
(1892, p. 641)

'I was obliged to, after we'd proved each other.'
(1897, p. 210)

'I was obliged to, after we'd proved each other by island custom.'
(1903, p. 210)

There is a significant shift between 1892 and 1897 in the characterization of Pierston at all three stages of his association with Avices I, II, III and Marcia. The opening chapter of 1892 shows Pearston, out of 'a sentimental feeling' for old love-letters, no longer having the 'heart to burn them' (1892, p. 425) as he had intended. Instead, in the opening encounter with Avice I in 1897, Pierston at no time displays any similar tendency to sentimentality, even though he becomes engaged to her; rather a kind of cool, idealized portrayal of a passion than the passion itself. With regard to the 'island custom' of pre-marital intercourse between engaged couples, it is Pearston who proposes it to Avice I but Pierston of 1897, on the contrary, is amused at Avice's naivety in thinking that he might want this. Nevertheless, Pearston, even after meeting Marcia, still feels 'bound to marry' Avice (1892, p. 458); whereas no such thought crosses the mind of the 1897 Pierston. He is, at first, a less likeable person than his fore-runner, at least until he is shocked by the news of Avice I's death into realizing what she had meant, or should have meant, to him.

At the end of Pierston's episode as a 'Young Man of Forty' with Avice II, when she had admitted to him that she had had to marry her husband because they had 'proved each other by island custom', Hardy gives Pierston an additional comment: 'You shouldn't have thought of such a thing. It is ridiculous and out of date nowadays' (1897, p. 210). This is now a more sophisticated character, but he does not differ from the earlier Pearston in being 'pale and distressed' at Avice II's confession of her predicament; and the reader warms to him when a 'proposal to her which crossed his mind was dismissed as disloyalty, particularly to an inexperienced fellow-islander', after she has told him that she likes him 'more and more' (1897, p. 212). This had not been present in 1892.

The third stage of Pierston's life and development shows the most marked change from 1892. In 1892, it is on his own initiative that he decides to return to England from Rome to check whether Marcia is still alive, and it is coincidental that he hears of the accidental death of Avice II's husband and decides to visit her, and hence becomes acquainted with Avice III. In 1897, though he still overhears a conversation in Rome among some American visitors which relates to Marcia, he decides not to follow it up, and it is only on receipt of a letter from Avice II stating that her husband has been killed and that she would like to see him that he decides to return to England. From then on, nearly all the initiative passes to Avice II in encouraging his courtship of Avice III. Though he does not understand it immediately, she hints that she has recalled him to meet Avice III (1897, p. 235); we are told her private thoughts that her plan 'will work of itself, without my telling' (1897, p. 242); the 'desultory courtship' is 'brought about by her mother's contrivance' (1897, p. 262); when Pierston tries for a fortnight to withdraw from the situation, Avice II is in a 'fever of anxiety lest after all he should not come to see Avice [III] again' (1897, p. 266) and explains openly that she wants to see her daughter settled with Pierston because she herself has a heart condition and is not certain how long she has to live to look after her daughter (1897, p. 267). Later, when Pierston rejoins the two Avices on the 'island' after returning from London, the now very ill Avice II is pitiful in her distress and anxiety 'to acquire him as a son-in-law' (1897, p. 288); as a result, this state of affairs 'destroyed any remaining scruples he [Pierston] might have had from perceiving that Avice [III]'s consent was rather an obedience than a desire' (1897, p. 288).

All these factors are new to 1897 and go a long way towards mitigating the censure the reader might feel towards an old character pursuing a girl forty years his junior: Hardy is now presenting Pierston in a much kindlier light than Pearston.

Nor does Jocelyn's loss of initiative end there: in 1892 it is he who promotes the renewed relationship between Avice III (his wife in that version) and Leverre to the point of making arrangements for a marriage between them; in 1897 the unmarried Avice III and Leverre elope without his or anybody's consent and (again to his credit from the reader's point of view) Pierston lays the blame for the situation on himself (1897, pp. 302–3).

That the reader is intended to observe a change in Pierston's attitude to the pursuit of his Well-Beloved is quite clearly signalled near the beginning of the third stage of his life in Part III.i, but the transfer from worship of an ideal to affection for an individual woman is taken more gradually in the later version: in the serial we are told that 'now his heart showed an extraordinary fidelity to the specimen' (1892, p. 643); this becomes 'now his heart showed its bent to be a growing fidelity to the specimen' (1897, p. 231).

There is one final change in the characterization of Pierston. In the last chapter of 1892, though Marcia nurses him through his illness and is 'watchful to tenderness' (in itself a much changed attitude from that of the younger

Marcia), his attitude towards her elderly appearance is harsh and totally unsympathetic:

The contrast of the ancient Marcia's aspect, both with this portrait [of Avice III] and with her own fine former self, brought into his brain a sudden sense of the grotesqueness of things. His wife was—not Avice, but that parchment-covered skull moving about his room. An irresistible fit of laughter, so violent as to be an agony, seized upon him   (1892, p. 775)

The behaviour of Jocelyn in 1897 is much more acceptable. He shows appreciation for Marcia's nursing and when she later reveals to him the ravages of age without her make-up, his response is generous:

'. . . Marcia, you are a brave woman. You have the courage of the great women of history. I can no longer love; but I admire you from my soul!'   (1897, pp. 329–30)

—and his proposal to her a little later shows more genuine human warmth than any of his earlier attempts, in spite of the limitation he himself places upon it:

'I have no love to give, you know, Marcia,' he said. 'But such friendship as I am capable of is yours till the end.'
                                                      (1897, p. 335)

The three stages of the novel have become an account of the education of Pierston in human relationships.

The division of the novel into three parts representing the three ages of Pierston and the three generations of Avices is the most immediately apparent feature of its structure. It provides a series of pegs on which to hang the story of Pierston's pursuit of his ideal and a basis for the sub-theme of the effects of the passage of time. That Hardy was already thinking in terms of a story in which the bones of the narrative would show through its skin is evident from several entries in the *Life* quoting extracts from his own notes prior to 1892:

'My art is to intensify the expression of things . . . so that the heart and inner meaning is made vividly visible.'
                                                      (3 January 1886, p. 177)

'Art is a disproportioning—(*i.e.* a distorting, throwing out of proportion)—of realities, to show more clearly the features that matter in those realities.'   (August 1890, p. 229)

'The story of a face which goes through three generations or
more, would make a fine novel or poem of the passage of Time.
The differences in personality to be ignored.'
                                        (19 February 1889, p. 217)

Hardy added a note to this last entry that 'This idea was
to some extent carried out in the novel *The Well-Beloved*,
the poem entitled "Heredity", etc.'

When Hardy revised his serial novel for the first book
version in 1897 and again in 1912, it is manifest that he
wished to draw further attention to the formal structure of
the story. In 1892, the three parts were entitled 'A Young
Man of Twenty', 'A Young Man of Forty' and 'A Young
Man of Fifty-nine'. In 1897 Part Third becomes 'A Young
Man Turned Sixty' and uniformity becomes absolute in
1912 when Part Third is changed again to 'A Young Man
of Sixty'. Even some of the passing references to time are
rounded out: the gap of 'a dozen years' since Pierston had
seen Marcia becomes 'a whole twenty years' (1897, p. 84);
the portrait of Avice I was taken 'twenty years before'
(1897, p. 113) instead of nineteen years; and there are
others. The reader is to be reminded, then, that here we
have a story based on tranches of time separated by
mathematically uniform intervals. Other elements of pattern are imposed upon the narrative: the names of the three
Avices, obviously: Avice II's 'real' name is Ann Avice but
Pierston insists that she (and later her daughter) be Avice.
Jocelyn's relationship with Marcia is another example: he
begins married life, in fact if not in law, with her and ends
with her. That this is all part of the pattern is made quite
explicit in the final chapter: when the question of marriage
again arises between them at the prompting of neighbours,
Pierston says that people want 'to round off other people's
histories in the best machine-made conventional manner';
and a little later Hardy comments that 'the zealous wishes
of the neighbours to give a geometrical shape to their story

were fulfilled almost in spite of the chief parties themselves'
(III.viii).

There is nothing intrinsically wrong with such patent
patterning. Novels are interpretations of life, and patterns
are fundamental to life, whether they are the scientifically
identifiable patterns of the snowflake and the DNA
molecule or the patterns existing only subjectively in the
imagination and comprehension of a particular human
being in observing the world's phenomena: the delight in
the reflection of trees in a still pool; the feeling of completion and fulfilment engendered by the closing sounds of a
symphony. The sculpturing of *The Well-Beloved* can be a
legitimate translation from reality provided credulity is not
strained by too unnatural devices; and each reader must
decide for himself or herself whether this is so. (So far as
old Jocelyn's courtship of the young Avice III is concerned,
it was and is not unknown for old men to marry young
girls, and Desmond Hawkins recounts the case of a Baron
Corneille du Fleurant who married in 1873 the granddaughter of the girl who had jilted him forty-one years
earlier.[9] Had Hardy read about this?)

I have suggested that the emphasis on time and its passing has most relevance in terms of the development of the
characterization of Jocelyn Pierston, but running
underneath that theme is a preoccupation with the effects
of the rolling years on places and people, made specific in
a number of instances. It is naturally in Part Third that
such references are most evident: after twenty years Avice
II is a 'sorry shadow of Avice the Second' who has had
'troubles to take the bloom off me' (III.i); Pierston himself
sees his reflection in a mirror as 'too grievously far,
chronologically, in advance of the person he felt himself to
be' (III.iv); and Marcia, with 'her forehead ploughed, her
cheek hollow, her hair white as snow' has been brought to
this state 'by the raspings, chisellings, scourgings, bakings,
freezings of forty invidious years' (III.viii). Hardy shows
an interest in the effect of age and experience on the human
face in other stories and poems, e.g. on Yeobright's in *The*

[9] *Thomas Hardy*, London, 1950, p. 34.

Return of the Native: 'His countenance was overlaid with legible meanings' (II.vi); and on Agnette's in 'The Revisitation': 'Time's transforming chisel / Had been tooling night and day for twenty years, and tooled too well' (lines 109–10).

The opening paragraphs of Part Third offer the most direct expression of the movement of time, though men suffer 'only a little more adulteration in their refreshments' and have only 'a trifle less dialect in their speech than of yore'; the Isle of Slingers 'looked just the same as before' though we are aware throughout the story of the relentless nibbling away of Portland stone from the quarries for transport to London; and the tides have continued to 'gnaw' at the Pebble-bank, but 'the pebbles remained undevoured'. The seeming immutability of Portland in spite of the quarrymen's activities adds a wider dimension to the novel's time-scale: the three small episodes in Jocelyn's life are set within the vast context of the passing of the ages: he is a tiny dot in a cosmic landscape.

This impression of a vision broadened far beyond the confines of the immediate world of Pierston is established very early in the story, in the second chapter of Part First. The paragraph beginning: 'The evening and night winds here were, to Pierston's mind, charged with a something that did not burden them elsewhere' was added in 1897 to the already very effective previous paragraph describing the sound of the sea against the pebbles on Chesil Beach. As an evocation of an atmosphere it is one of the finest passages in Hardy. The 'huge composite ghost' of those drowned in shipwreck over many centuries running 'a shapeless figure over the isle, shrieking for some good god who would disunite it again' is one of his more startling images. It has much in common with a passage in *Jude* where another wind seems to Jude to be a composite ghost, this time of the souls of past Oxford ('Christminster') scholars: 'In the gloom it was as if he ran against them without feeling their bodily frames' (II.i).

The effective use of imagery and symbolism is evident elsewhere in *The Well-Beloved*. Jocelyn is not the only dot on a landscape. When he realizes that Avice II is interested

in a soldier on sentry-go up at the fortifications, he sees
him as 'a small red spot . . . creeping backwards and forwards monotonously against the heavy sky' (II.ix). He sees
Avice II herself as 'a dot of a figure' (II.viii), but although
the reader again observes the comparison between the
puniness of humanity and the immensity of the universe,
it is clear that for Pierston (and for Hardy?) the
significance of one individual for another predominates
over the impact of the universe:

How incomparably the immaterial dream dwarfed the grandest
of substantial things, when here, between these three sublimities
—the sky, the rock, and the ocean—the minute personality of
this washer-girl filled his consciousness to its extremest boundary, and the stupendous inanimate scene shrank to a corner
therein.   (II.viii)

Hardy uses the same image in a number of other places:
'She was but a spot' ('On the Departure Platform', line 4);
'an insignificant speck' (*The Mayor of Casterbridge*,
Chapter xliii); and as early as *An Indiscretion in the Life
of an Heiress*, Hardy describes the face of the lady in the
first chapter as 'a solitary white spot against the black surface of the wainscot'. The most interesting example, in
terms of links between Hardy's last three novels, is in *Tess*:
near the end of the book, when Angel Clare observes Tess
running towards him to tell him that she has killed
d'Urberville, he sees her as 'a moving spot intruded on the
white vacuity of its perspective' (Chapter lvii). (In most
cases a man is observing a woman in the distance. In the
next and penultimate chapter of *Tess*, when Tess is lying
on the sacrificial altar amid the vastness of Stonehenge, the
'mere dot' which appears in the distance is the head of one
of the men coming to arrest her.)
Not surprisingly the sea plays a prominent part in a
novel whose action is based largely on Portland, and it is
employed symbolically in relation to the lives of various
characters in a number of places. One example which
Hardy revised in 1897 to express the analogy more clearly
occurs in the description of Avice II's labours in childbirth

in Part II, Chapter xiii. In the serial version 'The sea murmured—more than murmured' (1892, p. 642) but later, 'The sea moaned—more than moaned' (1897, p. 215); this links more precisely with the moaning of Avice II referred to in both versions. It is followed almost immediately by a 'louder roll' (1892, p. 642) of the tide which is changed to pursue the metaphor a stage further: it becomes a 'throe of its tide' (1897, p. 215). A few lines later, Hardy adds a new clause to extend the parallel: Pierston 'waited there between the travail of the sea without, and the travail of the woman within' (ibid.).

It can be a misleading exercise to look for links between an author's creative writing and his own life, but it would be difficult to ignore a number of points of interest in the case of *The Well-Beloved*. Hardy was in his late fifties when he produced the revised version of the story in 1897 and the following extract from the *Life* reminds the reader that the three parts of *The Well-Beloved* are entitled 'A Young Man of Twenty', 'A Young Man of Forty' and 'A Young Man of Sixty': 'He himself said humorously in later times that he was a child till he was sixteen, a youth till he was five-and-twenty, and a young man till he was nearly fifty' (p. 32).

There is a slight indication in a letter to Edmund Gosse dated 21 March 1897 that Hardy is aware he has incorporated some elements of himself in Pierston. He wrote: 'I hope we shall see Portland together again. But I, too, am getting old like Pierston!' He was also like Pierston in that, throughout his life, he showed himself susceptible to the attractions of women friends.

There are other autobiographical links which can be suggested, such as the identification of some of his London characters with persons actually known to him, but more interesting, if more conjectural, has to be the nature of the novel itself, appearing as it did when Hardy was terminating his novel-writing and already turning to the poetry he had always been longing to write. If Pierston is at least to some extent Hardy (and the slightly mocking tone in which Hardy refers to Jocelyn at times sounds very like self-mockery), then this association and the formal structure signal the abandoning of the prose form and the adoption of the poet's role, speaking in his own voice.

There was one curious autobiographical turn of events, a kind of echo to the story: at the age of seventy-three Hardy married a second wife nearly forty years younger than himself. Even the 'Young Man of Sixty' didn't quite achieve that.

NOTE ON THE TEXT

THE principal editions and printings of *The Well-Beloved* published in England in Hardy's lifetime are as follows, and will be identified by their dates:

1892 Serial version published weekly under the title *The Pursuit of the Well-Beloved* in the *Illustrated London News* from 1 October to 17 December 1892.

1897 The Wessex Novels Edition, Vol. XVII; London: Osgood, McIlvaine.

1898 Colonial Library Edition; London: Macmillan.

1903 The Wessex Novels Edition, Vol. XVII; London: Macmillan (also advertised by Macmillan as 'The Collected Edition').

1907 The Wessex Novels Pocket Edition, Vol. XVII; London: Macmillan.

1912 The Wessex Edition, Vol. XIII; London: Macmillan.

1920 The Mellstock Edition, Vol. XXI; London: Macmillan (de luxe edition limited to 500 copies).

The choice of copy-text in the case of *The Well-Beloved* is limited by the absence of a manuscript. In Hardy's personal notebooks its whereabouts or existence is listed in 1923 as 'unknown' and it has not been recovered subsequently. The first witness is therefore the serial version in the *Illustrated London News*. It was published in the United States at the same time in *Harper's Bazar*.

Hardy was not satisfied with it (he later called it 'experimental') and did not revise it for book publication until late in 1896; but the revision was very thorough and extensive. It was published as Volume XVII of the first uniform and complete edition of Hardy's novels, the rest of which had been issued by Osgood, McIlvaine in 1895 and 1896.

A second printing of *The Well-Beloved*, advertised as a second edition, followed very quickly.

The book was also published in 1897 in the United States and Canada by Harper of New York, but neither the variants in this nor in any later American edition have any known authority.

In 1898 Macmillan purchased a set of plates from Osgood, McIlvaine and published the book in their Colonial Library Edition. There was only one change from 1897 but it was continued in later editions: in the first paragraph of the Preface 'almost distinctive people' became 'well-nigh distinct people'.

After Hardy had transferred his work from Osgood, McIlvaine to Macmillan in 1902, *The Well-Beloved* was issued in the blue livery of Macmillan's 'Three-and-Sixpenny Library' in 1903 and reprinted in 1911, again as Volume XVII of the Wessex Novels and using the same plates. Alterations were few: a new penultimate paragraph was added to the Preface ('As for the story itself . . .') and there were four minor changes in wording in the latter part of the novel.

The pocket edition issued by Macmillan in 1907 was reprinted as required. Up to and including 1925 all pocket editions were reprints of 1903 and did not vary from it. In 1927 changes were made to conform to the 1912 Wessex Edition, but in a number of places the text remained the same as in 1903, generally in minor matters of punctuation.

As explained in the Introduction, for the 1912 Wessex Edition Hardy produced the only thoroughgoing revision of the novel after the substantial revision for the first book publication in 1897. He had also proposed to Macmillan a re-arrangement of the books and *The Well-Beloved* now became Volume XIII and was included in Group II: 'Romances and Fantasies'.

It was renumbered again for the Mellstock Edition of 1920, becoming Volume XXI in that edition. For all except *A Pair of Blue Eyes* this was largely a re-setting of the Wessex Edition, and in the case of *The Well-Beloved* there are only seven slight differences which might be attributed to the compositor, as they are trifling changes which were not maintained in subsequent reprints of 1912 and would therefore appear not to have authorial validation.

The definitive 1912 edition was reprinted in 1922 in the same format and subsequently in several different formats but from the same plates. The variants in these reprintings have no authority and in the case of *The Well-Beloved* are due to compositorial errors or plate batter.

As there is no evidence that Hardy carried out any further revision of *The Well-Beloved* for new editions or reprintings after 1912, most students of Hardy would accept the view that 1912 should be the choice of copy-text for substantives. The question of the choice of copy-text for accidentals does, however, require further consideration, in view of the preference of some editors for choosing the manuscript, or the earliest printed version in the absence of a manuscript, as being likely to contain the least accretion of compositorial interference with the authorial punctuation.

Since we do not have a manuscript, the editor is faced with the problem of balancing the authority of 1892 against that of 1912, and here several factors are relevant. The most crucial is the degree of attention given by Hardy to revising 1892 for 1897 and 1903 for 1912. If there is evidence of thorough revision by Hardy, then the later edition has the greater authority.

Any doubt about Hardy's authorship of revisions in general for the 1912 Wessex Edition is settled by the evidence of his revision of the 1906 *The Woodlanders* for use as printer's copy for 1912. This shows that Hardy carried out extensive revision, particularly of the punctuation. The question then arises as to whether the printers paid heed to his revisions. If they did, then it will be a reasonable assumption that whatever conclusions may be drawn in the case of *The Woodlanders* are likely to be applicable to Hardy's preparation of the other novels for the Wessex Edition. An examination of Hardy's emendations of a copy of *The Woodlanders* of 1906 at Dorchester and a comparison with a 1912 *The Woodlanders* showed that the printers had indeed followed Hardy's directions.

This means that, apart from a few errors in 1912 apparently missed by Hardy, the variants in 1912 are authorial.

It is, of course, desirable to be able to show that these conclusions do apply directly to *The Well-Beloved* (where we do not have the same concrete evidence) and not just by analogy; and something very near to conclusive proof does exist: *The Well-Beloved* of 1897 has had over 120 commas removed from the serial version of 1892, and the revised 1897 (and 1903) accidentals are largely—but not entirely—identical with 1912. These deletions bear the mark of Hardy, who sometimes punctuated to indicate a manner of speaking or to give a particular emphasis, not of a compositor, who would follow conventional usage. If this is accepted, then the fact that there are as many as seven, and quite frequently five or six, changes in accidentals on a single page indicates Hardy's close attention to this aspect as well as to substantives.

By 1897, and even more so by 1912, Hardy's status as a novelist and relationship with his printers were very different from what they had been in his early days. For the 1897 edition he took time to carry out the emendation of 1892 with great care, and he was in a position to see to it that the compositors took note of his intentions; and these intentions continue to a very large extent, as has already been indicated, to be reflected in 1912.

For these reasons 1912 has been chosen (with a few emendations) as the copy-text for both substantives and accidentals. The 1922 reprint would have been adopted as the last edition published in Hardy's lifetime containing his revisions, but it only differs from 1912 in minor printers' errors or plate batter.

I have entered into my text a very limited number of divergences from the copy-text for the following reasons only: to incorporate the emendations pencilled by Hardy in the margins of his own copy of the 1912 *The Well-Beloved*; to correct apparent plate batter or compositorial errors; to amend incorrect or unconventional usage where there appears to be no justification for it; and to restore an 1892 or other reading which appears to conform more closely with Hardy's intention than a later deviation which he seems to have overlooked in correcting his copy-text or proof. With regard to this last point, any attempt to interpret Hardy's intentions for him must involve hazardous conjecture, and therefore emendations on these grounds have been kept to a minimum, but in a few places use has been made of the evidence available in Hardy's emendations of the 1906 *The Woodlanders* and his corrections to the 1893 proofs of *Life's Little Ironies*. Particular trends in those alterations would seem to provide very strong indications of an author's intentions: when he is first composing his tale he may not give undue attention to such matters as accidentals; but when he is revising the manuscript or copy-text and undertaking several hundred amendments, he is giving clear signals of his own preferences, especially when the same features recur.

Anyone who has had the opportunity to examine in detail Hardy's work in emending his texts is likely to conclude that here is not only a gifted story-teller but also a skilled and careful craftsman.

An Appendix after the Explanatory Notes gives a detailed comparison of the revised text with the original 1892 text.

SELECT BIBLIOGRAPHY

THE Note on the Text gives details of the main editions and print-ings of *The Well-Beloved*. Except where they are replaced by full scholarly editions, the texts in the volumes of the Wessex Edition of 1912 are regarded as having been up to now the nearest to contain-ing Hardy's final intentions. The only scholarly editions so far published are *Tess of the d'Urbervilles*, edited by Simon Gatrell and Juliet Grindle (Oxford, 1983) and *The Woodlanders*, edited by Dale Kramer (Oxford, 1981). Other writings of Hardy are to be found in: Harold Orel (ed.), *Thomas Hardy's Personal Writings* (London, 1967); Richard H. Taylor (ed.), *The Personal Notebooks of Thomas Hardy* (London, 1978); and Richard Little Purdy and Michael Millgate (eds.), *The Collected Letters of Thomas Hardy* in seven volumes (Oxford, 1978–88). The first two volumes, published in 1978 and 1980 and covering the period from 1840 to 1901, are of most interest for references to matters concerning *The Well-Beloved* and the novels in general. Hardy's poem 'The Well Beloved' is well worth reading for the light it throws on his intentions in the novel.

Biographical considerations are important for a full understand-ing of *The Well-Beloved*. Hardy's autobiography, published as a bio-graphy under the authorship of his second wife, Florence Emily Hardy, first appeared in two volumes as *The Early Life of Thomas Hardy* (London, 1928) and *The Later Years of Thomas Hardy* (London, 1930); it was issued in one volume as *The Life of Thomas Hardy* (Lon-don, 1962). This conceals as much as it reveals, as Hardy intended it should, so it is valuable to have more recent biographical studies. Robert Gittings published *Young Thomas Hardy* (London) in 1975 and *The Older Hardy* (London) in 1978. Michael Millgate's *Thomas Hardy: A Biography* (Oxford) published in 1982 and his *Thomas Hardy: His Career as a Novelist* (London, 1971) are essential reading for any serious student of Hardy; so is the standard bibliographical work, R. L. Purdy's *Thomas Hardy: A Bibliographical Study* (Oxford, 1954). Michael Millgate has also edited *The Early Life* and *The Later Years* to produce as far as possible *The Life and Work of Thomas Hardy by Thomas Hardy* (London and Georgia, 1984).

There have been several articles dealing specifically with *The Well-Beloved*. Milton Chaikin's 'A Possible Source of Hardy's *The Well-*

Beloved' (in *Modern Language Notes*, LXXI, Nov. 1956) is of interest for the similarities he observes between the story elements in Hardy and those in de Maupassant's *Fort Comme la Mort*, published in English by Harper in 1889, three years before Hardy's first version. Others are: John Fowles, 'Hardy and the Hag' (in *Thomas Hardy After Fifty Years*, ed. L. St J. Butler, London, 1977), particularly interesting for its consideration of 'the fictionality of fiction' (see also the same author's Foreword to *The Magus* [revised, 1977] for a comment on *The Well-Beloved* as the most revealing of all modern novels about novelists'); Helmut E. Gerber, 'Hardy's *The Well-Beloved* as a Comment on the Well-Despised' (in *English Language Notes*, Vol. I, Colorado, 1963–4); J. Hillis Miller's Introduction to the New Wessex Edition of *The Well-Beloved* (London, 1975), especially for his comments about *The Well-Beloved* as 'one of the most important nineteenth-century novels about art' (and he also writes about 'the fictionality of fiction'); Milton L. Miller, 'A Comparison of *Remembrance of Things Past* with Thomas Hardy's *The Well-Beloved*' (in *Nostalgia: A Psychoanalytical Study of Marcel Proust*, Boston, 1956); and Michael Ryan, 'One Name of Many Shapes: "The Well-Beloved"' (in *Critical Approaches to the Fiction of Thomas Hardy*, ed. Dale Kramer, London, 1979).

Alma Priestley is another critic who compares Hardy's achievement with Proust's in 'Hardy's *The Well-Beloved*: a Study in Failure' (in *The Thomas Hardy Society Review*, Vol. I, No. 2, 1976) and provides a counterbalance to more favourable recent opinions of Hardy's last completed novel. Proust himself wrote approvingly about *The Well-Beloved* on several occasions: in particular in a letter of about December 1909 to Robert de Billy (in *Marcel Proust: Choix de Lettres*, Plon, 1965): and in 'La Prisonnière' (À *la Recherche du Temps Perdu*, éd. de la Pléiade, Paris, 1954, Vol. III, p. 376). Vols. I and II, 'Du Côté de Chez Swann' and 'A L'Ombre des Jeunes Filles en Fleurs', contain views on the subjectivity of love which it is interesting to compare with Hardy's.

As with all Hardy's novels, a knowledge of the geographical bases for his fictional settings increases enjoyment and understanding of the story. For this purpose Denys Kay-Robinson's *Hardy's Wessex Re-appraised* (Newton Abbot, 1972) is an excellent comprehensive illustrated survey of 'Hardy country'; for Portland in particular, T. R. Wightman's 'The Country of "The Well-Beloved"' (Dorchester, 1976) is essential. This is Number 12 in a series of very useful pamphlets published by the Thomas Hardy Society relating the fictional settings of each novel to the actual geographical locations.

Reference to Shelley's influence on Hardy can be found in a number of places, including Roy Morrell, *Thomas Hardy: The Will and the Way* (Kuala Lumpur, 1965); W. R. Rutland, *Thomas Hardy: A Study of his Writings and their Background* (Oxford, 1938); and particularly Phyllis Bartlett: ' "Seraph of Heaven": A Shelleyan Dream in Hardy's Fiction' (in *Publications of the Modern Language Association*, LXX, 1955). Roy Morrell has also written on 'Some Aspects of Hardy's Minor Novels' (in *Budmouth Essays on Thomas Hardy*, ed. F. B. Pinion, Dorchester, 1976).

More recent chapters and articles with some relevance to *The Well-Beloved* are to be found in the following: Rosemary Sumner, *Thomas Hardy: Psychological Novelist* (London, 1981); Richard Taylor, *The Neglected Hardy: Thomas Hardy's Lesser Novels* (London, 1982); David S. Werman and Theodore J. Jacobs, 'Thomas Hardy's *The Well-Beloved* and the Nature of Infatuation' (in *International Review of Psycho-Analysis*, 10, 1983); Glen Irvin, 'High Passion and High Church in Hardy's *Two on a Tower*' (in *English Literature in Transition 1880–1920*, Special Series No. 3, 1985); J. B. Bullen, *The Expressive Eye* (Oxford, 1986); Arnold E. Davidson, 'On Reading *The Well-Beloved* as a Parable of Art' (in *The Thomas Hardy Year Book*, No. 14, Guernsey, 1988); Martin Seymour-Smith, *Hardy* (London, 1994).

A continuing source of valuable information on Hardy is *The Thomas Hardy Journal*. It has published: Ralph W. V. Elliott, 'The Infatuated Artist: Thomas Hardy and *The Well-Beloved*' (in Vol. III, No. 2, 1987); Norman Page, '*The Well-Beloved* and Other Hardyan Fantasies' (in Vol. VIII, No. 3, 1992); Abdul Aziz M. Bulaila, ' "The Clay But Not the Potter": Love and Marriage in *The Well-Beloved*' (in Vol. IX, No. 2, 1993); Frank G. Healey, 'Proust and Hardy—an Update' (in Vol. X, No. 2, 1994).

A CHRONOLOGY
OF THOMAS HARDY

1840   2 June: Thomas Hardy born, first child of Thomas and Jemima (Hand) Hardy, five and a half months after their marriage. His father was a builder in a small but slowly developing way of business, thus setting the family apart socially from the 'work-folk' whom they clearly resembled in financial circumstances.

1848   Entered the newly opened Stinsford National School.

1849   Sent to Dorchester British School kept by Isaac Last.

1853   Last established an independent 'commercial academy', and Hardy became a pupil there. His education was practical and effective, including Latin, some French, theoretical and applied mathematics and commercial studies.

1856   11 July: articled to Dorchester architect John Hicks. Soon after this he became friendly with Horace Moule, an important influence on his life.

1860   Summer: Hardy's articles, having been extended for a year, completed. Employed by Hicks as an assistant.

1862   17 April: Without a position; travelled to London, but soon employed by Arthur Blomfield as a 'Gothic draughtsman'. November: Elected to the Architectural Association; began to find his feet in London.

1863   Won architectural prizes; began to consider some form of writing as a means of support.

1863–7   Possibly became engaged to Eliza Nicholls.

1865   March: 'How I Built myself a House' published in *Chambers' Journal*. Began to write poetry.

1866   Hardy's commitment to the Church and his religious belief seem to have declined though he probably experienced no dramatic loss of faith.

1867   Returned to Dorset. Began his first unpublished novel.

1868   Sent MS of *The Poor Man and the Lady* to four publishers, where it was read by Morley and Meredith, amongst others, but finally rejected.

1869   Worked in Weymouth for the architect Crickmay;
        began writing *Desperate Remedies*.

1870   In order to take 'a plan and particulars' of the church,
        Hardy journeyed to St Juliot, near Boscastle in North
        Cornwall; there he met Emma Lavinia Gifford, who
        became his wife four years later.

1871   *Desperate Remedies* published after Hardy had advan-
        ced £75.

1872   *Under the Greenwood Tree* published; the copyright
        sold to Tinsley for £30. Hardy moved temporarily to
        London to work in the offices of T. Roger Smith. Con-
        tracted to provide serial for *Tinsleys' Magazine* for £200
        (to include first edition rights). *A Pair of Blue Eyes*
        began to appear in September. Hardy decided to relin-
        quish architecture and concentrate on writing. Leslie
        Stephen requested a serial for the *Cornhill Magazine*.

1873   *A Pair of Blue Eyes* published in three volumes;
        Horace Moule, his close adviser and friend, committed
        suicide in Cambridge.

1874   *Far From the Madding Crowd* begun as a serial in *Corn-
        hill* under Leslie Stephen's editorship and published
        later in the year in two volumes. Hardy married Emma
        Gifford on 17 September; they honeymooned in Paris
        and returned to live in London.

1875   *Cornhill* serialized *The Hand of Ethelberta*. The
        Hardys moved from London to Swanage in Dorset.

1876   Further moves to Yeovil and Sturminster Newton,
        where Hardy began writing *The Return of the Native*.

1878   Return to London (Tooting). *The Return of the Native*
        serialized in *Belgravia* and published in three volumes,
        to which Hardy affixed a map of the novel's environ-
        ment. Made researches in the British Museum for the
        background of *The Trumpet-Major*.

1879   With 'The Distracted Young Preacher', began regularly
        to publish short stories.

1880   *Good Words* serialized *The Trumpet-Major*, which
        was also published in three volumes with covers
        designed by Hardy. In October he became seriously ill
        and believed himself close to death; the cause of his
        illness uncertain, but led to five months' total inactivity.

1881   *A Laodicean*, mostly written from his bed, published as a serial in *Harper's New Monthly Magazine* (the first in the new European edition), and in three volumes. The Hardys returned to Dorset, living at Wimborne Minster.

1882   Controversy with Pinero over Hardy's adaptation of *Far From the Madding Crowd* and Pinero's use of the same material. Hardy's third novel in three years, *Two on a Tower*, serialized in the *Atlantic Monthly* and issued in three volumes.

1883   The final move of his life—from Wimborne to Dorchester, though into temporary accommodation while his own house was being built.

1884   Made a Justice of the Peace and began to receive invitations from aristocracy. Began writing *The Mayor of Casterbridge*.

1885   Max Gate, designed by Hardy and built by his brother Henry, completed; on the outskirts of Dorchester, it remained his home for the rest of his life.

1886   *The Mayor of Casterbridge* serialized in the *Graphic* and brought out in two volumes; in the same year *The Woodlanders* began its run in *Macmillan's Magazine*. William Barnes, the Dorset poet and friend of Hardy, died.

1887   *The Woodlanders* issued in three volumes. The Hardys visited France and Italy. Began work on *Tess of the d'Urbervilles*.

1888   Hardy's first collection of short stories, *Wessex Tales*, published in two volumes. Also published the first of three significant essays on the theory of fiction, *The Profitable Reading of Fiction*.

1889   The novel that was to become *Tess* rejected by Tillotson's Fiction Bureau, which had commissioned it; subsequent further rejections fuelled the bitterness behind a second essay, *Candour in English Fiction*, published in January of the following year.

1890   *A Group of Noble Dames* appeared in the *Graphic*.

1891   *Tess of the d'Urbervilles* serialized in the *Graphic* and published in three volumes; *A Group of Noble Dames* brought out in one volume. The third important essay,

The Science of Fiction, appeared. A Copyright Bill passed through the United States Congress in time for *Tess* to benefit from its provisions, a factor of considerable financial significance in Hardy's career.

1892   Father died 20 July. *The Pursuit of the Well-Beloved* serialized in the *Illustrated London News*.

1893   Met Florence Henniker, subject of the intensest of his romantic attachments to artistic ladies. Wrote *The Spectre of the Real* in collaboration with her. Began writing *Jude the Obscure*.

1894   Third volume of short stories, *Life's Little Ironies*, published in one volume.

1895   First collected edition of Hardy's work begun, published by Osgood, McIlvaine; it included the first edition of *Jude the Obscure*, previously serialized in *Harper's New Monthly Magazine*. Some reviews of *Jude* quite savage, a contributory factor to Hardy's writing no further novels. Hardy dramatized *Tess*.

1896   The first group of major poems with identifiable dates written since the 1860s; they included the three *In Tenebris* poems and *Wessex Heights*.

1897   *The Well-Beloved*, substantially revised from the 1892 serialization, published as part of the Osgood, McIlvaine edition. Visited Switzerland.

1898   Hardy's first collection of verse published, *Wessex Poems*; comprising mainly poems written in the 1860s and 1890s, and illustrated by himself.

1899   Boer War began, to which Hardy responded in verse. The gradual physical separation between Hardy and Emma intensified, following the mental separation that set in after the publication of *Jude the Obscure*.

1901   *Poems of the Past and the Present* published.

1902   Changed publishers for the last time, to Macmillan.

1904   First part of *The Dynasts* appeared. 3 April: Hardy's mother died, leaving a tremendous gap in his life.

1905   Met Florence Dugdale. Received LL D from Aberdeen University.

1906   Part Two of *The Dynasts* published.

1908   *The Dynasts* completed with the publication of the

third part; it embodied Hardy's most complete statement of his philosophical outlook. Also published his *Select Poems of William Barnes*, undertaken as a memorial to his great predecessor. The first Dorchester dramatization of a Hardy novel, *The Trumpet-Major*. Meredith and Swinburne died, leaving Hardy as the greatest living English writer.

1909   Relationship with Florence Dugdale deepened. *Time's Laughingstocks*, Hardy's third volume of poems published.

1910   Awarded the Order of Merit, having previously refused a knighthood. Received the freedom of Dorchester.

1912   Second collected edition of Hardy's works begun, the Wessex Edition. Received the gold medal of the Royal Society of Literature. 27 November: Emma Hardy died; as a direct result Hardy began writing the poems of 1912–13.

1913   Visited Cornwall in search of his and Emma's youth. Awarded Litt.D. at Cambridge and became an Honorary Fellow of Magdalene College—a partial fulfilment of an early aspiration. His final collection of short stories published, *A Changed Man*.

1914   10 February: married Florence Dugdale. *Satires of Circumstance* published. First World War began; Hardy's attitude to the future of humanity coloured by it in a profound way.

1915   At the age of 75 Hardy began to become reclusive. Frank George, his chosen heir, killed at Gallipoli. Hardy's sister Mary died 24 November.

1916   *Selected Poems of Thomas Hardy* published.

1917   Hardy's fifth collection of verse published, *Moments of Vision*. He and Florence began work on what was eventually to become *The Life of Thomas Hardy*.

1919–20   The de luxe edition of Hardy's work issued, the Mellstock Edition.

1922   *Late Lyrics and Earlier*, with its important Preface, published.

1923   Florence Henniker died. The Prince of Wales visited Max Gate. Friendship with T. E. Lawrence developed. *The Queen of Cornwall* published.

1924   Hardy's adaptation of *Tess* acted in Dorchester with the last of his romantic attachments, Gertrude Bugler, in the title role.

1925   *Tess* acted in London, but not by Miss Bugler. *Human Shows Far Phantasies Songs and Trifles*, Hardy's seventh volume of verse, published.

1928   11 January: Hardy died. His final book of poems, *Winter Words*, published posthumously.

THE WELL-BELOVED

A SKETCH OF A TEMPERAMENT

'One shape of many names.'—P. B. SHELLEY.

PREFACE

THE peninsula carved by Time out of a single stone,
whereon most of the following scenes are laid, was for centuries immemorial the home of a curious and well-nigh
distinct people, cherishing strange beliefs and singular
customs, now for the most part obsolescent. Fancies, like
certain soft-wooded plants which cannot bear the silent
inland frosts, but thrive by the sea in the roughest of
weather, seem to grow up naturally here, in particular
amongst those natives who have no active concern in the
labours of the 'Isle.' Hence it is a spot apt to generate a type
of personage like the character imperfectly sketched in
these pages—a native of natives—whom some may choose
to call a fantast (if they honour him with their consideration so far), but whom others may see only as one that
gave objective continuity and a name to a delicate dream
which in a vaguer form is more or less common to all men,
and is by no means new to Platonic philosophers.

To those who know the rocky coign of England here
depicted—overlooking the great Channel Highway with all
its suggestiveness, and standing out so far into mid-sea that
touches of the Gulf Stream soften the air till February—it is
matter of surprise that the place has not been more frequently chosen as the retreat of artists and poets in search of
inspiration—for at least a month or two in the year, the
tempestuous rather than the fine seasons by preference. To be
sure, one nook therein is the retreat, at their country's expense,
of other geniuses from a distance; but their presence is hardly discoverable. Yet perhaps it is as well that the artistic visitors
do not come, or no more would be heard of little freehold
houses being bought and sold there for a couple of hundred
pounds—built of solid stone, and dating from the sixteenth
century and earlier, with mullions, copings, and corbels complete. These transactions, by the way, are carried out and
covenanted, or were till lately, in the parish church, in the face
of the congregation, such being the ancient custom of the Isle.

As for the story itself, it may be worth while to remark that, differing from all or most others of the series in that the interest aimed at is of an ideal or subjective nature, and frankly imaginative, verisimilitude in the sequence of events has been subordinated to the said aim.

The first publication of this tale in an independent form was in 1897; but it had appeared in the periodical press in 1892, under the title of 'The Pursuit of the Well-Beloved.' A few chapters of that experimental issue were rewritten for the present and final form of the narrative.

T. H.

August 1912.

CONTENTS

PART THIRD

A YOUNG MAN OF SIXTY

PART FIRST
A YOUNG MAN OF TWENTY

—'Now, if Time knows
That Her, whose radiant brows
Weave them a garland of my vows;

Her that dares be
What these lines wish to see:
I seek no further, it is She.'
                                        R. CRASHAW.

A SUPPOSITITIOUS
PRESENTMENT OF HER
I.—i.

A PERSON who differed from the local wayfarers was
climbing the steep road which leads through the sea-skirted
townlet definable as the Street of Wells, and forms a pass
into that Gibraltar of Wessex, the singular peninsula once
an island, and still called such, that stretches out like the
head of a bird into the English Channel. It is connected
with the mainland by a long thin neck of pebbles 'cast up
by rages of the se,' and unparalleled in its kind in Europe.

The pedestrian was what he looked like—a young man
from London and the cities of the Continent. Nobody
could see at present that his urbanism sat upon him only
as a garment. He was just recollecting with something of
self-reproach that a whole three years and eight months
had flown since he paid his last visit to his father at this
lonely rock of his birthplace, the intervening time having
been spent amid many contrasting societies, peoples, manners, and scenes.

What had seemed usual in the isle when he lived there
always looked quaint and odd after his later impressions.
More than ever the spot seemed what it was said once to
have been, the ancient Vindilia Island, and the Home of
the Slingers. The towering rock, the houses above houses,
one man's doorstep rising behind his neighbour's chimney,
the gardens hung up by one edge to the sky, the vegetables
growing on apparently almost vertical planes, the unity of
the whole island as a solid and single block of limestone
four miles long, were no longer familiar and commonplace
ideas. All now stood dazzlingly unique and white against
the tinted sea, and the sun flashed on infinitely stratified
walls of oolite,

> The melancholy ruins
> Of cancelled cycles, . . .

with a distinctiveness that called the eyes to it as strongly
as any spectacle he had beheld afar.

After a laborious clamber he reached the top, and walked
along the plateau towards the eastern village. The time being about two o'clock, in the middle of the summer season,
the road was glaring and dusty, and drawing near to his
father's house he sat down in the sun.

He stretched out his hand upon the rock beside him. It
felt warm. That was the island's personal temperature
when in its afternoon sleep as now. He listened, and heard
sounds: whirr-whirr, saw-saw-saw. Those were the
island's snores—the noises of the quarrymen and stone-
sawyers.

Opposite to the spot on which he sat was a roomy cottage or homestead. Like the island it was all of stone, not
only in walls but in window-frames, roof, chimneys,
fence, stile, pigsty and stable, almost door.

He remembered who had used to live there—and probably lived there now—the Caro family; the 'roan-mare'
Caros, as they were called to distinguish them from other
branches of the same pedigree, there being but half-a-
dozen christian and surnames in the whole island. He
crossed the road and looked in at the open doorway. Yes,
there they were still.

Mrs. Caro, who had seen him from the window, met
him in the entry, and an old-fashioned greeting took place
between them. A moment after a door leading from the
back rooms was thrown open, and a young girl about
seventeen or eighteen came bounding in.

'Why, *'tis* dear Joce!' she burst out joyfully. And running
up to the young man she kissed him.

The demonstration was sweet enough from the owner of
such an affectionate pair of bright hazel eyes and brown
tresses of hair. But it was so sudden, so unexpected by a
man fresh from towns, that he winced for a moment quite
involuntarily; and there was some constraint in the manner in which he returned her kiss, and said, 'My pretty little Avice, how do you do after so long?'

For a few seconds her impulsive innocence hardly noticed

his start of surprise; but Mrs. Caro, the girl's mother, had observed it instantly. With a pained flush she turned to her daughter.

'Avice—my dear Avice! Why—what are you doing? Don't you know that you've grown up to be a woman since Jocelyn—Mr. Pierston—was last down here? Of course you mustn't do now as you used to do three or four years ago!'

The awkwardness which had arisen was hardly removed by Pierston's assurance that he quite expected her to keep up the practice of her childhood, followed by several minutes of conversation on general subjects. He was vexed from his soul that his unaware movement should so have betrayed him. At his leaving he repeated that if Avice regarded him otherwise than as she used to do he would never forgive her; but though they parted good friends her regret at the incident was visible in her face. Jocelyn passed out into the road and onward to his father's house hard by. The mother and daughter were left alone.

'I was quite amazed at 'ee, my child!' exclaimed the elder. 'A young man from London and foreign cities, used now to the strictest company manners, and ladies who almost think it vulgar to smile broad! How could ye do it, Avice?'

'I—I didn't think about how I was altered!' said the conscience-stricken girl. 'I used to kiss him, and he used to kiss me before he went away.'

'But that was years ago, my dear!'

'O yes, and for the moment I forgot! He seemed just the same to me as he used to be.'

'Well, it can't be helped now. You must be careful in the future. He's got lots of young women, I'll warrant, and has few thoughts left for you. He's what they call a sculptor, and he means to be a great genius in that line some day, they do say.'

'Well, I've done it; and it can't be mended!' moaned the girl.

Meanwhile Jocelyn Pierston, the sculptor of budding fame, had gone onward to the house of his father, an inartistic man of trade and commerce merely, from whom, nevertheless, Jocelyn condescended to accept a yearly allowance pending the famous days to come. But the elder, having received no warning of his son's intended visit, was not at home to welcome him. Jocelyn looked round the familiar premises, glanced across the Common at the great yards within which eternal saws were going to and fro upon eternal blocks of stone—the very same saws and the very same blocks that he had seen there when last in the island, so it seemed to him—and then passed through the dwelling into the back garden.

Like all the gardens in the isle it was surrounded by a wall of dry-jointed spawls, and at its further extremity it ran out into a corner, which adjoined the garden of the Caros. He had no sooner reached this spot than he became aware of a murmuring and sobbing on the other side of the wall. The voice he recognized in a moment as Avice's, and she seemed to be confiding her trouble to some young friend of her own sex.

'O, what shall I *do*! what *shall* I do!' she was saying bitterly. 'So bold as it was—so shameless! How could I think of such a thing! He will never forgive me—never. Never like me again. He'll think me a forward hussy, and yet— and yet I quite forgot how much I had grown. But that he'll never believe!' The accents were those of one who had for the first time become conscious of her womanhood, as an unwonted possession which shamed and frightened her.

'Did he seem angry at it?' inquired the friend.

'O no—not angry! Worse. Cold and haughty. O, he's such a fashionable person now—not at all an island man. But there's no use in talking of it. I wish I was dead!'

Pierston retreated as quickly as he could. He grieved at the incident which had brought such pain to this innocent soul; and yet it was beginning to be a source of vague pleasure to him. He returned to the house, and when his father had come back and welcomed him, and they had shared a meal together, Jocelyn again when out, full of an earnest desire to soothe his young neighbour's sorrow in a way she little expected; though, to tell the truth, his affection for her was rather that of a friend than of a lover, and he felt by no means sure that the migratory, elusive idealization he called his Love who, ever since his boyhood, had flitted from human shell to human shell an indefinite number of times, was going to take up her abode in the body of Avice Caro.

THE INCARNATION IS
ASSUMED TO BE TRUE

I.—ii.

IT was difficult to meet her again, even though on this lump of rock the difficulty lay as a rule rather in avoidance than in meeting. But Avice had been transformed into a very different kind of young woman by the self-consciousness engendered of her impulsive greeting, and, notwithstanding their near neighbourhood, he could not encounter her, try as he would. No sooner did he appear an inch beyond his father's door than she was to earth like a fox; she bolted upstairs to her room.

Anxious to soothe her after his unintentional slight he could not stand these evasions long. The manners of the isle were primitive and straightforward, even among the well-to-do, and noting her disappearance one day he followed her into the house and onward to the foot of the stairs.

'Avice!' he called.

'Yes, Mr. Pierston.'

'Why do you run upstairs like that?'

'O—only because I wanted to come up for something.'

'Well, if you've got it, can't you come down again?'

'No, I can't very well.'

'Come, *dear* Avice. That's what you are, you know.'

There was no response.

'Well, if you won't, you won't!' he continued. 'I don't want to bother you.' And Pierston went away.

He was stopping to look at the old-fashioned flowers under the garden walls when he heard a voice behind him.

'Mr. Pierston—I wasn't angry with you. When you were gone I thought—you might mistake me, and I felt I could do no less than come and assure you of my friendship still.'

Turning he saw the blushing Avice immediately behind him.

'You are a good, dear girl!' said he, and, seizing her hand, set upon her cheek the kind of kiss that should have been the response to hers on the day of his coming.

'Darling Avice, forgive me for the slight that day! Say you do. Come, now! And then I'll say to you what I have never said to any other woman, living or dead: "Will you have me as your husband?" '

'Ah!—mother says I am only one of many!'

'You are not, dear. You knew me when I was young, and others didn't.'

Somehow or other her objections were got over, and though she did not give an immediate assent, she agreed to meet him later in the afternoon, when she walked with him to the southern point of the island called the Beal, or, by strangers, the Bill, pausing over the treacherous cavern known as Cave Hole, into which the sea roared and splashed now as it had done when they visited it together as children. To steady herself while looking in he offered her his arm, and she took it, for the first time as a woman, for the hundredth time as his companion.

They rambled on to the lighthouse, where they would have lingered longer if Avice had not suddenly remembered an engagement to recite poetry from a platform that very evening at the Street of Wells, the village commanding the entrance to the island—the village that has now advanced to be a town.

'Recite!' said he. 'Who'd have thought anybody or anything could recite down here except the reciter we hear away there—the never speechless sea.'

'O but we are quite intellectual now. In the winter particularly. But, Jocelyn—don't come to the recitation, will you? It would spoil my performance if you were there, and I want to be as good as the rest.'

'I won't if you really wish me not to. But I shall meet you at the door and bring you home.'

'Yes!' she said, looking up into his face. Avice was perfectly happy now; she could never have believed on that mortifying day of his coming that she would be so happy with him. When they reached the east side of the isle they parted, that she might be soon enough to take her place on the platform. Pierston went home, and after dark, when it was about the hour for accompanying her back, he went along the middle road northward to the Street of Wells.

He was full of misgiving. He had known Avice Caro so well of old that his feeling for her now was rather comradeship than love; and what he had said to her in a moment of impulse that morning rather appalled him in its consequences. Not that any of the more sophisticated and accomplished women who had attracted him successively would be likely to rise inconveniently between them. For he had quite disabused his mind of the assumption that the idol of his fancy was an integral part of the personality in which it had sojourned for a long or a short while.

To his Well-Beloved he had always been faithful; but she had had many embodiments. Each individuality known as Lucy, Jane, Flora, Evangeline, or whatnot, had been merely a transient condition of her. He did not recognize this as an excuse or as a defence, but as a fact simply. Essentially she was perhaps of no tangible substance; a spirit, a dream, a frenzy, a conception, an aroma, an epitomized sex, a light of the eye, a parting of the lips. God only knew what she really was; Pierston did not. She was indescribable.

Never much considering that she was a subjective phenomenon vivified by the weird influences of his descent and birthplace, the discovery of her ghostliness, of her independence of physical laws and failings, had occasionally given him a sense of fear. He never knew where she next would be, whither she would lead him, having herself instant access to all ranks and classes, to every abode of men. Sometimes at night he dreamt that she was 'the wile-weaving Daughter of high Zeus' in person, bent on tormenting him for his sins against her beauty in his art—the implacable Aphrodite herself indeed. He knew that he loved the masquerading creature wherever he found her, whether with blue eyes, black eyes, or brown;

whether presenting herself as tall, fragile, or plump. She was never in two places at once; but hitherto she had never been in one place long.

By making this clear to his mind some time before to-day, he had escaped a good deal of ugly self-reproach. It was simply that she who always attracted him, and led him whither she would as by a silken thread, had not remained the occupant of the same fleshly tabernacle in her career so far. Whether she would ultimately settle down to one he could not say.

Had he felt that she was becoming manifest in Avice, he would have tried to believe that this was the terminal spot of her migrations, and have been content to abide by his words. But did he see the Well-Beloved in Avice at all? The question was somewhat disturbing.

He had reached the brow of the hill, and descended towards the village, where in the long straight Roman street he soon found the lighted hall. The performance was not yet over; and by going round to the side of the building and standing on a mound he could see the interior as far down as the platform level. Avice's turn, or second turn, came on almost immediately. Her pretty embarrassment on facing the audience rather won him away from his doubts. She was, in truth, what is called a 'nice' girl; attractive, certainly, but above all things nice—one of the class with whom the risks of matrimony approximate most nearly to zero. Her intelligent eyes, her broad forehead, her thoughtful carriage, ensured one thing, that of all the girls he had known he had never met one with more charming and solid qualities than Avice Caro's. This was not a mere conjecture—he had known her long and thoroughly; her every mood and temper.

A heavy wagon passing without drowned her small soft voice for him; but the audience were pleased, and she blushed at their applause. He now took his station at the door, and when the people had done pouring out he found her within awaiting him.

They climbed homeward slowly by the Old Road, Pierston dragging himself up the steep by the wayside hand-rail and pulling Avice after him upon his arm. At the top they turned and stood still. To the left of them the sky was streaked like a fan with the lighthouse rays, and under their front, at periods of a quarter of a minute, there arose a deep, hollow stroke like the single beat of a drum, the intervals being filled with a long-drawn rattling, as of bones between huge canine jaws. It came from the vast concave of Deadman's Bay, rising and falling against the pebble dyke.

The evening and night winds here were, to Pierston's mind, charged with a something that did not burden them elsewhere. They brought it up from that sinister Bay to the west, whose movement she and he were hearing now. It was a presence—an imaginary shape or essence from the human multitude lying below: those who had gone down in vessels of war, East Indiamen, barges, brigs, and ships of the Armada—select people, common, and debased, whose interests and hopes had been as wide asunder as the poles, but who had rolled each other to oneness on that restless sea-bed. There could almost be felt the brush of their huge composite ghost as it ran a shapeless figure over the isle, shrieking for some good god who would disunite it again.

The twain wandered a long way that night amid these influences—so far as to the old Hope Churchyard, which lay in a ravine formed by a landslip ages ago. The church had slipped down with the rest of the cliff, and had long been a ruin. It seemed to say that in this last local stronghold of the Pagan divinities, where Pagan customs lingered yet, Christianity had established itself precariously at best. In that solemn spot Pierston kissed her.

The kiss was by no means on Avice's initiative this time. Her former demonstrativeness seemed to have increased her present reserve.

That day was the beginning of a pleasant month passed mainly in each other's society. He found that she could not only recite poetry at intellectual gatherings, but play the piano fairly, and sing to her own accompaniment.

He observed that every aim of those who had brought her up had been to get her away mentally as far as possible from her natural and individual life as an inhabitant of a peculiar island: to make her an exact copy of tens of thousands of other people, in whose circumstances there was nothing special, distinctive, or picturesque; to teach her to forget all the experiences of her ancestors; to drown the local ballads by songs purchased at the Budmouth fashionable music-sellers', and the local vocabulary by a governess-tongue of no country at all. She lived in a house that would have been the fortune of an artist, and learnt to draw London suburban villas from printed copies.

Avice had seen all this before he pointed it out, but, with a girl's tractability, had acquiesced. By constitution she was local to the bone, but she could not escape the tendency of the age.

The time for Jocelyn's departure drew near, and she looked forward to it sadly, but serenely, their engagement being now a settled thing. Pierston thought of the native custom on such occasions, which had prevailed in his and her family for centuries, both being of the old stock of the isle. The influx of 'kimberlins,' or 'foreigners' (as strangers from the mainland of Wessex were called), had led in a large measure to its discontinuance; but underneath the veneer of Avice's education many an old-fashioned idea lay slumbering, and he wondered if, in her natural melancholy at his leaving, she regretted the changing manners which made unpopular the formal ratification of a betrothal, according to the precedent of their sires and grandsires.

THE APPOINTMENT

I.—iii.

'WELL,' said he, 'here we are, arrived at the fag-end of my
holiday. What a pleasant surprise my old home, which I
have not thought worth coming to see for three or four
years, had in store for me!'

'You must go to-morrow?' she asked uneasily.

'Yes.'

Something seemed to overweigh them; something more
than the natural sadness of a parting which was not to be
long; and he decided that instead of leaving in the daytime
as he had intended, he would defer his departure till night,
and go by the mail-train from Budmouth. This would give
him time to look into his father's quarries, and enable her,
if she chose, to walk with him along the beach as far as to
Henry the Eighth's Castle above the sands, where they
could linger and watch the moon rise over the sea. She said
she thought she could come.

So after spending the next day with his father in the
quarries Jocelyn prepared to leave, and at the time appointed set out from the stone house of his birth in this stone
isle to walk to Budmouth-Regis by the path along the
beach, Avice having some time earlier gone down to see
some friends in the Street of Wells, which was halfway
towards the spot of their tryst. The descent soon brought
him to the pebble bank, and leaving behind him the last
houses of the isle, and the ruins of the village destroyed by
the November gale of 1824, he struck out along the narrow
thread of land. When he had walked a hundred yards he
stopped, turned aside to the pebble ridge which walled out
the sea, and sat down to wait for her.

Between him and the lights of the ships riding at anchor
in the roadstead two men passed slowly in the direction he
intended to pursue. One of them recognized Jocelyn, and
bade him good-night, adding, 'Wish you joy, sir, of your
choice, and hope the wedden will be soon?'

'Thank you, Seaborn. Well—we shall see what Christmas will do towards bringing it about.'

'My wife opened upon it this mornen: "Please God, I'll up and see that there wedden," says she, "knowing 'em both from their crawling days." '

The men moved on, and when they were out of Pierston's hearing the one who had not spoken said to his friend, 'Who was that young kimberlin? He don't seem one o' we.'

'O, he is, though, every inch o' en. He's Mr. Jocelyn Pierston, the stwone-merchant's only son up at East Quarriers. He's to be married to a stylish young body; her mother, a widow woman, carries on the same business as well as she can; but their trade is not a twentieth part of Pierston's. He's worth thousands and thousands, they say, though 'a do live on in the same wold way up in the same wold house. This son is doen great things in London as a' image-carver; and I can mind when, as a boy, 'a first took to carving soldiers out o' bits o' stwone from the softbed of his father's quarries; and then 'a made a set o' stwonen chess-men, and so 'a got on. He's quite the gent in London, they tell me; and the wonder is that 'a cared to come back here and pick up little Avice Caro—nice maid as she is notwithstanding. . . . Hullo! there's to be a change in the weather soon.'

Meanwhile the subject of their remarks waited at the appointed place till seven o'clock, the hour named between himself and his affianced, had struck. Almost at the moment he saw a figure coming forward from the last lamp at the bottom of the hill. But the figure speedily resolved itself into that of a boy, who, advancing to Jocelyn, inquired if he were Mr. Pierston, and handed him a note.

A LONELY PEDESTRIAN

I.–iv.

WHEN the boy had gone Jocelyn retraced his steps to the last lamp, and read, in Avice's hand:

MY DEAREST—I shall be sorry if I grieve you at all in what I am going to say about our arrangement to meet tonight in the Sandsfoot ruin. But I have fancied that my seeing you again and again lately is inclining your father to insist, and you as his heir to feel, that we ought to carry out Island Custom in our courting—your people being such old inhabitants in an unbroken line. Truth to say, mother supposes that your father, for natural reasons, may have hinted to you that we ought. Now, the thing is contrary to my feelings: it is nearly left off; and I do not think it good, even where there is property, as in your case, to justify it, in a measure. I would rather trust in Providence.

On the whole, therefore, it is best that I should not come—if only for appearances—and meet you at a time and place suggesting the custom, to others than ourselves, at least, if known.

I am sure that this decision will not disturb you much; that you will understand my modern feelings, and think no worse of me for them. And dear, if it were to be done, and we were unfortunate in the result, we might both have enough old family feeling to think, like our forefathers, and possibly your father, that we could not marry honourably; and hence we might be made unhappy.

However, you will come again shortly, will you not, dear Jocelyn?—and then the time will soon draw on when no more good-byes will be required.—Always and ever yours,

AVICE

Jocelyn, having read the letter, was surprised at the naïveté it showed, and at Avice and her mother's antiquated simplicity in supposing that to be still a grave and operating principle which was a bygone barbarism to himself and other absentees from the island. His father, as a money-maker, might have practical wishes on the matter of descendants which lent plausibility to the conjecture of Avice and her mother; but to Jocelyn he had never expressed himself in favour of the ancient ways, old-fashioned as he was.

Amused therefore at her regard of herself as modern, Jocelyn was disappointed, and a little vexed, that such an unforeseen reason should have deprived him of her company. How the old ideas survived under the new education!

The reader is asked to remember that the date, though recent in the history of the Isle of Slingers, was more than forty years ago.

Finding that the evening seemed louring, yet indisposed to go back and hire a vehicle, he went on quickly alone. In such an exposed spot the night wind was gusty, and the sea behind the pebble barrier kicked and flounced in complex rhythms, which could be translated equally well as shocks of battle or shouts of thanksgiving.

Presently on the pale road before him he discerned a figure, the figure of a woman. He remembered that a woman passed him while he was reading Avice's letter by the last lamp, and now he was overtaking her.

He did hope for a moment that it might be Avice, with a changed mind. But it was not she, nor anybody like her. It was a taller, squarer form than that of his betrothed, and although the season was only autumn she was wrapped in furs, or in thick and heavy clothing of some kind.

He soon advanced abreast of her, and could get glimpses of her profile against the roadstead lights. It was dignified, arresting, that of a very Juno. Nothing more classical had he ever seen. She walked at a swinging pace, yet with such ease and power that there was but little difference in their rate of speed for several minutes; and during this time he regarded and conjectured. However, he was about to pass her by when she suddenly turned and addressed him.

'Mr. Pierston, I think, of East Quarriers?'

He assented, and could just discern what a handsome, commanding, imperious face it was—quite of a piece with the proud tones of her voice. She was a new type altogether in his experience; and her accent was not so local as Avice's.

'Can you tell me the time, please?'

He looked at his watch by the aid of a light, and in telling her that it was a quarter past seven observed, by the momentary gleam of his match, that her eyes looked a little red and chafed, as if with weeping.

'Mr Pierston, will you forgive what will appear very strange to you, I dare say? That is, may I ask you to lend me some money for a day or two? I have been so foolish as to leave my purse on the dressing-table.'

It did appear strange: and yet there were features in the young lady's personality which assured him in a moment that she was not an impostor. He yielded to her request, and put his hand in his pocket. Here it remained for a moment. How much did she mean by the words 'some money'? The Junonian quality of her form and manner made him throw himself by an impulse into harmony with her, and he responded regally. He scented a romance. He handed her five pounds.

His munificence caused her no apparent surprise. 'It is quite enough, thank you,' she remarked quietly, as he announced the sum, lest she should be unable to see it for herself.

While overtaking and conversing with her he had not observed that the rising wind, which had proceeded from puffing to growling, and from growling to screeching, with the accustomed suddenness of its changes here, had at length brought what it promised by these vagaries—rain. The drops, which had at first hit their left cheeks like the pellets of a popgun, soon assumed the character of a raking fusillade from the bank adjoining, one shot of which was sufficiently smart to go through Jocelyn's sleeve. The tall girl turned, and seemed to be somewhat concerned at an onset which she had plainly not foreseen before her starting.

'We must take shelter,' said Jocelyn.

'But where?' said she.

To windward was the long, monotonous bank, too obtusely piled to afford a screen, over which they could hear the canine crunching of pebbles by the sea without; on their right stretched the inner bay or roadstead, the distant riding-lights of the ships now dim and glimmering; behind them a faint spark here and there in the lower sky showed where the island rose; before there was nothing definite, and could be nothing, till they reached a precarious wood bridge, a mile further on, Henry the Eighth's Castle being a little further still.

But just within the summit of the bank, whither it had apparently been hauled to be out of the way of the waves, was one of the local boats called lerrets, bottom upwards. As soon as they saw it the pair ran up the pebbly slope towards it by a simultaneous impulse. They then perceived that it had lain there a long time, and were comforted to find it capable of affording more protection than anybody would have expected from a distant view. It formed a shelter or store for the fishermen, the bottom of the lerret being tarred as a roof. By creeping under the bows, which overhung the bank on props to leeward, they made their way within, where, upon some thwarts, oars, and other fragmentary woodwork, lay a mass of dry netting—a whole seine. Upon this they scrambled and sat down, through inability to stand upright.

A CHARGE

I.–v.

THE rain fell upon the keel of the old lerret like corn thrown in handfuls by some colossal sower, and darkness set in to its full shade.

They crouched so close to each other that he could feel her furs against him. Neither had spoken since they left the roadway till she said, with attempted unconcern: 'This is unfortunate.'

He admitted that it was, and found, after a few further remarks had passed, that she certainly had been weeping, there being a suppressed gasp of passionateness in her utterance now and then.

'It is more unfortunate for you, perhaps, than for me,' he said, 'and I am very sorry that it should be so.'

She replied nothing to this, and he added that it was rather a desolate place for a woman, alone and afoot. . . . He hoped nothing serious had happened to drag her out at such an untoward time.

At first she seemed not at all disposed to show any candour on her own affairs, and he was left to conjecture as to her history and name, and how she could possibly have known him. But, as the rain gave not the least sign of cessation, he observed: 'I think we shall have to go back.'

'Never!' said she, and the firmness with which she closed her lips was audible in the word.

'Why not?' he inquired.

'There are good reasons.'

'I cannot understand how you should know me, while I have no knowledge of you.'

'O but you know me—about me, at least.'

'Indeed I don't. How should I? You are a kimberlin.'

'I am not. I am a real islander—or was, rather. . . . Haven't you heard of the Best-Bed Stone Company?'

'I should think so! They tried to ruin my father by

getting away his trade—or, at least, the founder of the company did—old Bencomb.'

'He's my father!'

'Indeed. I am sorry I should have spoken so disrespect-fully of him, for I never knew him personally. After mak-ing over his large business to the company, he retired, I believe, to London?'

'Yes. Our house, or rather his, not mine, is at South Kensington. We have lived there for years. But we have been tenants of Sylvania Castle, on the island here, this season. We took it for a month or two of the owner, who is away.'

'Then I have been staying quite near you, Miss Ben-comb. My father's is a comparatively humble residence hard by.'

'But he could afford a much bigger one if he chose.'

'You have heard so? I don't know. He doesn't tell me much of his affairs.'

'My father,' she burst out suddenly, 'is always scolding me for my extravagance! And he has been doing it to-day more than ever. He said I go shopping in town to simply a diabolical extent, and exceed my allowance!'

'Was that this evening?'

'Yes. And then it reached such a storm of passion bet-ween us that I pretended to retire to my room for the rest of the evening, but I slipped out; and I am never going back home again.'

'What will you do?'

'I shall go first to my aunt in London; and if she won't have me, I'll work for a living. I have left my father for ever! What I should have done if I had not met you I can-not tell—I must have walked all the way to London, I sup-pose. Now I shall take the train as soon as I reach the mainland.'

'If you ever do in this hurricane.'

'I must sit here till it stops.'

And there on the nets they sat. Pierston knew of old Bencomb as his father's bitterest enemy, who had made a great fortune by swallowing up the small stone-merchants, but had found Jocelyn's sire a trifle too big to digest—the latter being, in fact, the chief rival of the Best-Bed Company to that day. Jocelyn thought it strange that he should be thrown by fate into a position to play the son of the Montagues to this daughter of the Capulets.

As they talked there was a mutual instinct to drop their voices, and on this account the roar of the storm necessitated their drawing quite close together. Something tender came into their tones as quarter-hour after quarter-hour went on, and they forgot the lapse of time. It was quite late when she started up, alarmed at her position.

'Rain or no rain, I can stay no longer,' she said.

'Do come back,' said he, taking her hand. 'I'll return with you. My train has gone.'

'No; I shall go on, and get a lodging in Budmouth town, if ever I reach it.'

'It is so late that there will be no house open, except a little place near the station where you won't care to stay. However, if you are determined I will show you the way. I cannot leave you. It would be too awkward for you to go there alone.'

She persisted, and they started through the twanging and spinning storm. The sea rolled and rose so high on their left, and was so near them on their right, that it seemed as if they were traversing its bottom like the Children of Israel. Nothing but the frail bank of pebbles divided them from the raging gulf without, and at every bang of the tide against it the ground shook, the shingle clashed, the spray rose vertically, and was blown over their heads. Quantities of sea-water trickled through the pebble wall, and ran in rivulets across their path to join the sea within. The 'Island' was an island still.

They had not realized the force of the elements till now. Pedestrians had often been blown into the sea hereabout, and drowned, owing to a sudden breach in the bank; which, however, had something of a supernatural power in being able to close up and join itself together again after such disruption, like Satan's form when, cut in two by the sword of Michael,

'The ethereal substance closed,
      Not long divisible.'

Her clothing offered more resistance to the wind than
his, and she was consequently in the greater danger. It was
impossible to refuse his proffered aid. First he gave his
arm, but the wind tore them apart as easily as coupled
cherries. He steadied her bodily by encircling her waist
with his arm; and she made no objection.

Somewhere about this time—it might have been sooner,
it might have been later—he became conscious of a sensation which, in its incipient and unrecognized form, had
lurked within him from some unnoticed moment when he
was sitting close to his new friend under the lerret. Though
a young man, he was too old a hand not to know what this
was, and felt alarmed—even dismayed. It meant a possible
migration of the Well-Beloved. The thing had not, however, taken place; and he went on thinking how soft and
warm the lady was in her fur covering, as he held her so
tightly; the only dry spots in the clothing of either being
her left side and his right, where they excluded the rain by
their mutual pressure.

As soon as they had crossed the ferry-bridge there was
a little more shelter, but he did not relinquish his hold till
she requested him. They passed the ruined castle, and having left the island far behind them trod mile after mile till
they drew near to the outskirts of the neighbouring
watering-place. Into it they plodded without pause, crossing the harbour bridge about midnight, wet to the skin.

He pitied her, and, while he wondered at it, admired her
determination. The houses facing the bay now sheltered
them completely, and they reached the vicinity of the
new railway terminus (which the station was at this date)
without difficulty. As he had said, there was only one
house open hereabout, a little temperance inn, where the
people stayed up for the arrival of the morning mail and
passengers from the Channel boats. Their application for
admission led to the withdrawal of a bolt, and they stood
within the gaslight of the passage.

He could see now that though she was such a fine figure, quite as tall as himself, she was but in the bloom of young womanhood. Her face was certainly striking, though rather by its imperiousness than its beauty; and the beating of the wind and rain and spray had inflamed her cheeks to peony hues.

She persisted in the determination to go on to London by an early morning train, and he therefore offered advice on lesser matters only. 'In that case,' he said, 'you must go up to your room and send down your things, that they may be dried by the fire immediately, or they will not be ready. I will tell the servant to do this, and send you up something to eat.'

She assented to his proposal, without, however, showing any marks of gratitude; and when she had gone Pierston despatched her the light supper promised by the sleepy girl who was 'night porter' at this establishment. He felt ravenously hungry himself, and set about drying his clothes as well as he could, and eating at the same time.

At first he was in doubt what to do, but soon decided to stay where he was till the morrow. By the aid of some temporary wraps, and some slippers from the cupboard, he was contriving to make himself comfortable when the maid-servant came downstairs with a damp armful of woman's raiment.

Pierston withdrew from the fire. The maid-servant knelt down before the blaze and held up with extended arms one of the habiliments of the Juno upstairs, from which a cloud of steam began to rise. As she knelt, the girl nodded forward, recovered herself, and nodded again.

'You are sleepy, my girl,' said Pierston.

'Yes, sir; I have been up a long time. When nobody comes I lie down on the couch in the other room.'

'Then I'll relieve you of that; go and lie down in the other room, just as if we were not here. I'll dry the clothing and put the articles here in a heap, which you can take up to the young lady in the morning.'

The 'night porter' thanked him and left the room, and he soon heard her snoring from the adjoining apartment.

Then Jocelyn opened proceedings, overhauling the robes and extending them one by one. As the steam went up he fell into a reverie. He again became conscious of the change which had been initiated during the walk. The Well-Beloved was moving house—had gone over to the wearer of this attire.

In the course of ten minutes he adored her.

And how about little Avice Caro? He did not think of her as before.

He was not sure that he had ever seen the real Beloved in that friend of his youth, solicitous as he was for her welfare. But, loving her or not, he perceived that the spirit, emanation, idealism, which called itself his Love was flitting stealthily from some remoter figure to the near one in the chamber overhead.

Avice had not kept her engagement to meet him in the lonely ruin, fearing her own imaginings. But he, in fact, more than she, had been educated out of the island innocence that had upheld old manners; and this was the strange consequence of Avice's misapprehension.

ON THE BRINK

I.–vi.

MISS BENCOMB was leaving the hotel for the railway, which was quite near at hand, and had only recently been opened, as if on purpose for this event. At Jocelyn's suggestion she wrote a message to inform her father that she had gone to her aunt's, with a view to allaying anxiety and deterring pursuit. They walked together to the platform and bade each other goodbye; each obtained a ticket independently, and Jocelyn got his luggage from the cloakroom.

On the platform they encountered each other again, and there was a light in their glances at each other which said, as by a flash-telegraph: 'We are bound for the same town, why not enter the same compartment?'

They did.

She took a corner seat, with her back to the engine; he sat opposite. The guard looked in, thought they were lovers, and did not show other travellers into that compartment. They talked on strictly ordinary matters; what she thought he did not know, but at every stopping station he dreaded intrusion. Before they were halfway to London the event he had just begun to realize was a patent fact. The Beloved was again embodied; she filled every fibre and curve of this woman's form.

Drawing near the great London station was like drawing near Doomsday. How should he leave her in the turmoil of a crowded city street? She seemed quite unprepared for the rattle of the scene. He asked her where her aunt lived.

'Bayswater,' said Miss Bencomb.

He called a cab, and proposed that she should share it till they arrived at her aunt's, whose residence lay not much out of the way to his own. Try as he would he could not ascertain if she understood his feelings, but she assented to his offer and entered the vehicle.

'We are old friends,' he said, as they drove onward.

'Indeed, we are,' she answered, without smiling.

'But hereditarily we are mortal enemies, dear Juliet.'

'Yes—— What did you say?'

'I said Juliet.'

She laughed in a half-proud way, and murmured: 'Your father is my father's enemy, and my father is mine. Yes, it is so.' And then their eyes caught each other's glance. 'My queenly darling!' he burst out; 'instead of going to your aunt's, will you come and marry me?'

A flush covered her over, which seemed akin to a flush of rage. It was not exactly that, but she was excited. She did not answer, and he feared he had mortally offended her dignity. Perhaps she had only made use of him as a convenient aid to her intentions. However, he went on—

'Your father would not be able to reclaim you, then? After all, this is not so precipitate as it seems. You know all about me, my history, my prospects. I know all about you. Our families have been neighbours on that isle for hundreds of years, though you are now such a London product.'

'Will you ever be a Royal Academician?' she asked musingly, her excitement having calmed down.

'I hope to be—I *will* be, if you will be my wife.'

His companion looked at him long.

'Think what a short way out of your difficulty this would be,' he continued. 'No bother about aunts, no fetching home by an angry father.'

It seemed to decide her. She yielded to his embrace.

'How long will it take to marry?' Miss Bencomb asked by-and-by, with obvious self-repression.

'We could do it to-morrow. I could get to Doctors' Commons by noon to-day, and the licence would be ready by to-morrow morning.'

'I won't go to my aunt's: I will be an independent woman! I have been reprimanded as if I were a child of six. I'll be your wife if it is as easy as you say.'

They stopped the cab while they held a consultation. Pierston had rooms and a studio in the neighbourhood of Campden Hill; but it would be hardly desirable to take her thither till they were married. They decided to go to an hotel.

Changing their direction, therefore, they went back to the Strand, and soon ensconced themselves in one of the venerable old taverns of Covent Garden, a precinct which in those days was frequented by West-country people. Jocelyn then left her and proceeded on his errand eastward.

It was about three o'clock when, having arranged all preliminaries necessitated by this sudden change of front, he began strolling slowly back; he felt bewildered, and to walk was a relief. Gazing occasionally into this shop window and that, he called a hansom as by an inspiration, and directed the driver to 'Mellstock Gardens.' Arrived here he rang the bell of a studio, and in a minute or two it was answered by a young man in shirt-sleeves, about his own age, with a great smeared palette on his left thumb.

'O, you, Pierston! I thought you were in the country. Come in. I'm awfully glad of this. I am here in town finishing off a painting for an American, who wants to take it back with him.'

Pierston followed his friend into the painting-room, where a pretty young woman was sitting sewing. At a signal from the painter she disappeared without speaking.

'I can see from your face you have something to say; so we'll have it all to ourselves. You are in some trouble? What'll you drink?'

'O! it doesn't matter what, so that it is alcohol in some shape or form. . . . Now, Somers, you must just listen to me, for I *have* something to tell.'

Pierston had sat down in an arm-chair, and Somers had resumed his painting. When a servant had brought in brandy to soothe Pierston's nerves, and soda to take off the injurious effects of the brandy, and milk to take off the depleting effects of the soda, Jocelyn began his narrative, addressing it rather to Somers's Gothic chimney-piece, and Somers's Gothic clock, and Somers's Gothic rugs, than to Somers himself, who stood at his picture a little behind his friend.

'Before I tell you what has happened to me,' Pierston said, 'I want to let you know the manner of man I am.'

'Lord—I know already.'

'No, you don't. It is a sort of thing one doesn't like to talk of. I lie awake at night thinking about it.'

'No!' said Somers, with more sympathy, seeing that his friend was really troubled.

'I am under a curious curse, or influence. I am posed, puzzled and perplexed by the legerdemain of a creature—a deity rather; by Aphrodite, as a poet would put it, as I should put it myself in marble. . . . But I forget—this is not to be a deprecatory wail, but a defence—a sort of *Apologia pro vitâ meâ.*'

'That's better. Fire away!'

HER EARLIER INCARNATIONS

'YOU, Somers, are not, I know, one of those who continue to indulge in the world-wide, fond superstition that the Beloved One of any man always, or even usually, cares to remain in one corporeal nook or shell for any great length of time, however much he may wish her to do so. If I am wrong, and you do still hold to that ancient error—well, my story will seem rather queer.'

'Suppose you say the Beloved of some men, not of any man.'

'All right—I'll say one man, this man only, if you are so particular. We are a strange, visionary race down where I come from, and perhaps that accounts for it. The Beloved of this one man, then, has had many incarnations—too many to describe in detail. Each shape, or embodiment, has been a temporary residence only, which she has entered, lived in awhile, and made her exit from, leaving the substance, so far as I have been concerned, a corpse, worse luck! Now, there is no spiritualistic nonsense in this—it is simple fact, put in the plain form that the conventional public are afraid of. So much for the principle.'

'Good. Go on.'

'Well; the first embodiment of her occurred, so nearly as I can recollect, when I was about the age of nine. Her vehicle was a little blue-eyed girl of eight or so, one of a family of eleven, with flaxen hair about her shoulders, which attempted to curl, but ignominiously failed, hanging like chimney-crooks only. This defect used rather to trouble me; and was, I believe, one of the main reasons of my Beloved's departure from that tenement. I cannot remember with any exactness when the departure occurred. I know it was after I had kissed my little friend in a garden-seat on a hot noontide, under a blue gingham umbrella, which we had opened over us as we sat, that passers through East Quarriers might not observe our marks of affection, forgetting that our screen must attract more attention than our persons.

'When the whole dream came to an end through her father leaving the island, I thought my Well-Beloved had gone for ever (being then in the unpractised condition of Adam at sight of the first sunset). But she had not. Laura had gone for ever, but not my Beloved.

'For some months after I had done crying for the flaxen-haired edition of her, my Love did not reappear. Then she came suddenly, unexpectedly, in a situation I should never have predicted. I was standing on the kerbstone of the pavement in Budmouth-Regis, outside the Preparatory School, looking across towards the sea, when a middle-aged gentleman on horseback, and beside him a young lady, also mounted, passed down the street. The girl turned her head, and—possibly because I was gaping at her in awkward admiration, or smiling myself—smiled at me. Having ridden a few paces, she looked round again and smiled.

'It was enough, more than enough, to set me on fire. I understood in a moment the information conveyed to me by my emotion—the Well-Beloved had reappeared. This second form in which it had pleased her to take up her abode was quite a grown young woman's, darker in complexion than the first. Her hair, also worn in a knot, was of an ordinary brown, and so, I think, were her eyes, but the niceties of her features were not to be gathered so cursorily. However, there sat my coveted one, re-embodied; and, bidding my schoolmates a hasty farewell as soon as I could do so without suspicion, I hurried along the Esplanade in the direction she and her father had ridden. But they had put their horses to a canter, and I could not see which way they had gone. In the greatest misery I turned down a side street, but was soon elevated to a state of excitement by seeing the same pair galloping towards me. Flushing up to my hair, I stopped and heroically faced her as she passed. She smiled again, but, alas! upon my Love's cheek there was no blush of passion for me.'

Pierston paused, and drank from his glass, as he lived for a brief moment in the scene he had conjured up. Somers reserved his comments, and Jocelyn continued—

'That afternoon I idled about the streets, looking for her in vain. When I next saw one of the boys who had been with me at her first passing I stealthily reminded him of the incident, and asked if he knew the riders.

' "O yes," he said. "That was Colonel Targe and his daughter Elsie."

' "How old do you think she is?" said I, a sense of disparity in our ages disturbing my mind.

' "O—nineteen, I think they say. She's going to be married the day after to-morrow to Captain Popp, of the 501st, and they are ordered off to India at once."

The grief which I experienced at this intelligence was such that at dusk I went away to the edge of the harbour, intending to put an end to myself there and then. But I had been told that crabs had been found clinging to the dead faces of persons who had fallen in thereabout, leisurely eating them, and the idea of such an unpleasant contingency deterred me. I should state that the marriage of my Beloved concerned me little; it was her departure that broke my heart. I never saw her again.

Though I had already learnt that the absence of the corporeal matter did not involve the absence of the informing spirit, I could scarce bring myself to believe that in this case it was possible for her to return to my view without the form she had last inhabited.

'But she did.

'It was not, however, till after a good space of time, during which I passed through that bearish age in boys, their middle teens, when girls are their especial contempt. I was about seventeen, and was sitting one evening over a cup of tea in a confectioner's at the very same watering-place, when opposite me a lady took her seat with a little girl. We looked at each other awhile, the child made advances, till I said: "She's a good little thing."

The lady assented, and made a further remark.

' "She has the soft fine eyes of her mother," said I.

' "Do you think her eyes are good?" asks the lady, as if she had not heard what she had heard most—the last three words of my opinion.

' "Yes—for copies," said I, regarding her.

'After this we got on very well. She informed me that her husband had gone out in a yacht, and I said it was a pity he didn't take her with him for the airing. She gradually disclosed herself in the character of a deserted young wife, and later on I met her in the street without the child. She was going to the landing-stage to meet her husband, so she told me; but she did not know the way.

'I offered to show her, and did so. I will not go into particulars, but I afterwards saw her several times, and soon discovered that the Beloved (as to whose whereabouts I had been at fault so long) lurked here. Though why she had chosen this tantalizing situation of an inaccessible matron's form when so many others offered, it was beyond me to discover. The whole affair ended innocently enough, when the lady left the town with her husband and child: she seemed to regard our acquaintance as a flirtation; yet it was anything but a flirtation for me!

'Why should I tell the rest of the tantalizing tale! After this, the Well-Beloved put herself in evidence with greater and greater frequency, and it would be impossible for me to give you details of her various incarnations. She came nine times in the course of the two or three ensuing years. Four times she masqueraded as a brunette, twice as a pale-haired creature, and two or three times under a complexion neither light nor dark. Sometimes she was a tall, fine girl, but more often, I think, she preferred to slip into the skin of a lithe airy being, of no great stature. I grew so accustomed to these exits and entrances that I resigned myself to them quite passively, talked to her, kissed her, corresponded with her, ached for her, in each of her several guises. So it went on until a month ago. And then for the first time I was puzzled. She either had, or she had not, entered the person of Avice Caro, a young girl I had known from infancy. Upon the whole, I have decided that, after all, she did not enter the form of Avice Caro, because I retain so great a respect for her still.'

Pierston here gave in brief the history of his revived

comradeship with Avice, the verge of the engagement to which they had reached, and its unexpected rupture by him, merely through this meeting with a woman into whom the Well-Beloved unmistakably moved under his very eyes—by name Miss Marcia Bencomb. He described their spontaneous decision to marry off-hand; and then he put it to Somers whether he ought to marry or not—her or anybody else—in such circumstances.

'Certainly not,' said Somers. 'Though, if anybody, little Avice. But not even her. You are like other men, only rather worse. Essentially, all men are fickle, like you; but not with such perceptiveness.'

'Surely fickle is not the word? Fickleness means getting weary of a thing while the thing remains the same. But I have always been faithful to the elusive creature whom I have never been able to get a firm hold of, unless I have done so now. And let me tell you that her flitting from each to each individual has been anything but a pleasure for me—certainly not a wanton game of my instigation. To see the creature who has hitherto been perfect, divine, lose under your very gaze the divinity which has informed her, grow commonplace, turn from flame to ashes, from a radiant vitality to a relic, is anything but a pleasure for any man, and has been nothing less than a racking spectacle to my sight. Each mournful emptied shape stands ever after like the nest of some beautiful bird from which the inhabitant has departed and left it to fill with snow. I have been absolutely miserable when I have looked in a face for her I used to see there, and could see her there no more.'

'You ought not to marry,' repeated Somers.

'Perhaps I oughtn't to! Though poor Marcia will be compromised, I'm afraid, if I don't. . . . Was I not right in saying I am accursed in this thing? Fortunately nobody but myself has suffered on account of it till now. Knowing what to expect, I have seldom ventured on a close acquaintance with any woman, in fear of prematurely driving away the dear one in her; who, however, has in time gone off just the same.'

Pierston soon after took his leave. A friend's advice on such a subject weighs little. He quickly returned to Miss Bencomb.

She was different now. Anxiety had visibly brought her down a notch or two, undone a few degrees of that haughty curl which her lip could occasionally assume. 'How long you have been away!' she said with a show of impatience.

'Never mind, darling. It is all arranged,' said he. 'We shall be able to marry in a few days.'

'Not to-morrow?'

'We can't to-morrow. We have not been here quite long enough.'

'But how did the people at Doctors' Commons know that?'

'Well—I forgot that residence, real or assumed, was necessary, and unfortunately admitted that we had only just arrived.'

'O how stupid! But it can't be helped now. I think, dear, I should have known better, however!'

I.—viii.

THEY lived on at the hotel some days longer, eyed curiously by the chambermaids, and burst in upon every now and then by the waiters as if accidentally. When they were walking together, mostly in back streets for fear of being recognized, Marcia was often silent, and her imperious face looked gloomy.

'Dummy!' he said playfully, on one of these occasions.

'I am vexed that by your admissions at Doctors' Commons you prevented them giving you the licence at once! It is not nice, my living on with you like this!'

'But we are going to marry, dear!'

'Yes,' she murmured, and fell into reverie again. 'What a sudden resolve it was of ours!' she continued. 'I wish I could get my father and mother's consent to our marriage. . . . As we can't complete it for another day or two, a letter might be sent to them and their answer received? I have a mind to write.'

Pierston expressed his doubts of the wisdom of this course, which seemed to make her desire it the more, and the result was a tiff between them. 'Since we are obliged to delay it, I won't marry without their consent!' she cried at last passionately.

'Very well then, dear. Write,' he said.

When they were again indoors she sat down to a note, but after a while threw aside her pen despairingly. 'No: I cannot do it!' she said. 'I can't bend my pride to such a job. Will *you* write for me, Jocelyn?'

'I? I don't see why I should be the one, particularly as I think it premature.'

'But you have not quarrelled with my father as I have done.'

'Well no. But there is a long-standing antagonism, which would make it odd in me to be the writer. Wait till we are married, and then I will write. Not till then.'

'Then I suppose I must. You don't know my father. He might forgive me marrying into any other family without his knowledge, but he thinks yours such a mean one, and so resents the trade rivalry, that he would never pardon till the day of his death my becoming a Pierston secretly. I didn't see it at first.'

This remark caused an unpleasant jar on the mind of Pierston. Despite his independent artistic position in London, he was staunch to the simple old parent who had stubbornly held out for so many years against Bencomb's encroaching trade, and whose money had educated and maintained Jocelyn as an art-student in the best schools. So he begged her to say no more about his mean family, and she silently resumed her letter, giving an address at a post-office that their quarters might not be discovered, at least just yet.

No reply came by return of post; but, rather ominously, some letters for Marcia that had arrived at her father's since her departure were sent on in silence to the address given. She opened them one by one, till on reading the last, she exclaimed, 'Good gracious!' and burst into laughter.

'What is it?' asked Pierston.

Marcia began to read the letter aloud. It came from a faithful lover of hers, a youthful Jersey gentleman, who stated that he was soon going to start for England to claim his darling, according to her plighted word.

She was half risible, half concerned. 'What shall I do?' she said.

'Do? My dear girl, it seems to me that there is only one thing to do, and that a very obvious thing. Tell him as soon as possible that you are just on the point of marriage.'

Marcia thereupon wrote out a reply to that effect, Jocelyn helping her to shape the phrases as gently as possible.

'I repeat' (her letter concluded) 'that I had quite forgotten! I am deeply sorry; but that is the truth. I have told my intended husband everything, and he is looking over my shoulder as I write.'

Said Jocelyn when he saw this set down: 'You might

leave out the last few words. They are rather an extra stab for the poor boy.'

'Stab? It is not that, dear. Why does he want to come bothering me? Jocelyn, you ought to be very proud that I have put you in my letter at all. You said yesterday that I was conceited in declaring I might have married that science-man I told you of. But now you see there was yet another available.'

He, gloomily: 'Well, I don't care to hear about that. To my mind this sort of thing is decidedly unpleasant, though you treat it so lightly.'

'Well,' she pouted, 'I have only done half what you have done!'

'What's that?'

'I have only proved false through forgetfulness, but you have while remembering!'

'O yes; of course you can use Avice Caro as a retort. But don't vex me about her, and make me do such an unexpected thing as regret the falseness.'

She shut her mouth tight, and her face flushed.

The next morning there did come an answer to the letter asking her parents' consent to her union with him; but to Marcia's amazement her father took a line quite other than the one she had expected him to take. Whether she had compromised herself or whether she had not seemed a question for the future rather than the present with him, a native islander, born when old island marriage views prevailed in families; he was fixed in his disapproval of her marriage with a hated Pierston. He did not consent; he would not say more till he could see her: if she had any sense at all she would, if still unmarried, return to the home from which she had evidently been enticed. He would then see what he could do for her in the desperate circumstances she had made for herself; otherwise he would do nothing.

Pierston could not help being sarcastic at her father's evidently low estimate of him and his belongings; and Marcia took umbrage at his sarcasms.

'I am the one deserving of satire if anybody!' she said.

'I begin to feel I was a foolish girl to run away from a father for such a trumpery reason as a little scolding because I had exceeded my allowance.'

'I advised you to go back, Marcie.'

'In a sort of way: not in the right tone. You spoke most contemptuously of my father's honesty as a merchant.'

'I couldn't speak otherwise of him than I did, I'm afraid, knowing what——'

'What have you to say against him?'

'Nothing—to you, Marcie, beyond what is matter of common notoriety. Everybody knows that at one time he made it the business of his life to ruin my father; and the way he alludes to me in that letter shows that his enmity still continues.'

'That miser ruined by an open-handed man like my father!' said she. 'It is like your people's misrepresentations to say that!'

Marcia's eyes flashed, and her face burnt with an angry heat, the enhanced beauty which this warmth might have brought being killed by the rectilinear sternness of countenance that came therewith.

'Marcia—this temper is too exasperating! I could give you every step of the proceeding in detail—anybody could—the getting the quarries one by one, and everything, my father only holding his own by the most desperate courage. There is no blinking facts. Our parents' relations are an ugly fact in the circumstances of us two people who want to marry, and we are just beginning to perceive it; and how we are going to get over it I cannot tell.'

She said steadily: 'I don't think we shall get over it at all!'

'We may not—we may not—altogether,' Pierston murmured, as he gazed at the fine picture of scorn presented by his Juno's classical face and dark eyes.

'Unless you beg my pardon for having behaved so!'

Pierston could not quite bring himself to see that he had behaved badly to his too imperious lady, and declined to ask forgiveness for what he had not done.

She thereupon left the room. Later in the day she

re-entered and broke a silence by saying bitterly: 'I showed temper just now, as you told me. But things have causes, and it is perhaps a mistake that you should have deserted Avice for me. Instead of wedding Rosaline, Romeo must needs go eloping with Juliet. It was a fortunate thing for the affections of those two Veronese lovers that they died when they did. In a short time the enmity of their families would have proved a fruitful source of dissension; Juliet would have gone back to her people, he to his; the subject would have split them as much as it splits us.'

Pierston laughed a little. But Marcia was painfully serious, as he found at tea-time, when she said that since his refusal to beg her pardon she had been thinking over the matter, and had resolved to go to her aunt's after all—at any rate till her father could be induced to agree to their union. Pierston was as chilled by this resolve of hers as he was surprised at her independence in circumstances which usually make women the reverse. But he put no obstacles in her way, and, with a kiss strangely cold after their recent ardour, the Romeo of the freestone Montagues went out of the hotel, to avoid even the appearance of coercing his Juliet of the rival house. When he returned she was gone.

A correspondence began between these too-hastily pledged ones; and it was carried on in terms of serious reasoning upon their awkward situation on account of the family feud. They saw their recent love as what it was:

'Too rash, too unadvised, too sudden;
Too like the lightning . . .'

They saw it with an eye whose calmness, coldness, and, it must be added, wisdom, did not promise well for their reunion.

Their debates were clinched by a final letter from Marcia, sent from no other place than her recently left home in the Isle. She informed him that her father had appeared suddenly at her aunt's, and had induced her to go home with him. She had told her father all the circumstances of their elopement, and what mere accidents had caused it: he had persuaded her on what she had almost been convinced of by their disagreement; that all thought of their marriage should be at least postponed for the present; any awkwardness and even scandal being better than that they should immediately unite themselves for life on the strength of a two or three days' resultless passion, and be the wretched victims of a situation they could never change.

Pierston saw plainly enough that he owed it to her father being a born islander, with all the ancient island notions of matrimony lying underneath his acquired conventions, that the stone-merchant did not immediately insist upon the usual remedy for a daughter's precipitancy in such cases, but preferred to await issues.

But the young man still thought that Marcia herself, when her temper had quite cooled, and she was more conscious of her real position, would return to him, in spite of the family hostility. There was no social reason against such a step. In birth the pair were about on one plane; and though Marcia's family had gained a start in the accumulation of wealth, and in the beginnings of social distinction, which lent colour to the feeling that the advantages of the match would be mainly on one side, Pierston was a sculptor who might rise to fame; so that potentially their marriage could not be considered inauspicious for a woman who, beyond being the probable heiress to a considerable fortune, had no exceptional opportunities.

Thus, though disillusioned, he felt bound in honour to remain on call at his London address as long as there was the slightest chance of Marcia's reappearance, or of the arrival of some message requesting him to join her, that they might, after all, go to the altar together. Yet in the night he seemed to hear sardonic voices, and laughter in the wind at this development of his little romance, and during the slow and colourless days he had to sit and behold the mournful departure of his Well-Beloved from the form he had lately cherished, till she had almost vanished away. The exact moment of her complete withdrawal Pierston knew not, but not many lines of her were longer discernible in Marcia's remembered contours, nor many sounds of her in Marcia's recalled accents. Their acquaintance, though so fervid, had been too brief for such lingering.

There came a time when he learnt, through a trustworthy channel, two pieces of news affecting himself. One was the marriage of Avice Caro with her cousin, the other that the Bencombs had started on a tour round the world, which was to include a visit to a relation of Mr. Bencomb's who was a banker in San Francisco. Since retiring from his former large business the stone-merchant had not known what to do with his leisure, and finding that travel benefited his health he had decided to indulge himself thus. Although he was not so informed, Pierston concluded that Marcia had discovered that nothing was likely to happen as a consequence of their elopement, and that she had accompanied her parents. He was more than ever struck with what this signified—her father's obstinate antagonism to her union with one of his blood and name.

FAMILIAR PHENOMENA
IN THE DISTANCE

I.—ix.

BY degrees Pierston began to trace again the customary lines of his existence; and his profession occupied him much as of old. The next year or two only once brought him tidings, through some residents at his former home, of the movements of the Bencombs. The extended voyage of Marcia's parents had given them quite a zest for other scenes and countries; and it was said that her father, a man still in vigorous health except at brief intervals, was utilizing the outlook which his cosmopolitanism afforded him by investing capital in foreign undertakings. What he had supposed turned out to be true; Marcia was with them; no necessity for joining him had arisen; and thus the separation of himself and his nearly married wife by common consent was likely to be a permanent one.

It seemed as if he would scarce ever again discover the carnate dwelling-place of the haunting minion of his imagination. Having gone so near to matrimony with Marcia as to apply for a licence, he had felt for a long while morally bound to her by the incipient contract, and would not intentionally look about him in search of the vanished Ideality. Thus during the first year of Miss Bencomb's absence, when absolutely bound to keep faith with the elusive one's late incarnation if she should return to claim him, this man of the odd fancy would sometimes tremble at the thought of what would become of his solemn intention if the Phantom were suddenly to disclose herself in an unexpected quarter, and seduce him before he was aware. Once or twice he imagined that he saw her in the distance—at the end of a street, on the far sands of a shore, in a window, in a meadow, at the opposite side of a railway station; but he determinedly turned on his heel, and walked the other way.

During the many uneventful seasons that followed Marcia's stroke of independence (for which he was not without a secret admiration at times), Jocelyn threw into plastic creations that ever-bubbling spring of emotion which, without some conduit into space, will surge upwards and ruin all but the greatest men. It was probably owing to this, certainly not on account of any care or anxiety for such a result, that he was successful in his art, successful by a seemingly sudden spurt, which carried him at one bound over the hindrances of years.

He prospered without effort. He was A.R.A.

But recognitions of this sort, social distinctions, which he had once coveted so keenly, seemed to have no utility for him now. By the accident of being a bachelor, he was floating in society without any soul-anchorage or shrine that he could call his own; and, for want of a domestic centre round which honours might crystallize, they dispersed impalpably without accumulating and adding weight to his material wellbeing.

He would have gone on working with his chisel with just as much zest if his creations had been doomed to meet no mortal eye but his own. This indifference to the popular reception of his dream-figures lent him a curious artistic *aplomb* that carried him through the gusts of opinion without suffering them to disturb his inherent bias.

The study of beauty was his only joy for years onward. In the streets he would observe a face, or a fraction of a face, which seemed to express to a hair's breadth in mutable flesh what he was at that moment wishing to express in durable shape. He would dodge and follow the owner like a detective; in omnibus, in cab, in steam-boat, through crowds, into shops, churches, theatres, public-houses, and slums—mostly, when at close quarters, to be disappointed for his pains.

In these professional beauty-chases he sometimes cast his eye across the Thames to the wharves on the south side, and to that particular one whereat his father's tons of freestone were daily landed from the ketches of the south coast. He could occasionally discern the white blocks lying there, vast cubes so persistently nibbled by his parent from his island rock in the English Channel that it seemed as if in time it would be nibbled all away.

One thing it passed him to understand: on what field of observation the poets and philosophers based their assumption that the passion of love was intensest in youth and burnt lower as maturity advanced. It was possibly because of his utter domestic loneliness that, during the productive interval which followed the first years of Marcia's departure, when he was drifting along from five-and-twenty to eight-and-thirty, Pierston occasionally loved with an ardour—though, it is true, also with a self-control —unknown to him when he was green in judgment.

His whimsical isle-bred fancy had grown to be such an emotion that the Well-Beloved—now again visible—was always existing somewhere near him. For months he would find her on the stage of a theatre: then she would flit away, leaving the poor, empty carcase that had lodged her to mumm on as best it could without her—a sorry lay figure to his eyes, heaped with imperfections and sullied with commonplace. She would reappear, it might be, in an at first unnoticed lady, met at some fashionable evening-party, exhibition, bazaar, or dinner; to flit from her, in turn, after a few months, and stand as a graceful shop-girl at some large drapery warehouse into which he had strayed on an unaccustomed errand. Then she would forsake this figure and redisclose herself in the guise of some popular authoress, piano-player, or fiddleress, at whose shrine he would worship for perhaps a twelvemonth. Once she was a dancing-girl at the Royal Moorish Palace of Varieties, though during her whole continuance at that establishment he never once exchanged a word with her, nor did she first or last ever dream of his existence. He knew that a ten-minutes' conversation in the wings with the substance would send the elusive haunter scurrying fearfully away into some other even less accessible mask-figure.

She was a blonde, a brunette, tall, *petite*, *svelte*, straight-featured, full, curvilinear. Only one quality remained unalterable: her instability of tenure. In Börne's phrase, nothing was permanent in her but change.

'It is odd,' he said to himself, 'that this experience of mine, or idiosyncrasy, or whatever it is, which would be sheer waste of time for other men, creates sober business for me.' For all these dreams he translated into plaster, and found that by them he was hitting a public taste he had never deliberately aimed at, and mostly despised. He was, in short, in danger of drifting away from a solid artistic reputation to a popularity which might possibly be as brief as it would be brilliant and exciting.

'You will be caught some day, my friend,' Somers would occasionally observe to him. 'I don't mean to say entangled in anything discreditable, for I admit that you are in practice as ideal as in theory. I mean the process will be reversed. Some woman, whose Well-Beloved flits about as yours does now, will catch your eye, and you'll stick to her like a limpet, while she follows her Phantom and leaves you to ache as you will.'

'You may be right; but I think you are wrong,' said Pierston. 'As flesh she dies daily, like the Apostle's corporeal self; because when I grapple with the reality she's no longer in it, so that I cannot stick to one incarnation if I would.'

'Wait till you are older,' said Somers.

PART SECOND
A YOUNG MAN OF FORTY

'Since Love will needs that I shall love,
Of very force I must agree:
And since no chance may it remove,
In wealth and in adversity
I shall alway myself apply
To serve and suffer patiently.'

SIR T. WYATT.

THE OLD PHANTOM
BECOMES DISTINCT

II.—i.

IN the course of these long years Pierston's artistic emotions were abruptly suspended by the news of his father's sudden death at Sandbourne, whither the stone-merchant had gone for a change of air by the advice of his physician.

Mr. Pierston, senior, it must be admitted, had been something miserly in his home life, as Marcia had so rashly reminded his son. But he had never stinted Jocelyn. He had been rather a hard taskmaster, though as a paymaster trustworthy; a ready-money man, just and ungenerous. To everyone's surprise, the capital he had accumulated in the stone trade was of large amount for a business so unostentatiously carried on—much larger than Jocelyn had ever regarded as possible. While the son had been modelling and chipping his ephemeral fancies into perennial shapes, the father had been persistently chiselling for half a century at the crude original matter of those shapes, the stern, isolated rock in the Channel; and by the aid of his cranes and pulleys, his trolleys and his boats, had sent off his spoil to all parts of Great Britain. When Jocelyn had wound up everything and disposed of the business, as recommended by his father's will, he found himself enabled to add about eighty thousand pounds to the twelve thousand which he already possessed from professional and other sources.

After arranging for the sale of some freehold properties in the island other than quarries—for he did not intend to reside there—he returned to town. He often wondered what had become of Marcia. He had promised never to trouble her; nor for a whole twenty years had he done so; though he had often sighed for her as a friend of sterling common sense in practical difficulties.

Her parents were, he believed, dead; and she, he knew,

had never gone back to the isle. Possibly she had formed some new tie abroad, and had made it next to impossible to discover her by her old name.

A reposeful time ensued. Almost his first entry into society after his father's death occurred one evening, when, for want of knowing what better to do, he responded to an invitation sent by one of the few ladies of rank whom he numbered among his friends, and set out in a cab for the square wherein she lived during three or four months of the year.

The hansom turned the corner, and he obtained a raking view of the houses along the north side, of which hers was one, with the familiar linkman at the door. There were Chinese lanterns, too, on the balcony. He perceived in a moment that the customary 'small and early' reception had resolved itself on this occasion into something very like great and late. He remembered that there had just been a political crisis, which accounted for the enlargement of the Countess of Channelcliffe's assembly; for hers was one of the neutral or non-political houses at which party politics are more freely agitated than at the professedly party gatherings.

There was such a string of carriages that Pierston did not wait to take his turn at the door, but unobtrusively alighted some yards off and walked forward. He had to pause a moment behind the wall of spectators which barred his way, and as he paused some ladies in white cloaks crossed from their carriages to the door on the carpet laid for the purpose. He had not seen their faces, nothing of them but vague forms, and yet he was suddenly seized with a presentiment. Its gist was that he might be going to re-encounter the Well-Beloved that night: after her recent long hiding she meant to reappear and intoxicate him. That liquid sparkle of her eye, that lingual music, that turn of the head, how well he knew it all, despite the many superficial changes, and how instantly he would recognize it under whatever complexion, contour, accent, height, or carriage that it might choose to masquerade!

Pierston's other conjecture, that the night was to be a

lively political one, received confirmation as soon as he
reached the hall, where a simmer of excitement was
perceptible as surplus or overflow from above down the
staircase—a feature which he had always noticed to be present when any climax or sensation had been reached in the
world of party and faction.

'And where have you been keeping yourself so long,
young man?' said his hostess archly, when he had shaken
hands with her. (Pierston was always regarded as a young
man, though he was now about forty.) 'O yes, of course,
I remember,' she added, looking serious in a moment at
thought of his loss. The Countess was a woman with a
good-natured manner verging on that oft-claimed feminine
quality, humour, and was quickly sympathetic.

She then began to tell him of a scandal in the political
side to which she nominally belonged, one that had come
out of the present crisis; and that, as for herself, she had
sworn to abjure politics for ever on account of it, so that
he was to regard her forthwith as a more neutral
householder than ever. By this time some more people had
surged upstairs, and Pierston prepared to move on.

'You are looking for somebody—I can see that,' said she.

'Yes—a lady,' said Pierston.

'Tell me her name, and I'll try to think if she's here.'

'I cannot; I don't know it,' he said.

'Indeed! What is she like?'

'I cannot describe her, not even her complexion or
dress.'

Lady Channelcliffe looked a pout, as if she thought he
were teasing her, and he moved on in the current. The fact
was that, for a moment, Pierston fancied he had made the
sensational discovery that the One he was in search of
lurked in the person of the very hostess he had conversed
with, who was charming always, and particularly charming to-night; he was just feeling an incipient consternation
at the possibility of such a jade's trick in his Beloved, who
had once before chosen to embody herself as a married
woman, though, happily, at that time with no serious
results. However, he felt that he had been mistaken, and

that the fancy had been solely owing to the highly charged
electric condition in which he had arrived by reason of his
recent isolation.

The whole set of rooms formed one great utterance of
the opinions of the hour. The gods of party were present
with their embattled seraphim, but the brilliancy of manner and form in the handling of public questions was only
less conspicuous than the paucity of original ideas. No
principles of wise government had place in any mind, a
blunt and jolly personalism as to the Ins and Outs
animating all. But Jocelyn's interest did not run in this
stream: he was like a stone in a purling brook, waiting for
some peculiar floating object to be brought towards him
and to stick upon his mental surface.

Thus looking for the next new version of the fair figure,
he did not consider at the moment, though he had done so
at other times, that this presentiment of meeting her was,
of all presentiments, just the sort of one to work out its
own fulfilment.

He looked for her in the knot of persons gathered round
a past Prime Minister who was standing in the middle of
the largest room discoursing in the genial, almost jovial,
manner natural to him at these times. The two or three
ladies forming his audience had been joined by another in
black and white, and it was on her that Pierston's attention
was directed, as well as the great statesman's, whose first
sheer gaze at her, expressing 'Who are you?' almost
audibly, changed into an interested, listening look as the
few words she spoke were uttered—for the Minister differed from many of his standing in being extremely careful
not to interrupt a timid speaker, giving way in an instant
if anybody else began with him. Nobody knew better than
himself that all may learn, and his manner was that of an
unconceited man who could catch an idea readily, even if
he could not undertake to create one.

The lady told her little story—whatever it was Jocelyn
could not hear it—the statesman laughed: 'Haugh-haugh-
haugh!'

The lady blushed. Jocelyn, wrought up to a high tension

by the aforesaid presentiment that his Shelleyan 'One-shape-of-many-names' was about to reappear, paid little heed to the others, watching for a full view of the lady who had won his attention.

That lady remained for the present partially screened by her neighbours. A diversion was caused by Lady Channelcliffe bringing up somebody to present to the ex-Minister; the ladies got mixed, and Jocelyn lost sight of the one whom he was beginning to suspect as the stealthily returned absentee.

He looked for her in a kindly young lady of the house, his hostess's relation, who appeared to more advantage that night than she had ever done before—in a sky-blue dress, which had nothing between it and the fair skin of her neck, lending her an unusually soft and sylph-like aspect. She saw him, and they converged. Her look of 'What do you think of me *now*?' was suggested, he knew, by the thought that the last time they met she had appeared under the disadvantage of mourning clothes, on a wet day in a country-house, where everybody was cross.

'I have some new photographs, and I want you to tell me whether they are good,' she said. 'Mind you are to tell me truly, and no favour.'

She produced the pictures from an adjoining drawer, and they sat down together upon an ottoman for the purpose of examination. The portraits, taken by the last fashionable photographer, were very good, and he told her so; but as he spoke and compared them his mind was fixed on something else than the mere judgment. He wondered whether the elusive one were indeed in the frame of this girl.

He looked up at her. To his surprise, her mind, too, was on other things bent than on the pictures. Her eyes were glancing away to distant people, she was apparently considering the effect she was producing upon them by this cosy tête-à-tête with Pierston, and upon one in particular, a man of thirty, of military appearance, whom Pierston did not know. Quite convinced now that no phantom belonging to him was contained in the outlines of the present young lady, he could coolly survey her as he responded. They were both doing the same thing—each was pretending to be deeply interested in what the other was talking about, the attention of the two alike flitting away to other corners of the room even when the very point of their discourse was pending.

No, he had not seen Her yet. He was not going to see her, apparently, to-night; she was scared away by the twanging political atmosphere. But he still moved on searchingly, hardly heeding certain spectral imps other than Aphroditean, who always haunted these places, and jeeringly pointed out that under the white hair of this or that ribanded old man, with a forehead grown wrinkled over treaties which had swayed the fortunes of Europe, with a voice which had numbered sovereigns among its respectful listeners, might be a heart that would go inside a nut-shell; that beneath this or that white rope of pearl and pink bosom, might lie the half-lung which had, by hook or by crook, to sustain its possessor above-ground till the wedding-day.

At that moment he encountered his amiable host, and almost simultaneously caught sight of the lady who had at first attracted him and then had disappeared. Their eyes met, far off as they were from each other. Pierston laughed inwardly: it was only in ticklish excitement as to whether this was to prove a true *trouvaille*, and with no instinct to mirth; for when under the eyes of his Jill-o'-the-Wisp he was more inclined to palpitate like a sheep in a fair.

However, for the minute he had to converse with his host, Lord Channelcliffe, and almost the first thing that friend said to him was: 'Who is that pretty woman in the black dress with the white fluff about it and the pearl necklace?'

'I don't know,' said Jocelyn, with incipient jealousy: 'I was just going to ask the same thing.'

'O, we shall find out presently, I suppose. I daresay my wife knows.' They had parted, when a hand came upon his shoulder. Lord Channelcliffe had turned back for an instant: 'I find she is the granddaughter of my father's old

friend, the last Lord Hengistbury. Her name is Mrs.——
Mrs. Pine-Avon; she lost her husband two or three years
ago, very shortly after their marriage.'

Lord Channelcliffe became absorbed into some adjoining dignitary of the Church, and Pierston was left to pursue his quest alone. A young friend of his—the Lady
Mabella Buttermead, who appeared in a cloud of muslin
and was going on to a ball—had been brought against him
by the tide. A warm-hearted, emotional girl was Lady
Mabella, who laughed at the humorousness of being alive.
She asked him whither he was bent, and he told her.

'O yes, I know her very well!' said Lady Mabella eagerly.
'She told me one day that she particularly wished to meet
you. Poor thing—so sad—she lost her husband. Well, it
was a long time ago now, certainly. Women ought not to
marry and lay themselves open to such catastrophes,
ought they, Mr. Pierston? *I* never shall. I am determined
never to run such a risk! Now, do you think I shall?'

'Marry? O no; never,' said Pierston drily.

'That's very satisfying.' But Mabella was scarcely comfortable under his answer, even though jestingly returned,
and she added: 'But sometimes I think I may, just for the
fun of it. . . . Now we'll steer across to her, and catch her,
and I'll introduce you. But we shall never get to her at this
rate!'

'Never, unless we adopt "the ugly rush," like the citizens
who follow the Lord Mayor's Show.'

They talked, and inched towards the desired one, who,
as she discoursed with a neighbour, seemed to be of
those—

'Female forms, whose gestures beam with mind,'

seen by the poet in his Vision of the Golden City of Islam.

Their progress was continually checked. Pierston was as
he had sometimes seemed to be in a dream, unable to
advance towards the object of pursuit unless he could have
gathered up his feet into the air. After ten minutes given
to a preoccupied regard of shoulderblades, back hair, glit-
tering headgear, neck-napes, moles, hairpins, pearl-powder,

pimples, minerals cut into facets of many-coloured rays, necklace-clasps, fans, stays, the seven styles of elbow and arm, the thirteen varieties of ear; and by using the toes of his dress-boots as coulters with which he ploughed his way and that of Lady Mabella in the direction they were aiming at, he drew near to Mrs. Pine-Avon, who was drinking a cup of tea in the back drawing-room.

'My dear Nichola, we thought we should never get to you, because it is worse to-night, owing to these dreadful politics! But we've done it.' And she proceeded to tell her friend of Pierston's existence hard by.

It seemed that the widow really did wish to know him, and that Lady Mabella Buttermead had not indulged in one of the too frequent inventions in that kind. When the youngest of the trio had made the pair acquainted with each other she left them to talk to a younger man than the sculptor.

Mrs. Pine-Avon's black velvets and silks, with their white accompaniments, finely set off the exceeding fairness of her neck and shoulders, which, though unwhitened artificially, were without a speck or blemish of the least degree. The gentle, thoughtful creature she had looked from a distance she now proved herself to be; she held also sound rather than current opinions on the plastic arts, and was the first intellectual woman he had seen there that night, except one or two as aforesaid.

They soon became well acquainted, and at a pause in their conversation noticed the fresh excitement caused by the arrival of some late comers with more news. The latter had been brought by a rippling, bright-eyed lady in black, who made the men listen to her, whether they would or no.

'I am glad I am an outsider,' said Jocelyn's acquaintance, now seated on a sofa beside which he was standing. 'I wouldn't be like my cousin, over there, for the world. She thinks her husband will be turned out at the next election, and she's quite wild.'

'Yes; it is mostly the women who are the gamesters; the men only the cards. The pity is that politics are looked on as being a game for politicians, just as cricket is a game for cricketers; not as the serious duties of political trustees.'

'How few of us ever think or feel that "the nation of every country dwells in the cottage," as somebody says!'

'Yes. Though I wonder to hear you quote that.'

'O—I am of no party, though my relations are. There can be only one best course at all times, and the wisdom of the nation should be directed to finding it, instead of zigzagging in two courses, according to the will of the party which happens to have the upper hand.'

Having started thus, they found no difficulty in agreeing on many points. When Pierston went downstairs from that assembly at a quarter to one, and passed under the steaming nostrils of an ambassador's horses to a hansom which waited for him against the railing of the square, he had an impression that the Beloved had re-emerged from the shadows, without any hint or initiative from him—to whom, indeed, such re-emergence was an unquestionably awkward thing.

In this he was aware, however, that though it might be now, as heretofore, the Loved who danced before him, it was the Goddess behind her who pulled the string of that Jumping Jill. He had lately been trying his artist hand again on the Dea's form in every conceivable phase and mood. He had become a one-part man—a presenter of her only. But his efforts had resulted in failures. In her implacable vanity she might be punishing him anew for presenting her so deplorably.

II.—ii.

HE could not forget Mrs. Pine-Avon's eyes, though he remembered nothing of her other facial details. They were round, inquiring, luminous. How that chestnut hair of hers had shone: it required no tiara to set it off, like that of the dowager he had seen there, who had put ten thousand pounds upon her head to make herself look worse than she would have appeared with the ninepenny muslin cap of a servant woman.

Now the question was, ought he to see her again? He had his doubts. But, unfortunately for discretion, just when he was coming out of the rooms he had encountered an old lady of seventy, his friend Mrs. Brightwalton—the Honourable Mrs. Brightwalton—and she had hastily asked him to dinner for the day after the morrow, stating in the honest way he knew so well that she had heard he was out of town, or she would have asked him two or three weeks ago. Now, of all social things that Pierston liked it was to be asked to dinner off-hand, as a stopgap in place of some bishop, earl, or Under-Secretary who couldn't come, and when the invitation was supplemented by the tidings that the lady who had so impressed him was to be one of the guests, he had promised instantly.

At the dinner he took down Mrs. Pine-Avon upon his arm, and talked to nobody else during the meal. Afterwards they kept apart awhile in the drawing-room for form's sake; but eventually gravitated together again, and finished the evening in each other's company. When, shortly after eleven, he came away, he felt almost certain that within those luminous grey eyes the One of his eternal fidelity had verily taken lodgings—and for a long lease. But this was not all. At parting, he had, almost involuntarily, given her hand a pressure of a peculiar and indescribable kind; a little response from her, like a mere pulsation, of the same sort, told him that the impression she had made upon him was reciprocated. She was, in a word, willing to go on.

But was he able?

There had not been much harm in the flirtation thus far; but did she know his history, the curse upon his nature?—that he was the Wandering Jew of the love-world, how restlessly ideal his fancies were, how the artist in him had consumed the wooer, how he was in constant dread lest he should wrong some woman twice as good as himself by seeming to mean what he fain would mean but could not, how useless he was likely to be for practical steps towards householding, though he was all the while pining for domestic life. He was now over forty, she was probably thirty; and he dared not make unmeaning love with the careless selfishness of a younger man. It was unfair to go further without telling her, even though, hitherto, such explicitness had not been absolutely demanded.

He determined to call immediately on the New Incarnation.

She lived not far from the long, fashionable Hamptonshire Square, and he went thither with expectations of having a highly emotional time, at least. But somehow the very bell-pull seemed cold, although she had so earnestly asked him to come.

As the house spoke, so spoke the occupant, much to the astonishment of the sculptor. The doors he passed through seemed as if they had not been opened for a month; and, entering the large drawing-room, he beheld, in an armchair, in the far distance, a lady whom he journeyed across the carpet to reach, and ultimately did reach. To be sure it was Mrs. Nichola Pine-Avon, but frosted over indescribably. Raising her eyes in a slightly inquiring manner from the book she was reading, she leant back in the chair, as if soaking herself in luxurious sensations which had nothing to do with him, and replied to his greeting with a few commonplace words.

The unfortunate Jocelyn, though recuperative to a

degree, was at first terribly upset by this reception. He had distinctly begun to love Nichola, and he felt sick and almost resentful. But happily his affection was incipient as yet, and a sudden sense of the ridiculous in his own position carried him to the verge of risibility during the scene. She signified a chair, and began the critical study of some rings she wore.

They talked over the day's news, and then an organ began to grind outside. The tune was a rollicking air he had heard at some music-hall; and, by way of a diversion, he asked her if she knew the composition.

'No, I don't!' she replied.

'Now, I'll tell you all about it,' said he gravely. 'It is based on a sound old melody called "The Jilt's Hornpipe." Just as they turn Madeira into port in the space of a single night, so this old air has been taken and doctored, and twisted about, and brought out as a new popular ditty.'

'Indeed!'

'If you are in the habit of going much to the music-halls or the burlesque theatres——'

'Yes?'

'You would find this is often done, with excellent effect.'

She thawed a little, and then they went on to talk about her house, which had been newly painted, and decorated with greenish-blue satin up to the height of a person's head—an arrangement that somewhat improved her slightly faded, though still pretty, face, and was helped by the awnings over the windows.

'Yes; I have had my house some years,' she observed complacently, 'and I like it better every year.'

'Don't you feel lonely in it sometimes?'

'O never!'

However, before he rose she grew friendly to some degree, and when he left, just after the arrival of three opportune young ladies, she seemed regretful. She asked him to come again; and he thought he would tell the truth. 'No: I shall not care to come again,' he answered, in a tone inaudible to the young ladies.

She followed him to the door. 'What an uncivil thing to say!' she murmured in surprise.

'It is rather uncivil. Good-bye,' said Pierston.

As a punishment she did not ring the bell, but left him to find his way out as he could. 'Now what the devil this means I cannot tell,' he said to himself, reflecting stock-still for a moment on the stairs. And yet the meaning was staring him in the face.

Meanwhile one of the three young ladies had said, 'What interesting man was that, with his lovely head of hair? I saw him at Lady Channelcliffe's the other night.'

'Jocelyn Pierston.'

'O, Nichola, that *is* too bad! To let him go in that shabby way, when I would have given anything to know him! I have wanted to know him ever since I found out how much his experiences had dictated his statuary, and I discovered them by seeing in a Jersey paper of the marriage of a person supposed to be his wife, who ran off with him many years ago, don't you know, and then wouldn't marry him, in obedience to some novel social principles she had invented for herself.'

'O! didn't he marry her?' said Mrs. Pine-Avon, with a start. 'Why, I heard only yesterday that he did, though they have lived apart ever since.'

'Quite a mistake,' said the young lady. 'How I wish I could run after him!'

But Jocelyn was receding from the pretty widow's house with long strides. He went out very little during the next few days, but about a week later he kept an engagement to dine with Lady Iris Speedwell, whom he never neglected, because she was the brightest hostess in London.

By some accident he arrived rather early. Lady Iris had left the drawing-room for a moment to see that all was right in the dining-room, and when he was shown in there stood alone in the lamplight Nichola Pine-Avon. She had been the first arrival. He had not in the least expected to meet her there, further than that, in a general sense, at Lady Iris's you expected to meet everybody.

She had just come out of the cloak-room, and was so tender and even apologetic that he had not the heart to be other than friendly. As the other guests dropped in, the

pair retreated into a shady corner, and she talked beside
him till all moved off for the eating and drinking.

He had not been appointed to take her across to the
dining-room, but at the table found her exactly opposite.
She looked very charming between the candles, and then
suddenly it dawned upon him that her previous manner
must have originated in some false report about Marcia, of
whose existence he had not heard for years. Anyhow, he
was not disposed to resent an inexplicability in womankind, having found that it usually arose independently of
fact, reason, probability, or his own deserts.

So he dined on, catching her eyes and the few pretty
words she made opportunity to project across the table to
him now and then. He was courteously responsive only,
but Mrs. Pine-Avon herself distinctly made advances. He
re-admired her, while at the same time her conduct in her
own house had been enough to check his confidence—
enough even to make him doubt if the Well-Beloved really
resided within those contours, or had ever been more than
the most transitory passenger through that interesting and
accomplished soul.

He was pondering this question, yet growing decidedly
moved by the playful pathos of her attitude when, by
chance, searching his pocket for his handkerchief,
something crackled, and he felt there an unopened letter,
which had arrived at the moment he was leaving his house,
and he had slipped into his coat to read in the cab as he
drove along. Pierston drew it sufficiently forth to observe
by the post-mark that it came from his natal isle. Having
hardly a correspondent in that part of the world now he
began to conjecture on the possible sender.

The lady on his right, whom he had brought in, was a
leading actress of the town—indeed, of the United
Kingdom and America, for that matter—a creature in airy
clothing, translucent, like a balsam or sea-anemone,
without shadows, and in movement as responsive as some
highly lubricated, many-wired machine, which, if one
presses a particular spring, flies open and reveals its works.
The spring in the present case was the artistic commenda-

tion she deserved—and craved. At this particular moment she was engaged with the man on her own right, a representative of Family, who talked positively and hollowly, as if shouting down a vista of five hundred years from the Feudal past. The lady on Jocelyn's left, wife of a Lord Justice of Appeal, was in like manner talking to her companion on the outer side; so that, for the time, he was left to himself. He took advantage of the opportunity, drew out his letter, and read it as it lay upon his napkin, nobody observing him, so far as he was aware.

It came from the wife of one of his father's former workmen, and was concerning his son, whom she begged Jocelyn to recommend as candidate for some post in town that she wished him to fill. But the end of the letter was what arrested him—

You will be sorry to hear, Sir, that dear little Avice Caro, as we used to call her in her maiden days, is dead. She married her cousin, if you do mind, and went away from here for a good-few years, but was left a widow, and came back a twelvemonth ago; since when she faltered and faltered, and now she is gone.

SHE BECOMES AN
INACCESSIBLE GHOST

II.—iii.

By imperceptible and slow degrees the scene at the dinner-
table receded into the background, behind the vivid
presentment of Avice Caro, and the old, old scenes on Isle
Vindilia which were inseparable from her personality. The
dining-room was real no more, dissolving under the bold
stony promontory and the incoming West Sea. The handsome marchioness in geranium-red and diamonds, who
was visible to him on his host's right hand opposite,
became one of the glowing vermilion sunsets that he had
watched so many times over Deadman's Bay, with the
form of Avice in the foreground. Between his eyes and the
judge who sat next to Nichola, with a chin so raw that he
must have shaved every quarter of an hour during the day,
intruded the face of Avice, as she had glanced at him in
their last parting. The crannied features of the evergreen
society lady, who, if she had been a few years older, would
have been as old-fashioned as her daughter, shaped
themselves to the dusty quarries of his and Avice's parents,
down which he had clambered with Avice hundreds of
times. The ivy trailing about the table-cloth, the lights in
the tall candlesticks, and the bunches of flowers, were
transmuted into the ivies of the cliff-built Castle, the tufts
of seaweed, and the lighthouses on the isle. The salt airs of
the ocean killed the smell of the viands, and instead of the
clatter of voices came the monologue of the tide off the
Beal.

More than all, Nichola Pine-Avon lost the blooming
radiance which she had latterly acquired; she became a
woman of his acquaintance with no distinctive traits; she
seemed to grow material, a superficies of flesh and bone
merely, a person of lines and surfaces; she was a language
in living cipher no more.

When the ladies had withdrawn it was just the same. The soul of Avice—the only woman he had *never* loved of those who had loved him—surrounded him like a firmament. Art drew near to him in the person of one of the most distinguished of portrait painters; but there was only one painter for Jocelyn—his own memory. All that was eminent in European surgery addressed him in the person of that harmless and unassuming fogey whose hands had been inside the bodies of hundreds of living men; but the lily-white corpse of an obscure country-girl chilled the interest of discourse with such a king of operators.

Reaching the drawing-room he talked to his hostess. Though she had entertained three-and-twenty guests at her table that night she had known not only what every one of them was saying and doing throughout the repast, but what every one was thinking. So, being an old friend, she said quietly, 'What has been troubling you? Something has, I know. I have been travelling over your face and have seen it there.'

Nothing could less express the meaning his recent news had for him than a statement of its facts. He told of the opening of the letter and the discovery of the death of an old acquaintance.

'The only woman whom I never rightly valued, I may almost say!' he added; 'and therefore the only one I shall ever regret!'

Whether she considered it a sufficient explanation or not the woman of experiences accepted it as such. She was the single lady of his circle whom nothing erratic in his doings could surprise, and he often gave her stray ends of his confidence thus with perfect safety.

He did not go near Mrs. Pine-Avon again; he could not: and on leaving the house walked abstractedly along the streets till he found himself at his own door. In his room he sat down, and placing his hands behind his head thought his thoughts anew.

At one side of the room stood an escritoire, and from a lower drawer therein he took out a small box tightly nailed down. He forced the cover with the poker. The box

contained a variety of odds and ends, which Pierston had
thrown into it from time to time in past years for future
sorting—an intention that he had never carried out. From
the melancholy mass of papers, faded photographs, seals,
diaries, withered flowers, and such like, Jocelyn drew a little portrait, one taken on glass in the primitive days of
photography, and framed with tinsel in the commonest
way.

It was Avice Caro, as she had appeared during the summer month or two which he had spent with her on the
island twenty years before this time, her young lips pursed
up, her hands meekly folded. The effect of the glass was
to lend to the picture much of the softness characteristic of
the original. He remembered when it was taken—during
one afternoon they had spent together at a neighbouring
watering-place, when he had suggested her sitting to a
touting artist on the sands, there being nothing else for
them to do. A long contemplation of the likeness completed in his emotions what the letter had begun. He loved
the woman dead and inaccessible as he had never loved her
in life. He had thought of her but at distant intervals during the twenty years since that parting occurred, and only
as somebody he could have wedded. Yet now the times of
youthful friendship with her, in which he had learnt every
note of her innocent nature, flamed up into a yearning
and passionate attachment, embittered by regret beyond
words.

That kiss which had offended his dignity, which she
had so childishly given him before her consciousness of
womanhood had been awakened; what he would have
offered to have a quarter of it now!

Pierston was almost angry with himself for his feelings
of this night, so unreasonably, motivelessly strong were
they towards the lost young playmate. 'How senseless of
me!' he said, as he lay in his lonely bed. She had been
another man's wife almost the whole time since he was
estranged from her, and now she was a corpse. Yet the
absurdity did not make his grief the less: and the consciousness of the intrinsic, almost radiant, purity of this

new-sprung affection for a flown spirit forbade him to
check it. The flesh was absent altogether; it was love
rarefied and refined to its highest attar. He had felt nothing
like it before.

The next afternoon he went down to the club; not his
large club, where the men hardly spoke to each other, but
the homely one where they told stories of an afternoon,
and were not ashamed to confess among themselves to
personal weaknesses and follies, knowing well that such
secrets would go no further. But he could not tell this. So
volatile and intangible was the story that to convey it in
words would have been as hard as to cage a perfume.

They observed his altered manner, and said he was in
love. Pierston admitted that he was; and there it ended.
When he reached home he looked out of his bedroom window, and began to consider in what direction from where
he stood that darling little figure lay. It was straight across
there, under the young pale moon. The symbol signified
well. The divinity of the silver bow was not more excel-
lently pure than she, the lost, had been. Under that moon
was the island of Ancient Slingers, and on the island a
house, framed from mullions to chimney-top like the isle
itself, of stone. Inside the window, the moonlight irradiating
her winding-sheet, lay Avice, reached only by the faint
noises inherent in the isle; the tink-tink of the chisels in the
quarries, the surging of the tides in the Bay, and the muffled
grumbling of the currents in the never-pacified Race.

He began to divine the truth. Avice, the departed one,
though she had come short of inspiring a passion, had yet
possessed a ground-quality absent from her rivals, without
which it seemed that a fixed and full-rounded constancy to
a woman could not flourish in him. Like his own, her
family had been islanders for centuries—from Norman,
Anglian, Roman, Balearic-British times. Hence in her
nature, as in his, was some mysterious ingredient sucked
from the isle; otherwise a racial instinct necessary to the
absolute unison of a pair. Thus, though he might never
love a woman of the island race, for lack in her of the
desired refinement, he could not love long a kimberlin—a

woman other than of the island race, for her lack of this groundwork of character.

Such was Pierston's view of things. Another fancy of his, an artist's superstition merely, may be mentioned. The Caros, like some other local families, suggested a Roman lineage, more or less grafted on the stock of the Slingers. Their features recalled those of the Italian peasantry to any one as familiar as he was with them; and there were evidences that the Roman colonists had been populous and long-abiding in and near this corner of Britain. Tradition urged that a temple to Venus once stood at the top of the Roman road leading up into the isle; and possibly one to the love-goddess of the Slingers antedated this. What so natural as that the true star of his soul would be found nowhere but in one of the old island breed?

After dinner his old friend Somers came in to smoke, and when they had talked a little while Somers alluded casually to some place at which they would meet on the morrow.

'I shan't be there,' said Pierston.

'But you promised?'

'Yes. But I shall be at the island—looking at a dead woman's grave.' As he spoke his eyes turned, and remained fixed on a table near. Somers followed the direction of his glance to a photograph on a stand.

'Is that she?' he asked.

'Yes.'

'Rather a bygone affair, then?'

Pierston acknowledged it. 'She's the only sweetheart I ever slighted, Alfred,' he said. 'Because she's the only one I ought to have cared for. That's just the fool I have always been.'

'But if she's dead and buried, you can go to her grave at any time as well as now, to keep up the sentiment.'

'I don't know that she's buried.'

'But to-morrow—the Academy night! Of all days why go then?'

'I don't care about the Academy.'

'Pierston—you are our only inspired sculptor. You are

our Praxiteles, or rather our Lysippus. You are almost the only man of this generation who has been able to mould and chisel forms living enough to draw the idle public away from the popular paintings into the usually deserted Lecture-room, and people who have seen your last pieces of stuff say there has been nothing like them since sixteen hundred and——since the sculptors "of the great race" lived and died—whenever that was. Well, then, for the sake of others you ought not to rush off to that God-forgotten sea-rock just when you are wanted in town, all for a woman you last a saw a hundred years ago.'

'No—it was only nineteen and three quarters,' replied his friend, with abstracted literalness. He went the next morning.

Since the days of his youth a railway had been constructed along the pebble bank, so that, except when the rails were washed away by the tides, which was rather often, the peninsula was quickly accessible. At two o'clock in the afternoon he was rattled along by this new means of locomotion, under the familiar monotonous line of bran-coloured stones, and he soon emerged from the station, which stood as a strange exotic among the black lerrets, the ruins of the washed-away village, and the white cubes of oolite, just come to view after burial through unreckonable geologic years.

In entering upon the pebble beach the train had passed close to the ruins of Henry the Eighth's or Sandsfoot Castle, whither Avice was to have accompanied him on the night of his departure. Had she appeared the primitive betrothal, with its natural result, would probably have taken place; and, as no islander had ever been known to break that compact, she would have become his wife.

Ascending the steep incline to where the quarrymen were chipping just as they had formerly done, and within sound of the great stone saws, he looked southward towards the Beal.

The level line of the sea horizon rose above the surface of the isle, a ruffled patch in mid-distance as usual marking the Race, whence many a Lycidas had gone

'Visiting the bottom of the monstrous world';

but had not been blest with a poet as a friend. Against the stretch of water, where a school of mackerel twinkled in the afternoon light, was defined, in addition to the distant lighthouse, a church with its tower, standing about a quarter of a mile off, near the edge of the cliff. The churchyard gravestones could be seen in profile against the same vast spread of watery babble and unrest.

Among the graves moved the form of a man clothed in a white sheet, which the wind blew and flapped coldly every now and then. Near him moved six men bearing a long box, and two or three persons in black followed. The coffin, with its twelve legs, crawled across the isle, while around and beneath it the flashing lights from the sea and the school of mackerel were reflected; a fishing-boat, far out in the Channel, being momentarily discernible under the coffin also.

The procession wandered round to a particular corner, and halted, and paused there a long while in the wind, the sea behind them, the surplice of the priest still blowing. Jocelyn stood with his hat off: he was present, though he was a quarter of a mile off; and he seemed to hear the words that were being said, though nothing but the wind was audible.

He instinctively knew that it was none other than Avice whom he was seeing interred; *his* Avice, as he now began presumptuously to call her. Presently the little group withdrew from before the sea-shine, and disappeared.

He felt himself unable to go further in that direction, and turning aside went aimlessly across the open land, visiting the various spots that he had formerly visited with her. But, as if tethered to the churchyard by a cord, he was still conscious of being at the end of a radius whose pivot was the grave of Avice Caro; and as the dusk thickened he closed upon his centre and entered the churchyard gate.

Not a soul was now within the precincts. The grave, newly shaped, was easily discoverable behind the church, and when the same young moon arose which he had observed the previous evening from his window in London he could see the yet fresh footmarks of the mourners and bearers. The breeze had fallen to a calm with the setting of the sun: the lighthouse had opened its glaring eye, and, disinclined to leave a spot sublimed both by early association and present regret, he moved back to the church-wall, warm from the afternoon sun, and sat down upon a window-sill facing the grave.

SHE THREATENS TO RESUME
CORPOREAL SUBSTANCE

II.–iv.

THE lispings of the sea beneath the cliffs were all the sounds that reached him, for the quarries were silent now. How long he sat here lonely and thinking he did not know. Neither did he know, though he felt drowsy, whether inexpectant sadness—that gentle soporific—lulled him into a short sleep, so that he lost count of time and consciousness of incident. But during some minute or minutes he seemed to see Avice Caro herself, bending over and then withdrawing from her grave in the light of the moon.

She seemed not a year older, not a digit less slender, not a line more angular than when he had parted from her twenty years earlier, in the lane hard by. A renascent reasoning on the impossibility of such a phenomenon as this being more than a dream-fancy roused him with a start from his heaviness.

'I must have been asleep,' he said.

Yet she had seemed so real. Pierston however dismissed the strange impression, arguing that even if the information sent him of Avice's death should be false—a thing incredible—that sweet friend of his youth, despite the transfiguring effects of moonlight, would not now look the same as she had appeared nineteen or twenty years ago. Were what he saw substantial flesh, it must have been some other person than Avice Caro.

Having satisfied his sentiment by coming to the graveside there was nothing more for him to do in the island, and he decided to return to London that night. But some time remaining still on his hands Jocelyn by a natural instinct turned his feet in the direction of East Quarriers, the village of his birth and of hers. Passing the market-square he pursued the arm of road to 'Sylvania Castle,' a private mansion of comparativley modern date, in whose grounds stood the single plantation of trees of which the isle could boast. The cottages extended close to the walls of the enclosure, and one of the last of these dwellings had been Avice's, in which, as it was her freehold, she possibly had died.

To reach it he passed the gates of 'Sylvania,' and observed above the lawn wall a board announcing that the house was to be let furnished. A few steps further revealed the cottage which, with its quaint and massive stone features of two or three centuries' antiquity, was capable even now of longer resistance to the rasp of Time than ordinary new erections. His attention was drawn to the window, still unblinded, though a lamp lit the room. He stepped back against the wall opposite, and gazed in.

At a table covered with a white cloth a young woman stood putting tea-things away into a corner-cupboard. She was in all respects the Avice he had lost, the girl he had seen in the churchyard and had fancied to be the illusion of a dream. And though there was this time no doubt about her reality, the isolation of her position in the silent house lent her a curiously startling aspect. Divining the explanation he waited for footsteps, and in a few moments a quarryman passed him on his journey home. Pierston inquired of the man concerning the spectacle.

'O yes, sir; that's poor Mrs. Caro's only daughter, and it must be lonely for her there to-night, poor maid! Yes, good-now; she's the very daps of her mother—that's what everybody says.'

'But how does she come to be so lonely?'

'One of her brothers went to sea and was drowned, and t'other is in America.'

'They were quarryowners at one time?'

The quarryman 'pitched his nitch,' and explained to the seeming stranger that there had been three families thereabouts in the stone trade, who had got much involved with each other in the last generation. They were the Bencombs, the Pierstons, and the Caros. The Bencombs strained their utmost to out-lift the other two, and partially succeeded. They grew enormously rich, sold out, and disappeared altogether from the island which had been their making. The Pierstons kept a dogged middle course, throve without show or noise, and also retired in their turn. The Caros were pulled completely down in the competition with the other two, and when Widow Caro's daughter married her cousin Jim Caro, he tried to regain for the family its original place in the three-cornered struggle. He took contracts at less than he could profit by, speculated more and more, till at last the crash came; he was sold up, went away, and later on came back to live in this little cottage, which was his wife's by inheritance. There he remained till his death; and now his widow was gone. Hardships had helped on her end.

The quarryman proceeded on his way, and Pierston, deeply remorseful, knocked at the door of the minute freehold. The girl herself opened it, lamp in hand.

'Avice!' he said tenderly; 'Avice Caro!' even now unable to get over the strange feeling that he was twenty years younger, addressing Avice the forsaken.

'Ann, sir,' said she.

'Ah, your name is not the same as your mother's!'

'My second name is. And my surname. Poor mother married her cousin.'

'As everybody does here. . . . Well, Ann or otherwise, you are Avice to me. And you have lost her now?'

'I have, sir.'

She spoke in the very same sweet voice that he had listened to a score of years before, and bent eyes of the same familiar hazel inquiringly upon him.

'I knew your mother at one time,' he said; 'and learning of her death and burial I took the liberty of calling upon you. You will forgive a stranger doing that?'

'Yes,' she said dispassionately, and glancing round the room. 'This was mother's own house, and now it is mine. I am sorry not to be in mourning on the night of her funeral, but I have just been to put some flowers on her grave, and I took it off afore going that the damp mid not spoil the crape. You see, she was bad a long time, and I have to be careful, and do washing and ironing for a living. She hurt herside with wringing up the large sheets she had to wash for the Castle folks here.'

'I hope you won't hurt yourself doing it, my dear.'

'O no, that I shan't! There's Charl Woollat, and Sammy Scribben, and Ted Gibsey, and lots o' young chaps; they'll wring anything for me if they happen to come along. But I can hardly trust 'em. Sam Scribben t'other day twisted a linen tablecloth into two pieces, for all the world as if it had been a pipe-light. They never know when to stop in their wringing.'

The voice truly was his Avice's; but Avice the Second was clearly more matter-of-fact, unreflecting, less cultivated than her mother had been. This Avice would never recite poetry from any platform, local or other, with enthusiastic appreciation of its fire. There was a disappointment in his recognition of this; yet she touched him as few had done: he could not bear to go away. 'How old are you?' he asked.

'Going in nineteen.'

It was about the age of her double, Avice the First, when he and she had strolled together over the cliffs during the engagement. But he was now forty, if a day. She before him was a uneducated laundress, and he was a sculptor and a Royal Academician, with a fortune and a reputation. Yet why was it an unpleasant sensation to him just then to recollect that he was two score?

He could find no further excuse for remaining, and having still half-an-hour to spare he went round by the road to the other or west side of the last-century 'Sylvania Castle,' and came to the furthest house out there on the cliff. It was his early home. Used in the summer as a lodging-house for visitors, it now stood empty and silent, the evening wind swaying the euonymus and tamarisk boughs in the front—the only evergreen shrubs that could weather the whipping salt gales which sped past the walls. Opposite the house, far out at sea, the familiar light-ship winked from the sandbank, and all at once there came to him a wild wish—that, instead of having an artist's reputation, he could be living here an illiterate and unknown man,

wooing, and in a fair way of winning, the pretty laundress
in the cottage hard by.

THE RESUMPTION

TAKES PLACE

II.—v.

HAVING returned to London he mechanically resumed his customary life; but he was not really living there. The phantom of Avice, now grown to be warm flesh and blood, held his mind afar. He thought of nothing but the isle, and Avice the Second dwelling therein—inhaling its salt breath, stroked by its singing rains and by the haunted atmosphere of Roman Venus about and around the site of her perished temple there. The very defects in the country girl became charms as viewed from town.

Nothing now pleased him so much as to spend that portion of the afternoon which he devoted to out-door exercise, in haunting the purlieus of the wharves along the Thames, where the stone of his native rock was unshipped from the coasting-craft that had brought it thither. He would pass inside the great gates of these landing-places on the right or left bank, contemplate the white cubes and oblongs, imbibe their associations, call up the *genius loci* whence they came, and almost forget that he was in London.

One afternoon he was walking away from the mud-splashed entrance to one of the wharves, when his attention was drawn to a female form on the opposite side of the way, going towards the spot he had just left. She was somewhat small, slight, and graceful; her attire alone would have been enough to attract him, being simple and countrified to picturesqueness; but he was more than attracted by her strong resemblance to Avice Caro the younger—Ann Avice, as she had said she was called.

Before she had receded a hundred yards he felt certain that it was Avice indeed; and his unifying mood of the afternoon was now so intense that the lost and the found Avice seemed essentially the same person. Their external likeness to each other—probably owing to the cousinship between the elder and her husband—went far to nourish the fantasy. He hastily turned, and rediscovered the girl among the pedestrians. She kept on her way to the wharf, where, looking inquiringly around her for a few seconds, with the manner of one unaccustomed to the locality, she opened the gate and disappeared.

Pierston also went up to the gate and entered. She had crossed to the landing-place, beyond which a lumpy craft lay moored. Drawing nearer, he discovered her to be engaged in conversation with the skipper and an elderly woman—both come straight from the oolitic isle, as was apparent in a moment from their accent. Pierston felt no hesitation in making himself known as a native, the ruptured engagement between Avice's mother and himself twenty years before having been known to few or none now living.

The present embodiment of Avice recognized him, and with the artless candour of her race and years explained the situation, though that was rather his duty as an intruder than hers.

'This is Cap'n Kibbs, sir, a distant relation of father's,' she said. 'And this is Mrs. Kibbs. We've come up from the island wi'en just for a trip, and are going to sail back wi'en Wednesday.'

'O, I see. And where are you staying?'

'Here—on board.'

'What, you live on board entirely?'

'Yes.'

'Lord, sir,' broke in Mrs. Kibbs, 'I should be afeard o' my life to tine my eyes among these here kimberlins at night-time; and even by day, if so be I venture into the streets, I nowhen forget how many turnings to the right and to the left 'tis to get back to Job's vessel—do I, Job?'

The skipper nodded confirmation.

'You are safer ashore than afloat,' said Pierston, 'especially in the Channel, with these winds and those heavy blocks of stone.'

'Well,' said Cap'n Kibbs, after privately clearing something from his mouth, 'as to the winds, there idden much danger in them at this time o' year. 'Tis the ocean-bound steamers that make the risk to craft like ours. If you happen to be in their course, under you go—cut clane in two pieces, and they never lying-to to haul in your carcases, and nobody to tell the tale.'

Pierston turned to Avice, wanting to say much to her, yet not knowing what to say. He lamely remarked at last: 'You go back the same way, Avice?'

'Yes, sir.'

'Well, take care of yourself afloat.'

'O yes.'

'I hope—I may see you again soon—and talk to you.'

'I hope so, sir.'

He could not get further, and after a while Pierston left them, and went away thinking of Avice more than ever.

The next day he mentally timed them down the river, allowing for the pause to take in ballast, and on the Wednesday pictured the sail down the open sea. That night he thought of the little craft under the bows of the huge steam-vessels, powerless to make itself seen or heard, and Avice, now growing inexpressibly dear, sleeping in her little berth at the mercy of a thousand chance catastrophes.

Honest perception had told him that this Avice, fairer than her mother in face and form, was her inferior in soul and understanding. Yet the fervour which the first could never kindle in him was, almost to his alarm, burning up now. He began to have misgivings as to some queer trick that his migratory Beloved was about to play him, or rather the capricious Divinity behind that ideal lady.

A gigantic satire upon the mutations of his nymph during the past twenty years seemed looming in the distance. A forsaking of the accomplished and well-connected Mrs. Pine-Avon for the little laundress, under the traction of some mystic magnet which had nothing to do with reason—surely that was the form of the satire.

But it was recklessly pleasant to leave the suspicion unrecognized as yet, and follow the lead.

In thinking how best to do this Pierston recollected that, as was customary when the summer-time approached,

Sylvania Castle had been advertised for letting furnished. A solitary dreamer like himself, whose wants all lay in an artistic and ideal direction, did not require such gaunt accommodation as the aforesaid residence offered; but the spot was all, and the expenses of a few months of tenancy therein he could well afford. A letter to the agent was dispatched that night, and in a few days Jocelyn found himself the temporary possessor of a place which he had never seen the inside of since his childhood, and had then deemed the abode of unpleasant ghosts.

THE PAST SHINES
IN THE PRESENT

II.—vi.

IT was the evening of Pierston's arrival at Sylvania Castle, a dignified manor-house in a nook by the cliffs, with modern castellations and battlements; and he had walked through the rooms, about the lawn, and into the surrounding plantation of elms, which on this island of treeless rock lent a unique character to the enclosure. In name, nature, and accessories the property within the girdling wall formed a complete antithesis to everything in its precincts. To find other trees between Pebble-bank and Beal, it was necessary to recede a little in time—to dig down to a loose stratum of the underlying stone-beds, where a forest of conifers lay as petrifactions, their heads all in one direction, as blown down by a gale in the Secondary geologic epoch.

Dusk had closed in, and he now proceeded with what was, after all, the real business of his sojourn. The two servants who had been left to take care of the house were in their own quarters, and he went out unobserved. Crossing a hollow overhung by the budding boughs he approached an empty garden-house of Elizabethan design, which stood on the outer wall of the grounds, and commanded by a window the fronts of the nearest cottages. Among them was the home of the resuscitated Avice.

He had chosen this moment for his outlook through knowing that the villagers were in no hurry to pull down their blinds at nightfall. And, as he had divined, the inside of the young woman's living-room was visible to him as formerly, illuminated by the rays of its own lamp.

A subdued thumping came every now and then from the apartment. She was ironing linen on a flannel table-cloth, a row of such apparel hanging on a clothes-horse by the fire. Her face had been pale when he encountered her, but now it was warm and pink with her exertions and the heat of the stove. Yet it was in perfect and passionless repose, which imparted a Minerva cast to the profile. When she glanced up, her lineaments seemed to have all the soul and heart that had characterized her mother's, and had been with her a true index of the spirit within. Could it be possible that in this case the manifestation was fictitious? He had met with many such examples of hereditary persistence without the qualities signified by the traits. He unconsciously hoped that it was at least not entirely so here.

The room was less furnished than when he had last beheld it. The 'bo-fet,' or double corner-cupboard, where the china was formerly kept, had disappeared, its place being taken by a plain board. The tall old clock, with its ancient oak carcase, arched brow, and humorous mouth, was also not to be seen, a cheap, white-dialled specimen doing its work. What these displacements might betoken saddened his humanity less than it cheered his primitive instinct in pointing out how her necessities might bring them together.

Having fixed his residence near her for some lengthy time he felt in no hurry to obtrude his presence just now, and went indoors. That this girl's frame was doomed to be a real embodiment of that olden seductive one—that Protean dream-creature, who had never seen fit to irradiate the mother's image till it became a mere memory after dissolution—he doubted less every moment.

There was an uneasiness in recognizing such. There was something abnormal in his present proclivity. A certain sanity had, after all, accompanied his former idealizing passions: the Beloved had seldom informed a personality which, while enrapturing his soul, simultaneously shocked his intellect. A change, perhaps, had come.

It was a fine morning on the morrow. Walking in the grounds towards the gate he saw Avice entering his hired castle with a broad oval wicker-basket covered with a white cloth, which burden she bore round to the back door. Of course, she washed for his own household: he had not thought of that. In the morning sunlight she appeared

rather as a sylph than as a washerwoman; and he could not
but think that the slightness of her figure was as ill adapted
to this occupation as her mother's had been.

But, after all, it was not the washerwoman that he saw
now. In front of her, on the surface of her, was shining out
that more real, more inter-penetrating being whom he
knew so well! The occupation of the subserving minion,
the blemishes of the temporary creature who formed the
background, were of the same account in the presentation
of the indispensable one as the supporting posts and
framework in a pyrotechnic display.

She left the house and went homeward by a path of
which he was not aware, having probably changed her
course because she had seen him standing there. It meant
nothing, for she had hardly become acquainted with him;
yet that she should have avoided him was a new experience.
He had no opportunity for a further study of her by distant
observation, and hit upon a pretext for bringing her face
to face with him. He found fault with his linen, and
directed that the laundress should be sent for.

'She is rather young, poor little thing,' said the
housemaid apologetically. 'But since her mother's death
she has enough to do to keep above water, and we make
shift with her. But I'll tell her, sir.'

'I will see her myself. Send her in when she comes,' said
Pierston.

One morning, accordingly, when he was answering a
spiteful criticism of a late work of his, he was told that she
waited his pleasure in the hall. He went out.

'About the washing,' said the sculptor stiffly. 'I am a
very particular person, and I wish no preparation of lime
to be used.'

'I didn't know folks used it,' replied the maiden, in a
scared and reserved tone, without looking at him.

'That's all right. And then, the mangling smashes the
buttons.'

'I haven't got a mangle, sir,' she murmured.

'Ah! that's satisfactory. And I object to so much borax
in the starch.'

'I don't put any,' Avice returned in the same close way; 'never heard the name o't afore!'

'O I see.'

All this time Pierston was thinking of the girl—or as the scientific might say, Nature was working her plans for the next generation under the cloak of a dialogue on linen. He could not read her individual character, owing to the confusing effect of her likeness to a woman whom he had valued too late. He could not help seeing in her all that he knew of another, and veiling in her all that did not harmonize with his sense of metempsychosis.

The girl seemed to think of nothing but the business in hand. She had answered to the point, and was hardly aware of his sex or of his shape.

'I knew your mother, Avice,' he said. 'You remember my telling you so?'

'Yes.'

'Well—I have taken this house for two or three months, and you will be very useful to me. You still live just outside the wall?'

'Yes, sir,' said the self-contained girl.

Demurely and dispassionately she turned to leave—this pretty creature with features so still. There was something strange in seeing move off thus that form which he knew passing well, she who was once so throbbingly alive to his presence that, not many yards from this spot, she had flung her arms round him and given him a kiss which, despised in its freshness, had revived in him latterly as the dearest kiss of all his life. And now this 'daps' of her mother (as they called her in the dialect here), this perfect copy, why did she turn away?

'Your mother was a refined and well-informed woman, I think I remember?'

'She was, sir; everybody said so.'

'I hope you resemble her.'

She archly shook her head, and drew warily away.

'O! one thing more, Avice. I have not brought much linen, so you must come to the house every day.'

'Very good, sir.'

'You won't forget that?'

'O no.'

Then he let her go. He was a town man and she an artless islander, yet he had opened himself out like a sea-anemone, without disturbing the epiderm of her nature. It was monstrous that a maiden who had assumed the personality of her of his tenderest memory should be so impervious. Perhaps it was he who was wanting. Avice might be Passion masking as Indifference, because he was so many years older in outward show.

This brought him to the root of it. In his heart he was not a day older than when he had wooed the mother at the daughter's present age. His record moved on with the years, his sentiments stood still.

When he beheld those of his fellows who were defined as buffers and fogeys—imperturbable, matter-of-fact, slightly ridiculous beings, past masters in the art of populating homes, schools, and colleges, and present adepts in the science of giving away brides—how he envied them, assuming them to feel as they appeared to feel, with their commerce and their politics, their glasses and their pipes. They had got past the distracting currents of passionateness, and were in the calm waters of middle-aged philosophy. But he, their contemporary, was tossed like a cork hither and thither upon the crest of every fancy, precisely as he had been tossed when he was half his present age, with the burden now of double pain to himself in his growing vision of all as vanity.

Avice had gone, and he saw her no more that day. Since he could not again call upon her, she was as inaccessible as if she had entered the military citadel on the hill-top beyond them.

In the evening he went out and paced down the lane to the Red King's castle overhanging the cliff, beside whose age the castle he occupied was but a thing of yesterday. Below the castle precipice lay enormous blocks, which had fallen from it, and several of them were carved over with names and initials. He knew the spot and the old trick well, and by searching in the faint moon-rays he found a pair of

names which, as a boy, he himself had cut. They were
'AVICE' and 'JOCELYN'—Avice Caro's and his own. The let-
ters were now nearly worn away by the weather and the
brine. But close by, in quite fresh letters, stood 'ANN
AVICE,' coupled with the name 'ISAAC.' They could not
have been there more than two or three years, and the
'Ann Avice' was probably Avice the Second. Who was
Isaac? Some boy admirer of her child-time doubtless.

He retraced his steps, and passed the Caros' house
towards his own. The revivified Avice animated the dwelling, and the light within the room fell upon the window.
She was just inside that blind.

Whenever she unexpectedly came to the castle he
started, and lost placidity. It was not at her presence as
such, but at the new condition, which seemed to have
something sinister in it. On the other hand, the most
abrupt encounter with him moved her to no emotion as it
had moved her prototype in the old days. She was indifferent to, almost unconscious of, his propinquity. He was
no more than a statue to her; she was a growing fire to
him.

A sudden Sapphic terror of love would ever and anon
come upon the sculptor, when his matured reflecting
powers would insist upon informing him of the fearful
lapse from reasonableness that lay in this infatuation. It
threw him into a sweat. What if now, at last, he were
doomed to do penance for his past emotional wanderings
(in a material sense) by being chained in fatal fidelity to an
object that his intellect despised? One night he dreamt that
he saw dimly masking behind that young countenance 'the
Weaver of Wiles' herself, 'with all her subtle face laughing
aloud.'

However, the Well-Beloved was alive again; had been
lost and was found. He was amazed at the change of front
in himself. She had worn the guise of strange women; she
had been a woman of every class, from the dignified
daughter of some ecclesiastic or peer to a Nubian Almeh
with her handkerchief, undulating to the beats of the

THE PAST SHINES
IN THE PRESENT

II.—vi.

IT was the evening of Pierston's arrival at Sylvania Castle, a dignified manor-house in a nook by the cliffs, with modern castellations and battlements; and he had walked through the rooms, about the lawn, and into the surrounding plantation of elms, which on this island of treeless rock lent a unique character to the enclosure. In name, nature, and accessories the property within the girdling wall formed a complete antithesis to everything in its precincts. To find other trees between Pebble-bank and Beal, it was necessary to recede a little in time—to dig down to a loose stratum of the underlying stone-beds, where a forest of conifers lay as petrifactions, their heads all in one direction, as blown down by a gale in the Secondary geologic epoch.

Dusk had closed in, and he now proceeded with what was, after all, the real business of his sojourn. The two servants who had been left to take care of the house were in their own quarters, and he went out unobserved. Crossing a hollow overhung by the budding boughs he approached an empty garden-house of Elizabethan design, which stood on the outer wall of the grounds, and commanded by a window the fronts of the nearest cottages. Among them was the home of the resuscitated Avice.

He had chosen this moment for his outlook through knowing that the villagers were in no hurry to pull down their blinds at nightfall. And, as he had divined, the inside of the young woman's living-room was visible to him as formerly, illuminated by the rays of its own lamp.

A subdued thumping came every now and then from the apartment. She was ironing linen on a flannel table-cloth, a row of such apparel hanging on a clothes-horse by the fire. Her face had been pale when he encountered her, but now it was warm and pink with her exertions and the heat of the stove. Yet it was in perfect and passionless repose, which imparted a Minerva cast to the profile. When she glanced up, her lineaments seemed to have all the soul and heart that had characterized her mother's, and had been with her a true index of the spirit within. Could it be possible that in this case the manifestation was fictitious? He had met with many such examples of hereditary persistence without the qualities signified by the traits. He unconsciously hoped that it was at least not entirely so here.

The room was less furnished than when he had last beheld it. The 'bo-fet,' or double corner-cupboard, where the china was formerly kept, had disappeared, its place being taken by a plain board. The tall old clock, with its ancient oak carcase, arched brow, and humorous mouth, was also not to be seen, a cheap, white-dialled specimen doing its work. What these displacements might betoken saddened his humanity less than it cheered his primitive instinct in pointing out how her necessities might bring them together.

Having fixed his residence near her for some lengthy time he felt in no hurry to obtrude his presence just now, and went indoors. That this girl's frame was doomed to be a real embodiment of that olden seductive one—that Protean dream-creature, who had never seen fit to irradiate the mother's image till it became a mere memory after dissolution—he doubted less every moment.

There was an uneasiness in recognizing such. There was something abnormal in his present proclivity. A certain sanity had, after all, accompanied his former idealizing passions: the Beloved had seldom informed a personality which, while enrapturing his soul, simultaneously shocked his intellect. A change, perhaps, had come.

It was a fine morning on the morrow. Walking in the grounds towards the gate he saw Avice entering his hired castle with a broad oval wicker-basket covered with a white cloth, which burden she bore round to the back door. Of course, she washed for his own household: he had not thought of that. In the morning sunlight she appeared tom-tom; but all these embodiments had been endowed with a certain smartness, either of the flesh or spirit: some with wit, a few with talent, and even genius. But the new impersonation had apparently nothing beyond sex and prettiness. She knew not how to sport a fan or handkerchief, hardly how to pull on a glove.

But her limited life was innocent, and that went far. Poor little Avice! her mother's image: there it all lay. After all, her parentage was as good as his own; it was misfortune that had sent her down to this. Odd as it seemed to him, her limitations were largely what he loved her for. Her rejuvenating power over him had ineffable charm. He felt as he had felt when standing beside her predecessor; but, alas! he was twenty years further on towards the shade.

THE NEW BECOMES
ESTABLISHED

II.—vii.

A FEW mornings later he was looking through an upper back window over a screened part of the garden. The door beneath him opened, and a figure appeared tripping forth. She went round out of sight to where the gardener was at work, and presently returned with a bunch of green stuff fluttering in each hand. It was Avice, her dark hair now braided up snugly under a cap. She sailed on with a rapt and unconscious face, her thoughts a thousand removes from him.

How she had suddenly come to be an inmate of his own house he could not understand, till he recalled the fact that he had given the castle servants a whole holiday to attend a review of the yeomanry in the watering-place over the bay, on their stating that they could provide a temporary substitute to stay in the house. They had evidently called in Avice. To his great pleasure he discovered their opinion of his requirements to be such a mean one that they had called in no one else.

The Spirit, as she seemed to him, brought his lunch into the room where he was writing, and he beheld her uncover it. She went to the window to adjust a blind which had slipped, and he had a good view of her profile. It was not unlike that of one of the three goddesses in Rubens's 'Judgment of Paris,' and in contour was nigh perfection. But it was in her full face that the vision of her mother was most apparent.

'Did you cook all this, Avice?' he asked, arousing himself.

She turned and half-smiled, merely murmuring, 'Yes, sir.'

Well he knew the arrangement of those white teeth. In the junction of two of the upper ones there was a slight irregularity; no stranger would have noticed it, nor would he, but that he knew of the same mark in her mother's mouth, and looked for it here. Till Avice the Second had revealed it this moment by her smile, he had never beheld that mark since the parting from Avice the First, when she had smiled under his kiss as the copy had done now.

Next morning, when dressing, he heard her through the ricketty floor of the building engaged in conversation with the other servants. Having by this time regularly installed herself as the exponent of the Long-pursued—as one who, by no initiative of his own, had been chosen by some superior Power as the vehicle of her next début, she attracted him by the cadences of her voice; she would suddenly drop it to a rich whisper of roguishness, when the slight rural monotony of its narrative speech disappeared, and soul and heart—or what seemed soul and heart—resounded. The charm lay in the intervals, using that word in its musical sense. She would say a few syllables in one note, and end her sentence in a soft modulation upwards, then downwards, then into her own note again. The curve of sound was as artistic as any line of beauty ever struck by his pencil—as satisfying as the curves of her who was the World's Desire.

The subject of her discourse he cared nothing about—it was no more his interest than his concern. He took special pains that in catching her voice he might not comprehend her words. To the tones he had a right, none to the articulations. By degrees he could not exist long without this sound.

On Sunday evening he found that she went to church. He followed behind her over the open road, keeping his eye on the little hat with its bunch of cock's feathers as on a star. When she had passed in Pierston observed her position and took a seat behind her.

Engaged in the study of her ear and the nape of her white neck, he suddenly became aware of the presence of a lady still further ahead in the aisle, whose attire, though of black materials in the quietest form, was of a cut which rather suggested London than this *Ultima Thule*. For the minute he forgot, in his curiosity, that Avice intervened. The lady turned her head somewhat, and, though she was veiled with unusual thickness for the season, he seemed to recognize Nichola Pine-Avon in the form.

Why should Mrs. Pine-Avon be there? Pierston asked himself, if it should, indeed, be she.

The end of the service saw his attention again concentrated on Avice to such a degree that at the critical moment of moving out he forgot the mysterious lady in front of her, and found that she had left the church by the side-door. Supposing it to have been Mrs. Pine-Avon, she would probably be discovered staying at one of the hotels at the watering-place over the bay, and to have come along the Pebble-bank to the island as so many did, for an evening drive. For the present, however, the explanation was not forthcoming; and he did not seek it.

When he emerged from the church the great placid eye of the lighthouse at the Beal Point was open, and he moved thitherward a few steps to escape Nichola, or her double, and the rest of the congregation. Turning at length, he hastened homeward along the now deserted trackway, intending to overtake the revitalized Avice. But he could see nothing of her and concluded that she had walked too fast for him. Arrived at his own gate he paused a moment, and perceived that Avice's little freehold was still in darkness. She had not come.

He retraced his steps, but could not find her, the only persons on the road being a man and his wife, as he knew them to be though he could not see them, from the words of the man—

'If you had not a'ready married me, you'd cut my acquaintance! That's a pretty thing for a wife to say!'

The remark struck his ear unpleasantly, and by-and-by he went back again. Avice's cottage was now lighted: she must have come round by the other road. Satisfied that she was safely domiciled for the night he opened the gate of Sylvania Castle and retired to his room also.

Eastward from the grounds the cliffs were rugged and

the view of the opposite coast picturesque in the extreme. A little door from the lawn gave him immediate access to the rocks and shore on this side. Without the door was a dip-well of pure water, which possibly had supplied the inmates of the adjoining and now ruinous Red King's castle at the time of its erection. On a sunny morning he was meditating here when he discerned a figure on the shore below spreading white linen upon the pebbly strand.

Jocelyn descended. Avice, as he had supposed, had now returned to her own occupation. Her shapely pink arms, though slight, were plump enough to show dimples at the elbows, and were set off by her purple cotton print, which the shore-breeze licked and tantalized. He stood near, without speaking. The wind dragged a shirt-sleeve from the 'popple' or pebble which held it down. Pierston stooped and put a heavier one in its place.

'Thank you,' she said quietly. She turned up her hazel eyes, and seemed gratified to perceive that her assistant was Pierston. She had plainly been so wrapped in her own thoughts—gloomy thoughts, by their signs—that she had not considered him till then.

The young girl continued to converse with him in friendly frankness, showing neither ardour nor shyness. As for love—it was evidently further from her mind than even death and dissolution.

When one of the sheets became intractable Jocelyn said, 'Do you hold it down, and I'll put the popples.'

She acquiesced, and in placing a pebble his hand touched hers.

It was a young hand, rather long and thin, a little damp and coddled from her slopping. In setting down the last stone he laid it, by a pure accident, rather heavily on her fingers.

'I am very, very sorry!' Jocelyn exclaimed. 'O, I have bruised the skin, Avice!' He seized her fingers to examine the damage done.

'No, sir, you haven't!' she cried luminously, allowing him to retain her hand without the least objection. 'Why—that's where I scratched it this morning with a pin. You didn't hurt me a bit with the popple-stone!'

Although her gown was purple, there was a little black crape bow upon each arm. He knew what it meant, and it saddened him. 'Do you ever visit your mother's grave?' he asked.

'Yes, sir, sometimes. I am going there to-night to water the daisies.'

She had now finished here, and they parted. That evening, when the sky was red, he emerged by the garden-door and passed her house. The blinds were not down, and he could see her sewing within. While he paused she sprang up as if she had forgotten the hour, and tossed on her hat. Jocelyn strode ahead and round the corner, and was halfway up the straggling street before he discerned her little figure behind him.

He hastened past the lads and young women with clinking buckets who were drawing water from the fountains by the wayside, and took the direction of the church. With the disappearance of the sun the lighthouse had again set up its flame against the sky, the dark church rising in the foreground. Here he allowed her to overtake him.

'You loved your mother much?' said Jocelyn.

'I did, sir; of course I did,' said the girl, who tripped so lightly that it seemed he might have carried her on his hand.

Pierston wished to say, 'So did I,' but did not like to disclose events which she, apparently, never guessed. Avice fell into thought, and continued—

'Mother had a very sad life for some time when she was about as old as I. I should not like mine to be as hers. Her young man proved false to her because she wouldn't agree to meet him one night, and it grieved mother almost all her life. I wouldn't ha' fretted about him, if I'd been she. She would never name his name, but I know he was a wicked, cruel man; and I hate to think of him.'

After this he could not go into the churchyard with her, and walked onward alone to the south of the isle. He was wretched for hours. Yet he would not have stood where he did stand in the ranks of an imaginative profession if he had not been at the mercy of every haunting of the fancy that can beset man. It was in his weaknesses as a citizen and a national-unit that his strength lay as an artist, and he felt it childish to complain of susceptibilities not only innate but cultivated.

But he was paying dearly enough for his Liliths. He saw a terrible vengeance ahead. What had he done to be tormented like this? The Beloved, after flitting from Nichola Pine-Avon to the phantom of a dead woman whom he never adored in her lifetime, had taken up her abode in the living representative of the dead, with a permanence of hold which the absolute indifference of that little brown-eyed representative only seemed to intensify.

Did he really wish to proceed to marriage with this chit of a girl? He did: the wish had come at last. It was true that as he studied her he saw defects in addition to her social insufficiencies. Judgment, hoodwinked as it was, told him that she was colder in nature, commoner in character, than that well-read, bright little woman Avice the First. But twenty years make a difference in ideals, and the added demands of middle-age in physical form are more than balanced by its concessions as to the spiritual content. He looked at himself in the glass, and felt glad at those inner deficiencies in Avice which formerly would have impelled him to reject her.

There was a strange difference in his regard of his present folly and of his love in his youthful time. Now he could be mad with method, knowing it to be madness: then he was compelled to make believe his madness wisdom. In those days any flash of reason upon his loved one's imperfections was blurred over hastily and with fear. Such penetrative vision now did not cool him. He knew he was the creature of a tendency; and passively acquiesced.

To use a practical eye, it appeared that, as he had once thought, this Caro family—though it might not for centuries, or ever, furbish up an individual nature which would exactly, ideally, supplement his own imperfect one and round with it the perfect whole—was yet the only family he had ever met, or was likely to meet, which possessed the materials for her making. It was as if the

Caros had found the clay but not the potter, while other families whose daughters might attract him had found the potter but not the clay.

HIS OWN SOUL

CONFRONTS HIM

II.—viii.

FROM his roomy castle and its grounds and the cliffs hard
by he could command every move and aspect of her who
was the rejuvenated Spirit of the Past to him—in the
effulgence of whom all sordid details were disregarded.

Among other things he observed that she was often anxious
when it rained. If, after a wet day, a golden streak appeared
in the sky over Deadman's Bay, under a lid of cloud, her
manner was joyous and her tread light.

This puzzled him; and he found that if he endeavoured
to encounter her at these times she shunned him—
stealthily and subtly, but unmistakably. One evening,
when she had left her cottage and tripped off in the direction of the under-hill townlet, he set out by the same route,
resolved to await her return along the high roadway which
stretched between that place and East Quarriers.

He reached the top of the old road where it makes a sudden descent to the townlet, but she did not appear. Turning back, he sauntered along till he had nearly reached his
own house again. Then he retraced his steps, and in the
dim night he walked backwards and forwards on the bare
and lofty convex of the isle; the stars above and around
him, the lighthouse on duty at the distant point, the
lightship winking from the sandbank, the combing of the
pebble-beach by the tide beneath, the church away south-
westward, where the island fathers lay.

He walked the wild summit till his legs ached, and his
heart ached—till he seemed to hear on the upper wind the
stones of the slingers whizzing past, and the voices of the
invaders who annihilated them, and married their wives
and daughters, and produced Avice as the ultimate flower
of the combined stocks. Still she did not come. It was more
than foolish to wait, yet he could not help waiting. At

length he discerned a dot of a figure, which he knew to be hers rather by its motion than by its shape.

How incomparably the immaterial dream dwarfed the grandest of substantial things, when here, between those three sublimities—the sky, the rock, and the ocean—the minute personality of this washer-girl filled his consciousness to its extremest boundary, and the stupendous inanimate scene shrank to a corner therein.

But all at once the approaching figure had disappeared. He looked about; she had certainly vanished. At one side of the road was a low wall, but she could not have gone behind that without considerable trouble and singular conduct. He looked behind him; she had reappeared further on the road.

Jocelyn Pierston hurried after; and, discerning his movement, Avice stood still. When he came up, she was slily shaking with restrained laughter.

'Well, what does this mean, my dear girl?' he asked.

Her inner mirth escaping in spite of her she turned askance and said: 'When you was following me to Street o' Wells, two hours ago, I looked round and saw you, and huddied behind a stone! You passed and brushed my frock without seeing me. And when, on my way backalong, I saw you waiting hereabout again, I slipped over the wall, and ran past you! If I had not stopped and looked round at 'ee, you would never have catched me!'

'What did you do that for, you elf!'

'That you shouldn't find me.'

'That's not exactly a reason. Give another, dear Avice,' he said, as he turned and walked beside her homeward.

She hesitated. 'Come!' he urged again.

''Twas because I thought you wanted to be my young man,' she answered.

'What a wild thought of yours! Supposing I did, wouldn't you have me?'

'Not now. . . . And not for long, even if it had been sooner than now.'

'Why?'

'If I tell you, you won't laugh at me or let anybody else know?'

'Never.'

'Then I will tell you,' she said quite seriously. "Tis because I get tired of my lovers as soon as I get to know them well. What I see in one young man for a while soon leaves him and goes into another yonder, and I follow, and then what I admire fades out of him and springs up somewhere else; and so I follow on, and never fix to one. I have loved *fifteen* a'ready! Yes, fifteen, I am almost ashamed to say,' she repeated, laughing. 'I can't help it, sir, I assure you. Of course it is really, to *me*, the same one all through, only I can't catch him!' She added anxiously, 'You won't tell anybody o' this in me, will you, sir? Because if it were known I am afraid no man would like me.'

Pierston was surprised into stillness. Here was this obscure and almost illiterate girl engaged in the pursuit of the impossible ideal, just as he had been himself doing for the last twenty years. She was doing it quite involuntarily, by sheer necessity of her organization, puzzled all the while at her own instinct. He suddenly thought of its bearing upon himself, and said, with a sinking heart—

'Am I—one of them?'

She pondered critically.

'You was——for a week; when I first saw you.'

'Only a week?'

'About that.'

'What made the being of your fancy forsake my form and go elsewhere?'

'Well—though you seemed handsome and gentlemanly at first——'

'Yes?'

'I found you too old soon after.'

'You are a candid young person.'

'But you asked me, sir!' she expostulated.

'I did; and, having been answered, I won't intrude upon you longer. So cut along home as fast as you can. It is getting late.'

When she had passed out of earshot he also followed homewards. This seeking of the Well-Beloved was, then,

of the nature of a knife which could cut two ways. To be
the seeker was one thing: to be one of the corpses from
which the ideal inhabitant had departed was another; and
this was what he had become now, in the mockery of new
days.

The startling parallel in the idiosyncrasies of Avice and
himself—evinced by the elusiveness of the Beloved with
her as with him—meant probably that there had been
some remote ancestor common to both families, from
whom the trait had latently descended and recrudesced.
But the result was none the less disconcerting.

Drawing near his own gate he smelt tobacco, and could
discern two figures in the side lane leading past Avice's
door. They did not, however, enter her house, but strolled
onward to the narrow pass conducting to Red-King Castle
and the sea. He was in momentary heaviness at the
thought that they might be Avice with a worthless lover,
but a faintly argumentative tone from the man informed
him that they were the same married couple going
homeward whom he had encountered on a previous
occasion.

The next day he gave the servants a half-holiday to get
the pretty Avice into the castle again for a few hours, the
better to observe her. While she was pulling down the
blinds at sunset a whistle of peculiar quality came from
some point on the cliffs outside the lawn. He observed that
her colour rose slightly, though she bustled about as if she
had noticed nothing.

Pierston suddenly suspected that she had not only fifteen
past admirers but a current one. Still, he might be
mistaken. Stimulated now by ancient memories and present tenderness to use every effort to make her his wife,
despite her conventional unfitness, he strung himself up to
sift this mystery. If he could only win her—and how could
a country girl refuse such an opportunity?—he could pack
her off to school for two or three years, marry her, enlarge
her mind by a little travel, and take his chance of the rest.
As to her want of ardour for him—so sadly in contrast
with her sainted mother's affection—a man twenty years

older than his bride could expect no better, and he would
be well content to put up with it in the pleasure of possess-
ing one in whom seemed to linger as an aroma all the
charm of his youth and his early home.

JUXTAPOSITIONS

II.—ix.

IT was a sad and leaden afternoon, and Pierston paced up
the long, steep pass or Street of the Wells. On either side
of the road young girls stood with pitchers at the fountains
which bubbled there, and behind the houses forming the
propylæa of the rock rose the massive forehead of the
Isle—crested at this part with its enormous ramparts as
with a mural crown.

As you approach the upper end of the street all progress
seems about to be checked by the almost vertical face of
the escarpment. Into it your track apparently runs point-
blank: a confronting mass which, if it were to slip down,
would overwhelm the whole town. But in a moment you
find that the road, the old Roman highway into the peninsula, turns at a sharp angle when it reaches the base of the
scarp, and ascends in the stiffest of inclines to the right. To
the left there is also another ascending road, modern,
almost as steep as the first, and perfectly straight. This is
the road to the forts.

Pierston arrived at the forking of the ways, and paused
for breath. Before turning to the right, his proper and picturesque course, he looked up the uninteresting left road to
the fortifications. It was new, long, white, regular, taper-
ing to a vanishing point, like a lesson in perspective. About
a quarter of the way up a girl was resting beside a basket
of white linen: and by the shape of her hat and the nature
of her burden he recognized her.

She did not see him, and abandoning the right-hand
course he slowly ascended the incline she had taken. He
observed that her attention was absorbed by something
aloft. He followed the direction of her gaze. Above them
towered the green-grey mountain of grassy stone, here
levelled at the top by military art. The skyline was broken
every now and then by a little peg-like object—a sentry-
box; and near one of these a small red spot kept creeping

backwards and forwards monotonously against the heavy sky.

Then he divined that she had a soldier-lover.

She turned her head, saw him, and took up her clothes-basket to continue the ascent. The steepness was such that to climb it unencumbered was a breathless business; the linen made her task a cruelty to her. 'You'll never get to the forts with that weight,' he said. 'Give it to me.'

But she would not, and he stood still, watching her as she panted up the way; for the moment an irradiated being, the epitome of a whole sex: by the beams of his own infatuation

> '. . . robed in such exceeding glory
> That he beheld her not';

beheld her not as she really was, as she was even to himself sometimes. But to the soldier what was she? Smaller and smaller she waned up the rigid mathematical road, still gazing at the soldier aloft, as Pierston gazed at her. He could just discern sentinels springing up at the different coigns of vantage that she passed, but seeing who she was they did not intercept her; and presently she crossed the drawbridge over the enormous chasm surrounding the forts, passed the sentries there also, and disappeared through the arch into the interior. Pierston could not see the sentry now, and there occurred to him the hateful idea that this scarlet rival was meeting and talking freely to her, the unprotected orphan girl of his sweet original Avice; perhaps, relieved of duty, escorting her across the interior, carrying her basket, her tender body encircled by his arm.

'What the devil are you staring at, as if you were in a trance?'

Pierston turned his head: and there stood his old friend Somers—still looking the long-leased bachelor that he was.

'I might say what the devil do you do here? if I weren't so glad to see you.'

Somers said that he had come to see what was detaining his friend in such an out-of-the-way place at that time of year, and incidentally to get some fresh air into his own lungs. Pierston made him welcome, and they went towards Sylvania Castle.

'You were staring, as far as I could see, at a pretty little washerwoman with a basket of clothes?' resumed the painter.

'Yes; it was that to you, but not to me. Behind the mere pretty island-girl (to the world) is, in my eye, the Idea, in Platonic phraseology—the essence and epitome of all that is desirable in this existence. . . . I am under a doom, Somers. Yes, I am under a doom. To have been always following a phantom whom I saw in woman after woman while she was at a distance, but vanishing away on close approach, was bad enough; but now the terrible thing is that the phantom does *not* vanish, but stays to tantalize me even when I am near enough to see what it is! That girl holds me, *though* my eyes are open, and *though* I see that I am a fool!'

Somers regarded the visionary look of his friend, which rather intensified than decreased as his years wore on, but made no further remark. When they reached the castle Somers gazed round upon the scenery, and Pierston, signifying the quaint little Elizabethan cottage, said: 'That's where she lives.'

'What a romantic place!—and this island altogether. A man might love a scarecrow or turnip-lantern here.'

'But a woman mightn't. Scenery doesn't impress them, though they pretend it does. This girl is as fickle as——'

'You once were.'

'Exactly—from your point of view. She has told me so—candidly. And it hits me hard.'

Somers stood still in sudden thought. 'Well—that *is* a strange turning of the tables!' he said. 'But you wouldn't really marry her, Pierston?'

'I would—to-morrow. Why shouldn't I? What are fame and name and society to me—a descendant of wreckers and smugglers, like her. Besides, I know what she's made of, my boy, to her innermost fibre; I know the perfect and pure quarry she was dug from: and that gives a man confidence.'

different figure from her who, sitting in her chair with such finished composure, had snubbed him in her drawing-room in Hamptonshire Square.

'You are surprised at this? Of course you are!' she said, in a low, pleading voice, languidly lifting her heavy eyelids, while he was holding her hand. 'But I couldn't help it! I know I have done something to offend you—have I not? O! what can it be, that you have come away to this outlandish rock, to live with barbarians in the midst of the London season?'

'You have not offended me, dear Mrs. Pine-Avon,' he said. 'How sorry I am that you should have supposed it! Yet I am glad, too, that your fancy should have done me the good turn of bringing you here to see me.'

'I am staying at Budmouth-Regis,' she explained.

'Then I did see you at a church-service here a little while back?'

She blushed faintly upon her pallor, and she sighed. Their eyes met. 'Well,' she said at last, 'I don't know why I shouldn't show the virtue of candour. You know what it means. I was the stronger once; now I am the weaker. Whatever pain I may have given you in the ups and downs of our acquaintance I am sorry for, and would willingly repair all errors of the past of—being amenable to reason in the future.'

It was impossible that Jocelyn should not feel a tender impulsion towards this attractive and once independent woman, who from every worldly point of view was an excellent match for him—a superior match, indeed, except in money. He took her hand again and held it awhile, and a faint wave a gladness seemed to flow through her. But no—he could go no further. That island girl, in her coquettish Sunday frock and little hat with its bunch of cock's feathers held him as by strands of Manila rope. He dropped Nichola's hand.

'I am leaving Budmouth to-morrow,' she said. 'That was why I felt I must call. You did not know I had been there all through the Whitsun holidays?'

'I did not, indeed; or I should have come to see you.'

'I didn't like to write. I wish I had, now!'

'I wish you had, too, dear Mrs. Pine-Avon.'

But it was 'Nichola' that she wanted to be. As they reached the landau he told her that he should be back in town himself again soon, and would call immediately. At the moment of his words Avice Caro, now alone, passed close along by the carriage on the other side, towards her house hard at hand. She did not turn head or eye to the pair: they seemed to be in her view objects of indifference.

Pierston became cold as a stone. The chill towards Nichola that the presence of the girl,—sprite, witch, troll that she was—brought with it came like a doom. He knew what a fool he was, as he had said. But he was powerless in the grasp of the idealizing passion. He cared more for Avice's finger-tips than for Mrs. Pine-Avon's whole personality.

Perhaps Nichola saw it, for she said mournfully: 'Now I have done all I could! I felt that the only counterpoise to my cruelty to you in my drawing-room would be to come as a suppliant to yours.'

'It is most handsome and noble of you, my very dear friend!' said he, with an emotion of courtesy rather than of enthusiasm.

Then adieux were spoken, and she drove away. But Pierston saw only the retreating Avice, and knew that he was helpless in her hands. The church of the island had risen near the foundations of the Pagan temple, and a Christian emanation from the former might be wrathfully torturing him through the very false gods to whom he had devoted himself both in his craft, like Demetrius of Ephesus, and in his heart. Perhaps Divine punishment for his idolatries had come.

SHE FAILS TO VANISH STILL

II.—x.

PIERSTON had not turned far back towards the castle when he was overtaken by Somers and the man who carried his painting lumber. They paced together to the door; the man deposited the articles and went away, and the two walked up and down before entering.

'I met an extremely interesting woman in the road out there,' said the painter.

'Ah, she is! A sprite, a sylph; Psyche indeed!'

'I was struck with her.'

'It shows how beauty will out through the homeliest guise.'

'Yes, it will; though not always. And this case doesn't prove it, for the lady's attire was in the latest and most approved taste.'

'O, you mean the lady who was driving?'

'Of course. What, were you thinking of the pretty little cottage-girl outside here? I did meet her, but what's she? Very well for one's picture, though hardly for one's fireside. This lady——'

'Is Mrs. Pine-Avon. A kind, proud woman, who'll do what people with no pride would not condescend to think of. She is leaving Budmouth to-morrow, and she drove across to see me. You know how things seemed to be going with us at one time? But I am no good to any woman. She's been very generous towards me, which I've not been to her. . . . She'll ultimately throw herself away upon some wretch unworthy of her, no doubt.'

'Do you think so?' murmured Somers. After a while he said abruptly, 'I'll marry her myself, if she'll have me. I like the look of her.'

'I wish you would, Alfred, or rather could! She has long had an idea of slipping out of the world of fashion into the world of art. She is a woman of individuality and earnest instincts. I am in real trouble about her. I won't say she can be won—it would be ungenerous of me to say that. But try. I can bring you together easily.'

'I'll marry her, if she's willing!' With the phlegmatic dogmatism that was part of him, Somers added: 'When you have decided to marry, take the first nice woman you meet. They are all alike.'

'Well—you don't know her yet,' replied Jocelyn, who could give praise where he could not give love.

'But you do, and I'll take her on the strength of your judgment. Is she really handsome?—I had but the merest glance. But I know she is, or she wouldn't have caught your discriminating eye.'

'You may take my word for it; she looks as well at hand as afar.'

'What colour are her eyes?'

'Her eyes? I don't go much in for colour, being professionally sworn to form. But, let me see—grey; and her hair rather light than dark brown.'

'I wanted something darker,' said Somers airily. 'There are so many fair models among native Englishwomen. Still, blondes are useful property! . . . Well, well; this is flippancy. But I liked the look of her.'

Somers had gone back to town. It was a wet day on the little peninsula: but Pierston walked out as far as the garden-house of his hired castle, where he sat down and smoked. This erection being on the boundary-wall of his property his ear could now and then catch the tones of Avice's voice from her open-doored cottage in the lane which skirted his fence; and he noticed that there were no modulations in it. He knew why that was. She wished to go out, and could not. He had observed before that when she was planning an outing a particular note would come into her voice during the preceding hours: a dove's round-ness of sound; no doubt the effect upon her voice of her thoughts of her lover, or lovers. Yet the latter it could not be. She was pure and single-hearted: half an eye could see that. Whence, then, the two men? Possibly the quarrier was a relation.

There seemed reason in this when, going out into the lane he encountered one of the red-jackets he had been thinking of. Soldiers were seldom seen in this outer part of the isle: their beat from the forts, when on pleasure, was in the opposite direction, and this man must have had a special reason for coming hither. Pierston surveyed him. He was a round-faced, good-humoured fellow to look at, having two little pieces of moustache on his upper lip, like a pair of minnows rampant, and small black eyes, over which the Glengarry cap straddled flat. It was a hateful idea that her tender cheek should be kissed by the lips of this heavy young man who had never been sublimed by a single battle, even with defenceless savages.

The soldier went before her house, looked at the door, and moved on down the crooked way to the cliffs, where there was a path back to the forts. But he did not adopt it, returning by the way he had come. This showed his wish to pass the house again. She gave no sign, however, and the soldier disappeared.

Pierston could not be satisfied that Avice was in the house, and he crossed over to the front of her little freehold and tapped at the door, which stood ajar.

Nobody came: hearing a slight movement within he crossed the threshold. Avice was there alone, sitting on a low stool in a dark corner, as though she wished to be unobserved by any casual passer-by. She looked up at him without emotion or apparent surprise; but he could then see that she was crying. The view, for the first time, of distress in an unprotected young girl towards whom he felt drawn by ties of extraordinary delicacy and tenderness, moved Pierston beyond measure. He entered without ceremony.

'Avice, my dear girl!' he said. 'Something is the matter!'

She looked assent, and he went on: 'Now tell me all about it. Perhaps I can help you. Come, tell me.'

'I can't!' she murmured. 'Grammer Stockwool is upstairs, and she'll hear!' Mrs. Stockwool was the old woman who had come to live with the girl for company since her mother's death.

'Then come into my garden opposite. There we shall be quite private.'

She rose, put on her hat, and accompanied him to the door. Here she asked him if the lane were empty, and on his assuring her that it was she crossed over and entered with him through the garden-wall.

The place was a shady and secluded one, though through the boughs the sea could be seen quite near at hand, its moanings being distinctly audible. A water-drop from a tree fell here and there, but the rain was not enough to hurt them.

'Now let me hear it,' he said soothingly. 'You may tell me with the greatest freedom. I was a friend of your mother's, you know. That is, I knew her; and I'll be a friend of yours.'

The statement was risky, if he wished her not to suspect him of being her mother's false one. But that lover's name appeared to be unknown to the present Avice.

'I can't tell you, sir,' she replied unwillingly; 'except that it has to do with my own changeableness. The rest is the secret of somebody else.'

'I am sorry for that,' said he.

'I am getting to care for one I ought not to think of, and it means ruin. I ought to get away!'

'You mean from the island?'

'Yes.'

Pierston reflected. His presence in London had been desired for some time; yet he had delayed going because of his new solicitudes here. But to go and take her with him would afford him opportunity of watching over her, tending her mind, and developing it; while it might remove her from some looming danger. It was a somewhat awkward guardianship for him, as a lonely man, to carry out; still, it could be done. He asked her abruptly if she would really like to go away for a while.

'I like best to stay here,' she answered. 'Still, I should not mind going somewhere, because I think I ought to.'

'Would you like London?'

Avice's face lost its weeping shape. 'How could that be?' she said.

'I have been thinking that you could come to my house and make yourself useful in some way. I rent just now one of those new places called flats, which you may have heard of; and I have a studio at the back.'

'I haven't heard of 'em,' she said without interest.

'Well, I have two servants there, and as my man has a holiday you can help them for a month or two.'

'Would polishing furniture be any good? I can do that.'

'I haven't much furniture that requires polishing. But you can clear away plaster and clay messes in the studio, and chippings of stone, and help me in modelling, and dust all my Venus failures, and hands and heads and feet and bones, and other objects.'

She was startled, yet attracted by the novelty of the proposal.

'Only for a time?' she said.

'Only for a time. As short as you like, and as long.'

The deliberate manner in which, after the first surprise, Avice discussed the arrangements that he suggested, might have told him how far was any feeling for himself beyond friendship, and possibly gratitude, from agitating her breast. Yet there was nothing extravagant in the discrepancy between their ages, and he hoped, after shaping her to himself, to win her. What had grieved her to tears she would not more particularly tell.

She had naturally not much need of preparation, but she made even less preparation than he would have expected her to require. She seemed eager to be off immediately, and not a soul was to know of her departure. Why, if she were in love and at first averse to leave the island, she should be so precipitate now he failed to understand.

But he took great care to compromise in no way a girl in whom his interest was as protective as it was passionate. He accordingly left her to get out of the island alone, awaiting her at a station a few miles up the railway, where, discovering himself to her through the carriage-window, he entered the next compartment, his frame pervaded by a glow which was almost joy at having for the first time in his charge one who inherited the flesh and bore the name

so early associated with his own, and at the prospect of
putting things right which had been wrong through many
years.

THE IMAGE PERSISTS

II.—xi.

IT was dark when the four-wheeled cab wherein he had brought Avice from the station stood at the entrance to the pile of flats of which Pierston occupied one floor—rarer then as residences in London than they are now. Leaving Avice to alight and get the luggage taken in by the porter Pierston went upstairs. To his surprise his floor was silent, and on entering with a latchkey the rooms were all in darkness. He descended to the hall, where Avice was standing helpless beside the luggage, while the porter was outside with the cabman.

'Do you know what has become of my servants?' asked Jocelyn.

'What—and ain't they there, saur? Ah, then my belief is that what I suspected is thrue! You didn't leave your wine-cellar unlocked, did you, saur, by no mistake?'

Pierston considered. He thought he might have left the key with his elder servant, whom he had believed he could trust, especially as the cellar was not well stocked.

'Ah, then it was so! She's been very queer, saur, this last week or two. O yes, sending messages down the spakin'-tube which were like madness itself, and ordering us this and that, till we would take no notice at all. I see them both go out last night, and possibly they went for a holiday not expecting ye, or maybe for good! Shure, if ye'd written, saur, I'd ha' got the place ready, ye being out of a man, too, though it's not me duty at all!'

When Pierston got to his floor again he found that the cellar door was open; some bottles were standing empty that had been full, and many abstracted altogether. All other articles in the house, however, appeared to be intact. His letter to his housekeeper lay in the box as the postman had left it.

By this time the luggage had been sent up in the lift; and Avice, like so much more luggage, stood at the door, the hall-porter behind offering his assistance.

'Come here, Avice,' said the sculptor. 'What shall we do now? Here's a pretty state of affairs!'

Avice could suggest nothing, till she was struck with the bright thought that she should light a fire.

'Light a fire?—ah, yes. . . . I wonder if we could manage. This is an odd coincidence—and awkward!' he murmured. 'Very well, light a fire.'

'Is this the kitchen, sir, all mixed up with the parlours?'

'Yes.'

'Then I think I can do all that's wanted here for a bit; at any rate, till you can get help, sir. At least, I could if I could find the fuel-house. 'Tis no such big place as I thought!'

'That's right: take courage!' said he with a tender smile. 'Now, I'll dine out this evening, and leave the place for you to arrange as best you can with the help of the porter's wife downstairs.'

This Pierston accordingly did, and so their common residence began. Feeling more and more strongly that some danger awaited her in her native island he determined not to send her back till the lover or lovers who seemed to trouble her should have cooled off. He was quite willing to take the risk of his action thus far in his solicitous regard for her.

It was a dual solitude, indeed; for, though Pierston and Avice were the only two people in the flat, they did not keep each other company, the former being as scrupulously fearful of going near her now that he had the opportunity as he had been prompt to seek her when he had none. They lived in silence, his messages to her being frequently written on scraps of paper deposited where she could see them. It was not without a pang that he noted her unconsciousness of their isolated position—a position to which, had she experienced any reciprocity of sentiment, she would readily have been alive.

Considering that, though not profound, she was hardly a matter-of-fact girl as that phrase is commonly understood, she was exasperating in the matter-of-fact quality of her responses to the friendly remarks which would escape him in spite of himself, as well as in her general conduct. Whenever he formed some culinary excuse for walking across the few yards of tessellated hall which separated his room from the kitchen, and spoke through the doorway to her, she answered, 'Yes, sir,' or 'No, sir,' without turning her eyes from the particular work that she was engaged in.

In the usual course he would have obtained a couple of properly qualified servants immediately; but he lived on with the one, or rather the less than one, that this cottage-girl afforded. It had been his almost invariable custom to dine at one of his clubs. Now he sat at home over the miserable chop or steak to which he limited himself in dread lest she should complain of there being too much work for one person, and demand to be sent home. A charwoman came every two or three days, effecting an extraordinary consumption of food and alcoholic liquids: yet it was not for this that Pierston dreaded her presence, but lest, in conversing with Avice, she should open the girl's eyes to the oddity of her situation. Avice could see for herself that there must have been two or three servants in the flat during his former residence there: but his reasons for doing without them seemed never to strike her.

His intention had been to keep her occupied exclusively at the studio, but accident had modified this. However, he sent her round one morning, and entering himself shortly after found her engaged in wiping the layers of dust from the casts and models.

The colour of the dust never ceased to amaze her. 'It is like the hold of a Budmouth collier,' she said, 'and the beautiful faces of these clay people are quite spoilt by it.'

'I suppose you'll marry some day, Avice?' remarked Pierston, as he regarded her thoughtfully.

'Some do and some don't,' she said, with a reserved smile, still attending to the casts.

'You are very off-hand,' said he.

She archly weighed that remark without further speech. It was tantalizing conduct in the face of his instinct to

cherish her; especially when he regarded the charm of her
bending profile; the well-characterized though softly lined
nose, the round chin with, as it were, a second leap in its
curve to the throat, and the sweep of the eye-lashes over
the rosy cheek during the sedulously lowered glance. How
futilely he had laboured to express the character of that
face in clay, and, while catching it in substance, had yet
lost something that was essential!

That evening after dusk, in the stress of writing letters,
he sent her out for stamps. She had been absent some
quarter of an hour when, suddenly drawing himself up
from over his writing-table, it flashed upon him that he
had absolutely forgotten her total ignorance of London.

The head post-office, to which he had sent her because
it was late, was two or three streets off, and he had made
his request in the most general manner, which she had ac-
ceded to with alacrity enough. How could he have done
such an unreflecting thing?

Pierston went to the window. It was half-past nine
o'clock, and owing to her absence the blinds were not
down. He opened the casement and stepped out upon the
balcony. The green shade of his lamp screened its rays
from the gloom without. Over the opposite square the
moon hung, and to the right there stretched a long street,
filled with a diminishing array of lamps, some single, some
in clusters, among them an occasional blue or red one.
From a corner came the notes of a piano-organ strumming
out a stirring march of Rossini's. The shadowy black
figures of pedestrians moved up, down, and across the em-
browned roadway. Above the roofs was a bank of livid
mist, and higher a greenish-blue sky, in which stars were
visible, though its lower part was still pale with daylight,
against which rose chimney-pots in the form of elbows,
prongs, and fists.

From the whole scene proceeded a ground rumble, miles
in extent, upon which individual rattles, voices, a tin whistle, the bark of a dog, rode like bubbles on a sea. The
whole noise impressed him with the sense that no one in
its enormous mass ever required rest.

In this illimitable ocean of humanity there was a unit of existence, his Avice, wandering alone.

Pierston looked at his watch. She had been gone half an hour. It was impossible to distinguish her at this distance, even if she approached. He came inside, and putting on his hat determined to go out and seek her. He reached the end of the street, and there was nothing of her to be seen. She had the option of two or three routes from this point to the post-office; yet he plunged at random into one, till he reached the office to find it quite deserted. Almost distracted now by his anxiety for her he retreated as rapidly as he had come, regaining home only to find that she had not returned.

He recollected telling her that if she should ever lose her way she must call a cab and drive home. It occurred to him that this was what she would do now. He again went out upon the balcony; the dignified street in which he lived was almost vacant, and the lamps stood like placed sentinels awaiting some procession which tarried long. At a point under him where the road was torn up there stood a red light, and at the corner two men were talking in leisurely repose, as if sunning themselves at noonday. Lovers of a feline disposition, who were never seen by daylight, joked and darted at each other in and out of area gates.

His attention was fixed on the cabs, and he held his breath as the hollow clap of each horse's hoofs drew near the front of the house, only to go onward into the square. The two lamps of each vehicle afar dilated with its near approach, and seemed to swerve towards him. It was Avice surely? No, it passed by.

Almost frantic he again descended and let himself out of the house, moving towards a more central part, where the roar still continued. Before emerging into the noisy thoroughfare he observed a small figure approaching leisurely along the opposite side, and hastened across to find it was she.

A GRILLE DESCENDS BETWEEN

II.—xii.

'O AVICE!' he cried, with the tenderly subdued scolding of a mother. 'What is this you have done to alarm me so!'

She seemed unconscious of having done anything, and was altogether surprised at his anxiety. In his relief he did not speak further till he asked her suddenly if she would take his arm since she must be tired.

'O no, sir!' she assured him, 'I am not a bit tired, and I don't require any help at all, thank you.'

They went upstairs without using the lift, and he let her and himself in with his latchkey. She entered the kitchen, and he, following, sat down in a chair there.

'Where have you been?' he said, with almost angered concern on his face. 'You ought not to have been absent more than ten minutes.'

'I knew there was nothing for me to do, and thought I should like to see a little of London,' she replied naïvely. 'So when I had got the stamps I went on into the fashionable streets, where ladies are all walking about just as if it were daytime! 'Twas for all the world like coming home by night from Martinmas Fair at the Street o' Wells, only more genteel.'

'O Avice, Avice, you must not go out like this! Don't you know that I am responsible for your safety? I am your—well, guardian, in fact, and am bound by law and morals, and I don't know what-all, to deliver you up to your native island without a scratch or blemish. And yet you indulge in such a midnight vagary as this!'

'But I am sure, sir, the gentlemen in the street were more respectable than they are anywhere at home! They were dressed in the latest fashion, and would have scorned to do me any harm; and as to their love-making, I never heard anything so polite before.'

'Well, you must not do it again. I'll tell you some day why. What's that you have in your hand?'

'A mouse-trap. There are lots of mice in this kitchen—
sooty mice, not clean like ours—and I thought I'd try to
catch them. That was what I went so far to buy, as there
were no shops open just about here. I'll set it now.'

She proceeded at once to do so, and Pierston remained
in his seat regarding the operation, which seemed entirely
to engross her. It was extraordinary, indeed, to observe
how she wilfully limited her interests; with what content
she received the ordinary things that life offered, and persistently refused to behold what an infinitely extended life
lay open to her through him. If she had only said the word
he would have got a licence and married her the next morning. Was it possible that she did not perceive this tendency
in him? She could hardly be a woman if she did not; and
in her airy, elusive, off-hand demeanour she was very
much of a woman indeed.

'It only holds one mouse,' he said absently.

'But I shall hear it throw in the night, and set it again.'

He sighed, and left her to her own resources and retired
to rest, though he felt no tendency to sleep. At some small
hour of the darkness, owing, possibly, to some intervening
door being left open, he heard the mouse-trap click.
Another light sleeper must have heard it too, for almost
immediately after the pit-pat of naked feet, accompanied
by the brushing of drapery, was audible along the passage
towards the kitchen. After her absence in that apartment
long enough to reset the trap, he was startled by a scream
from the same quarter. Pierston sprang out of bed, jumped
into his dressing-gown, and hastened in the direction of the
cry.

Avice, barefooted and wrapped in a shawl, was standing
in a chair; the mouse-trap lay on the floor, the mouse running round and round in its neighbourhood.

'I was trying to take en out,' said she excitedly, 'and he
got away from me!'

Pierston secured the mouse while she remained standing
on the chair. Then, having set the trap anew, his feeling
burst out petulantly—

'A girl like you to throw yourself away upon such a

commonplace fellow as that quarryman! Why do you do it?'

Her mind was so intently fixed upon the matter in hand that it was some moments before she caught his irrelevant subject. 'Because I am a foolish girl,' she said quietly.

'What! Don't you love him?' said Jocelyn, with a surprised stare up at her as she stood, in her concern appearing the very Avice who had kissed him twenty years earlier.

'It is not much use to talk about that,' said she.

'Then, is it the soldier?'

'Yes, though I have never spoken to him.'

'Never spoken to the soldier?'

'Never.'

'Has either one treated you badly—deceived you?'

'No. Certainly not.'

'Well, I can't make you out; and I don't wish to know more than you choose to tell me. Come, Avice, why not tell me exactly how things are?'

'Not now, sir!' she said, her pretty pink face and brown eyes turned in simple appeal to him from her pedestal. 'I will tell you all to-morrow; an that I will!'

He retreated to his own room and lay down meditating. Some quarter of an hour after she had retreated to hers the mouse-trap clicked again, and Pierston raised himself on his elbow to listen. The place was so still and the jerry-built door-panels so thin that he could hear the mouse jumping about inside the wires of the trap. But he heard no footstep this time. As he was wakeful and restless he again arose, proceeded to the kichen with a light, and removing the mouse reset the trap. Returning he listened once more. He could see in the far distance the door of Avice's room; but that thoughtful housewife had not heard the second capture. From the room came a soft breathing like that of an infant.

He entered his own chamber and reclined himself gloomily enough. Her lack of all consciousness of him, the aspect of the deserted kitchen, the cold grate, impressed him with a deeper sense of loneliness than he had ever felt before.

Foolish he was, indeed, to be so devoted to this young woman. Her defencelessness, her freedom from the least thought that there lurked a danger in their propinquity, were in fact secondary safeguards, not much less strong than that of her being her mother's image, against risk to her from him. Yet it was out of this that his depression came.

At sight of her the next morning Pierston felt that he must put an end to such a state of things. He sent Avice off to the studio, wrote to an agent for a couple of servants, and then went round to his work. Avice was busy righting all that she was allowed to touch. It was the girl's delight to be occupied among the models and casts, which for the first time she regarded with the wistful interest of a soul struggling to receive ideas of beauty vaguely discerned yet ever eluding her. That brightness in her mother's mind which might have descended to the second Avice with the maternal face and form, had been dimmed by admixture with the mediocrity of her father's, and by one who remembered like Pierston the dual organization the opposites could be often seen wrestling internally.

They were alone in the studio, and his feelings found vent. Putting his arms round her he said, 'My darling, sweet little Avice! I want to ask you something—surely you guess what? I want to know this: will you be married to me, and live here with me always and ever?'

'O, Mr. Pierston, what nonsense!'

'Nonsense?' said he, shrinking somewhat.

'Yes, sir.'

'Well, why? Am I too old? Surely there's no serious difference?'

'O no—I should not mind that if it came to marrying. The difference is not much for husband and wife, though it is rather much for keeping company.'

She struggled to get free, and when in the movement she knocked down the Empress Faustina's head he did not try to retain her. He saw that she was not only surprised but a little alarmed.

'You haven't said why it is nonsense!' he remarked tartly.

'Why, I didn't know you was thinking of me like that. I hadn't any thought of it! And all alone here! What shall I do?'

'Say yes, my pretty Avice! We'll then go out and be married at once, and nobody be any the wiser.'

She shook her head. 'I couldn't, sir.'

'It would be well for you. You don't like me, perhaps?'

'Yes I do—very much. But not in that sort of way— quite. Still, I might have got to love you in time, if——'

'Well, then, try,' he said warmly. 'Your mother did!'

No sooner had the words slipped out than Pierston would have recalled them. He had felt in a moment that they jeopardized his cause.

'Mother loved you?' said Avice, incredulously gazing at him.

'Yes,' he murmured.

'You were not her false young man, surely? That one who——'

'Yes, yes! Say no more about it.'

'Who ran away from her?'

'Almost.'

'Then I can *never*, *never* like you again! I didn't know it was a gentleman—I—I thought——'

'It wasn't a gentleman, then.'

'O, sir, please go away! I can't bear the sight of 'ee at this moment! Perhaps I shall get to—to like you as I did; but——'

'No; I'm d——d if I'll go away!' said Pierston, thoroughly irritated. 'I have been candid with you; you ought to be the same with me!'

'What do you want me to tell?'

'Enough to make it clear to me why you don't accept this offer. Everything you have said yet is a reason for the reverse. Now, my dear, I am not angry.'

'Yes you are.'

'No I'm not. Now what is your reason?'

'The name of it is Isaac Pierston, down home.'

'How?'

'I mean he courted me, and led me on to island custom,

and then I went to chapel one morning and married him in secret, because mother didn't care about him; and I didn't either by that time. And then he quarrelled with me; and just before you and I came to London he went away to Guernsey. Then I saw a soldier; I never knew his name, but I fell in love with him because I am so quick at that! Still, as it was wrong, I tried not to think of him, and wouldn't look at him when he passed. But it made me cry very much that I mustn't. I was then very miserable, and you asked me to come to London. I didn't care what I did with myself, and I came.'

'Heaven above us!' said Pierston, his pale and distressed face showing with what a shock this announcement had come. 'Why have you done such extraordinary things? Or, rather, why didn't you tell me of this before? Then, at the present moment you are the wife of a man who is in Guernsey, whom you do not love at all; but instead of him love a soldier whom you have never spoken to; while I have nearly brought scandal upon us both by your letting me love you. Really, you are a very wicked woman!'

'No, I am not!' she pouted.

Still, Avice looked pale and rather frightened, and did not lift her eyes from the floor. 'I said it was nonsense in you to want to have me!' she went on, 'and, even if I hadn't been married to that horrid Isaac Pierston, I couldn't have married you after you told me that you was the man who ran away from my mother.'

'I have paid the penalty!' he said sadly. 'Men of my sort always get the worst of it somehow. Though I never did your mother any harm. Now, Avice—I'll call you dear Avice for your mother's sake and not for your own—I must see what I can do to help you out of the difficulty that unquestionably you are in. Why can't you love your husband now you have married him?'

Avice looked aside at the statuary as if the subtleties of her organization were not very easy to define.

'Was he that black-bearded typical local character I saw you walking with one Sunday? The same surname as mine; though, of course, you don't notice that in a place where there are only half-a-dozen surnames?'

'Yes, that was Ike. It was that evening we disagreed. He scolded me, and I answered him (you must have heard us); and the next day he went away.'

'Well, as I say, I must consider what it will be best to do for you in this. This first thing, it seems to me, will be to get your husband home.'

She impatiently shrugged her shoulders. 'I don't like him!'

'Then why did you marry him?'

'I was obliged to, after we'd proved each other by island custom.'

'You shouldn't have thought of such a thing. It is ridiculous and out of date nowadays.'

'Ah, he's so old-fashioned in his notions that he doesn't think like that. However, he's gone.'

'Ah—it is only a tiff between you, I dare say. I'll start him in business if he'll come. . . . Is the cottage at home still in your hands?'

'Yes, it is my freehold. Grammer Stockwool is taking care o' it for me.'

'Good. And back there you go straightway, my pretty madam, and wait till your husband comes to make it up with you.'

'I won't go!—I don't want him to come!' she sobbed. 'I want to stay here with you, or anywhere, except where he can come!'

'You will get over that. Now, go back to the flat, there's a dear Avice, and be ready in one hour, waiting in the hall for me.'

'I don't want to!'

'But I say you shall!'

She found it was no use to disobey. Precisely at the moment appointed he met her there himself, burdened only with a valise and umbrella, she with a box and other things. Directing the porter to put Avice and her belongings into a four-wheeled cab for the railway-station, he walked onward from the door, and kept looking behind till he saw the cab approaching. He then entered beside the astonished girl, and onward they went together.

They sat opposite each other in an empty compartment, and the tedious railway journey began. Regarding her closely now by the light of her revelation he wondered at himself for never divining her secret. Whenever he looked at her the girl's eyes grew rebellious, and at last she wept.

'I don't want to go to him!' she sobbed in a miserable voice.

Pierston was almost as much distressed as she. 'Why did you put yourself and me in such a position?' he said bitterly. 'It is no use to regret it now! And I can't say that I do. It affords me a way out of a trying position. Even if you had not been married to him you would not have married me!'

'Yes, I would, sir.'

'What! You would? You said you wouldn't not long ago.'

'I like you better now! I like you more and more!'

Pierston sighed, for emotionally he was not much older than she. That hitch in his development, rendering him the most lopsided of God's creatures, was his standing misfortune. A proposal to her which crossed his mind was dismissed as disloyalty, particularly to an inexperienced fellow-islander and one who was by race and traditions almost a kinswoman.

Little more passed between the twain on that wretched, never-to-be-forgotten day. Aphrodite, Ashtaroth, Freyja, or whoever the love-queen of his isle might have been, was punishing him sharply, as she knew but too well how to punish her votaries when they reverted from the ephemeral to the stable mood. When was it to end—this curse of his heart not ageing while his frame moved naturally onward? Perhaps only with life.

His first act the day after depositing her in her own house was to go to the chapel where, by her statement, the marriage had been solemnized, and make sure of the fact. Perhaps he felt an illogical hope that she might be free, even then, in the tarnished condition which such freedom would have involved. However, there stood the words distinctly: Isaac Pierston, Ann Avice Caro, son and daughter of So-and-so, married on such a day, signed by the contracting parties, the officiating minister, and the two witnesses.

SHE IS ENSHROUDED
FROM SIGHT

II.—xiii.

ONE evening in early winter, when the air was dry and gusty, the dark little lane which divided the grounds of Sylvania Castle from the cottage of Avice, and led down to the adjoining ruin of Red-King Castle, was paced by a solitary man. The cottage was the centre of his beat; its western limit being the gates of the former residence, its eastern the drawbridge of the ruin. The few other cottages thereabout—all as if carved from the solid rock—were in darkness, but from the upper window of Avice's tiny freehold glimmered a light. Its rays were repeated from the far-distant sea by the lightship lying moored over the mysterious Shambles quicksand, which brought tamelessness and domesticity into due position as balanced opposites.

The sea moaned—more than moaned—among the boulders below the ruins, a throe of its tide being timed to regular intervals. These sounds were accompanied by an equally periodic moan from the interior of the cottage chamber; so that the articulate heave of water and the articulate heave of life seemed but differing utterances of the selfsame troubled terrestrial Being—which in one sense they were.

Pierston—for the man in the lane was he—would look from lightship to cottage window; then back again, as he waited there between the travail of the sea without, and the travail of the woman within. Soon an infant's wail of the very feeblest was also audible in the house. He started from his easy pacing, and went again westward, standing at the elbow of the lane a long time. Then the peace of the sleeping village which lay that way was broken by light wheels and the trot of a horse. Pierston went back to the cottage gate and awaited the arrival of the vehicle.

It was a light cart, and a man jumped down as it stopped. He was in a broad-brimmed hat, under which no more of him could be perceived than that he wore a black beard clipped like a yew fence—a typical aspect in the island.

'You are Avice's husband?' asked the sculptor quickly.

The man replied that he was, in the local accent. 'I've just come in by to-day's boat,' he added. 'I couldn't git here avore. I had contracted for the job at Peter-Port, and had to see to't to the end.'

'Well,' said Pierston, 'your coming means that you are willing to make it up with her?'

'Ay, I don't know but I be,' said the man. 'Mid so well do that as anything else!'

'If you do, thoroughly, a good business in your old line awaits you here in the island.'

'Wi' all my heart, then,' said the man. His voice was energetic, and, though slightly touchy, it showed, on the whole, a disposition to set things right.

The driver of the trap was paid off, and Jocelyn and Isaac Pierston—undoubtedly scions of a common stock in this isle of intermarriages, though they had no proof of it—entered the house. Nobody was in the ground-floor room, in the centre of which stood a square table, in the centre of the table a little wool mat, and in the centre of the mat a lamp, the apartment having the appearance of being rigidly swept and set in order for an event of interest.

The woman who lived in the house with Avice now came downstairs, and to the inquiry of the comers she replied that matters were progressing favourably, but that nobody could be allowed to go upstairs just then. After placing chairs and viands for them she retreated, and they sat down, the lamp between them—the lover of the sufferer above, who had no right to her, and the man who had every right to her, but did not love her. Engaging in desultory and fragmentary conversation they listened to the trampling of feet on the floor-boards overhead— Pierston full of anxiety and attentiveness, Ike awaiting the course of nature calmly.

Soon they heard the feeble bleats repeated, and then the local practitioner descended and entered the room.

'How is she now?' said Pierston, the more taciturn Ike looking up with him for the answer that he felt would serve for two as well as for one.

'Doing well, remarkably well,' replied the professional gentleman, with a manner of having said it in other places; and his vehicle not being at the door he sat down and shared some refreshment with the others. When he had departed Mrs. Stockwool again stepped down, and informed them that Ike's presence had been made known to his wife.

The truant quarrier seemed rather inclined to stay where he was and finish the mug of ale, but Pierston quickened him, and he ascended the staircase. As soon as the lower room was empty Pierston leant with his elbows on the table, and covered his face with his hands.

Ike was absent no great time. Descending with a proprietary mien that had been lacking before, he invited Jocelyn to ascend likewise, since she had stated that she would like to see him. Jocelyn went up the crooked old steps, the husband remaining below.

Avice, though white as the sheets, looked brighter and happier than he had expected to find her, and was apparently very much fortified by the pink little lump at her side. She held out her hand to him.

'I just wanted to tell 'ee,' she said, striving against her feebleness, 'I thought it would be no harm to see you, though 'tis rather soon—to tell 'ee how very much I thank you for getting me settled again with Ike. He is very glad to come home again, too, he says. Yes, you've done a good many kind things for me, sir.'

Whether she were really glad, or whether the words were expressed as a matter of duty, Pierston did not attempt to learn.

He merely said that he valued her thanks. 'Now, Avice,' he added tenderly, 'I resign my guardianship of you. I hope to see your husband in a sound little business here in a very short time.'

'I hope so—for baby's sake,' she said, with a bright sigh. 'Would you—like to see her, sir?'

'The baby? O yes . . . *your* baby! You must christen her Avice.'

'Yes—so I will!' she murmured readily, and disclosed the infant with some timidity. 'I hope you forgive me, sir, for concealing my thoughtless marriage!'

'If you forgive me for making love to you.'

'Yes. How were you to know! I wish——'

Pierston bade her good-bye, kissing her hand; turned from her and the incipient being whom he was to meet again under very altered conditions, and left the bed-chamber with a tear in his eye.

'Here endeth that dream!' said he.

Hymen, in secret or overt guise, seemed to haunt Pierston just at this time with undignified mockery which savoured rather of Harlequin than of the torch-bearer. Two days after parting in a lone island from the girl he had so disinterestedly loved he met in Piccadilly his friend Somers, wonderfully spruced up, and hastening along with a preoccupied face.

'My dear fellow,' said Somers, 'what do you think! I was charged not to tell you, but, hang it! I may just as well make a clean breast of it now as later.'

'What—you are not going to . . .' began Pierston, with divination.

'Yes. What I said on impulse six months back I am about to carry out in cold blood. Nichola and I began in jest and ended in earnest. We are going to take one another next month for good and all.'

PART THIRD
A YOUNG MAN OF SIXTY

'In me thou seest the glowing of such fire,
That on the ashes of his youth doth lie
As the death-bed whereon it must expire,
Consumed with that which it was nourished by.'
                                    W. SHAKESPEARE.

SHE RETURNS FOR
THE NEW SEASON

III.—i.

TWENTY years had spread their films over the events which wound up with the reunion of the second Avice and her husband; and the hoary peninsula called an island looked just the same as before; though many who had formerly projected their daily shadows upon its unrelieved summer whiteness ceased now to disturb the colourless sunlight there.

The general change, nevertheless, was small. The silent ships came and went from the wharf, the chisels clinked in the quarries; file after file of whitey-brown horses, in strings of eight or ten, painfully dragged down the hill the square blocks of stone on the antediluvian wooden wheels just as usual. The lightship winked every night from the quicksands to the Beal Lantern, and the Beal Lantern glared through its eyeglass on the ship. The canine gnawing audible on the Pebble-bank had been repeated ever since at each tide, but the pebbles remained undevoured.

Men drank, smoked, and spat in the inns with only a little more adulteration in their refreshments and a trifle less dialect in their speech than of yore. But one figure had never been seen on the Channel rock in the interval, the form of Pierston the sculptor, whose first use of the chisel that rock had instigated.

He had lived abroad a great deal, and, in fact, at this very date he was staying at an hotel in Rome. Though he had not once set eyes on Avice since parting from her in the room with her firstborn, he had managed to obtain tidings of her from time to time during the interval. In this way Pierston learnt that, shortly after their resumption of a common life in her house, Ike had ill-used her, till fortunately, the business to which Jocelyn had assisted him chancing to prosper, he became immersed in its details,

and allowed Avice to pursue her household courses without
interference, initiating that kind of domestic reconciliation
which is so calm and durable, having as its chief ingredient
neither hate nor love, but an all-embracing indifference.

At first Pierston had sent her sums of money privately,
fearing lest her husband should deny her material com-
forts; but he soon found, to his great relief, that such help
was unnecessary, social ambition prompting Ike to set up
as quite a gentleman-islander, and to allow Avice a scope
for show which he would never have allowed in mere
kindness.

Being in Rome, as aforesaid, Pierston returned one evening to his hotel to dine, after spending the afternoon
among the busts in the long gallery of the Vatican. The
unconscious habit, common to so many people, of tracing
likes in unlikes had often led him to discern, or to fancy
he discerned, in the Roman atmosphere, in its lights and
shades, and particularly in its reflected or secondary lights,
something resembling the atmosphere of his native promontory. Perhaps it was that in each case the eye was
mostly resting on stone—that the quarries of ruins in the
Eternal City reminded him of the quarries of maiden rock
at home.

This being in his mind when he sat down to dinner at the
common table, he was surprised to hear an American
gentleman, who sat opposite, mention the name of
Pierston's birthplace. The American was talking to a friend
about a lady—an English widow, whose acquaintance they
had renewed somewhere in the Channel Islands during a
recent tour, after having known her as a young woman
who came to San Francisco with her father and mother
many years before. Her father was then a rich man just
retired from the business of a stone-merchant in the Isle of
Slingers; but he had engaged in large speculations, and had
lost nearly all his fortune. Jocelyn further gathered that the
widowed daughter's name was Mrs. Leverre; that she had
a step-son, her husband having been a Jersey gentleman,
a widower; and that the step-son seemed to be a promising
and interesting young man.

Pierston was instantly struck with the perception that these and other allusions, though general, were in accord with the history of his long-lost Marcia. He hardly felt any desire to hunt her up after nearly two score years of separation, but he was impressed enough to resolve to exchange a word with the strangers as soon as he could get opportunity.

He could not well attract their attention through the plants upon the wide table, and even if he had been able he was disinclined to ask questions in public. He waited on till dinner was over, and when the strangers withdrew Pierston withdrew in their rear.

They were not in the drawing-room, and he found that they had gone out. There was no chance of overtaking them, but Pierston, waked to restlessness by their remarks, wandered up and down the adjoining Piazza di Spagna, thinking they might return. The streets below were immersed in shade, the front of the church of the Trinità de' Monti at the top was flooded with orange light, the gloom of evening gradually intensifying upon the broad, long flight of steps, which foot-passengers incessantly ascended and descended with the insignificance of ants; the dusk wrapped up the house to the left, in which Shelley had lived, and that to the right, in which Keats had died.

Getting back to the hotel he learnt that the Americans had only dropped in to dine, and were staying elsewhere. He saw no more of them; and on reflection he was not deeply concerned, for what earthly woman, going off in a freak as Marcia had done, and keeping silence so long, would care for a belated friendship with him now in the sere, even if he were to take the trouble to discover her.

Thus much Marcia. The other thread of his connection with the ancient Isle of Slingers was stirred by a letter he received from Avice a little after this date, in which she stated that her husband Ike had been killed in his own quarry by an accident within the past year; that she herself had been ill, and though well again, and left amply provided for, she would like to see him if he ever came that way.

As she had not communicated for several long years, her expressed wish to see him now was likely to be prompted by something more, something newer, than memories of him. Yet the manner of her writing precluded all suspicion that she was thinking of him as an old lover whose suit events had now made practicable. He told her he was sorry to hear that she had been ill, and that he would certainly take an early opportunity of going down to her home on his next visit to England.

He did more. Her request had revived thoughts of his old home and its associations, and instead of awaiting other reasons for a return he made her the operating one. About a week later he stood once again at the foot of the familiar steep whereon the houses at the entrance to the Isle were perched like grey pigeons on a roof-side.

At Top-o'-Hill—as the summit of the rock was mostly called—he stood looking at the busy doings in the quarries beyond, where the numerous black hoisting-cranes scattered over the central plateau had the appearance of a swarm of crane-flies resting there. He went a little further, made some general inquiries about the accident which had carried off Avice's husband in the previous year, and learnt that though now a widow, she had plenty of friends and sympathizers about her, which rendered any immediate attention to her on his part unnecessary. Considering, therefore, that there was no great reason why he should call on her so soon, and without warning, he turned back. Perhaps after all her request had been dictated by a momentary feeling only, and a considerable strangeness to each other must naturally be the result of a score of dividing years. Descending to the bottom he took his seat in the train on the shore, which soon carried him along the Bank, and round to the watering-place five miles off, at which he had taken up his quarters for a few days.

Here, as he stayed on, his local interests revived. Whenever he went out he could see the island that was once his home lying like a great snail upon the sea across the bay. It was the spring of the year; local steamers had begun to run, and he was never tired of standing on the thinly occupied deck of one of these as it skirted the island and revealed to him on the cliffs far up its height the ruins of Red-King Castle, behind which the little village of East Quarriers lay.

Thus matters went on, if they did not rather stand still, for several days before Pierston redeemed his vague promise to seek Avice out. And in the meantime he was surprised by the arrival of another letter from her by a roundabout route. She had heard, she said, that he had been on the island, and imagined him therefore to be staying somewhere near. Why did he not call as he had told her he would do? She was always thinking of him, and wishing to see him.

Her tone was anxious, and there was no doubt that she really had something to say which she did not want to write. He wondered what it could be, and started the same afternoon.

Avice, who had been little in his mind of late years, began to renew for herself a distinct position therein. He was fully aware that since his earlier manhood a change had come over his regard of womankind. Once the individual had been nothing more to him than the temporary abiding-place of the typical or ideal; now his heart showed its bent to be a growing fidelity to the specimen, with all her pathetic flaws of detail; which flaws, so far from sending him further, increased his tenderness. This maturer feeling, if finer and higher, was less convenient than the old. Ardours of passion could be felt as in youth without the recuperative intervals which had accompanied evanescence.

The first sensation was to find that she had long ceased to live in the little freehold cottage she had occupied of old. In answer to his inquiries he was directed along the road to the west of the modern castle, past the entrance on that side, and onward to the very house that had once been his own home. There it stood as of yore, facing up the Channel, a comfortable roomy structure, euonymus and other shrubs, which alone would stand in the teeth of the salt wind, living on at about the same stature in front of it; but the paint-work much renewed. A thriving man had resided there of late, evidently.

The widow in mourning who received him in the front parlour was, alas! but the sorry shadow of Avice the Second. How could he have fancied otherwise after twenty years? Yet he had been led to fancy otherwise, almost without knowing it, by feeling himself unaltered. Indeed, curiously enough, nearly the first words she said to him were: 'Why—you are just the same!'

'Just the same. Yes, I am, Avice,' he answered sadly; for this inability to ossify with the rest of his generation threw him out of proportion with the time. Moreover, while wearing the aspect of comedy, it was of the nature of tragedy.

'It is well to be you, sir,' she went on. 'I have had troubles to take the bloom off me!'

'Yes; I have been sorry for you.'

She continued to regard him curiously, with humorous interest; and he knew what was passing in her mind: that this man, to whom she had formerly looked up as to a person far in advance of her along the lane of life, seemed now to be a well-adjusted contemporary, the pair of them observing the world with fairly level eyes.

He had come to her with warmth for a vision which, on reaching her, he found to have departed; and, though fairly weaned by the natural reality, he was so far staunch as to linger hankeringly. They talked of past days, his old attachment, which she had then despised, being now far more absorbing and present to her than to himself.

She unmistakably won upon him as he sat on. A curious closeness between them had been produced in his imagination by the discovery that she was passing her life within the house of his own childhood. Her similar surname meant little here; but it was also his, and, added to the identity of domicile, lent a strong suggestiveness to the accident.

'This is where I used to sit when my parents occupied the house,' he said, placing himself beside that corner of the fireplace which commanded a view through the window. 'I could see a bough of tamarisk wave outside at that time, and, beyond the bough, the same abrupt grassy waste towards the sea, and at night the same old lightship blinking far out there. Place yourself on the spot to please me.'

She set her chair where he indicated, and Pierston stood close beside her, directing her gaze to the familiar objects he had regarded thence as a boy. Her head and face—the latter thoughtful and worn enough, poor thing, to suggest a married life none too comfortable—were close to his breast, and, with a few inches further incline, would have touched it.

'And now you are the inhabitant; I the visitor,' he said. 'I am glad to see you here—so glad, Avice! You are fairly well provided for—I think I may assume that?' He looked round the room at the solid mahogany furniture, and at the modern piano and show bookcase.

'Yes, Ike left me comfortable. 'Twas he who thought of moving from my cottage to this larger house. He bought it, and I can live here as long as I choose to.'

Apart from the decline of his adoration to friendship, there seemed to be a general convergence of positions which suggested that he might make amends for the desertion of Avice the First by proposing to this Avice when a meet time should arrive. If he did not love her as he had done when she was a slim thing catching mice in his rooms in London, he could surely be content at his age with comradeship. After all she was only forty to his sixty. The feeling that he really could be thus content was so convincing that he almost believed the luxury of getting old and reposeful was coming to his restless, wandering heart at last.

'Well, you have come at last, sir,' she went on; 'and I am grateful to you. I did not like writing, and yet I wanted to be straightforward. Have you guessed at all why I wished to see you so much that I could not help sending twice to you?'

'I have tried, but cannot.'

'Try again. It is a pretty reason, which I hope you'll forgive.'

'I am sure I shan't unriddle it. But I'll say this on my own account before you tell me. I have always taken a lingering interest in you, which you must value for what it is worth. It originated, so far as it concerns you personally, with the sight of you in that cottage round the corner, nineteen or twenty years ago, when I became tenant of the castle opposite. But that was not the very beginning. The very beginning was a score of years before that, when I, a young fellow of one-and-twenty, coming home here, from London, to see my father, encountered a tender woman as like you as your double; was much attracted by her as I saw her day after day flit past this window; till I made it my business to accompany her in her walks awhile. I, as you know, was not a staunch fellow, and it all ended badly. But, at any rate you, her daughter, and I are friends.'

'Ah! there she is!' suddenly exclaimed Avice, whose attention had wanderd somewhat from his retrospective discourse. She was looking from the window towards the cliffs, where, upon the open ground quite near at hand, a slender female form was seen rambling along. 'She is out for a walk,' Avice continued. 'I wonder if she is going to call here this afternoon? She is living at the castle opposite as governess.'

'O, she's——'

'Yes. Her education was very thorough—better even than her grandmother's. I was the neglected one, and her father and myself both vowed that there should be no complaint on that score about her. We christened her Avice, to keep up the name, as you requested. I wish you could speak to her—I am sure you would like her.'

'Is that the baby?' faltered Jocelyn.

'Yes, the baby.'

The person signified, now much nearer, was a still more modernized, up-to-date edition of the two Avices of that blood with whom he had been involved more or less for the last forty years. A ladylike creature was she—almost elegant. She was altogether finer in figure than her mother or grandmother had ever been, which made her more of a woman in appearance than in years. She wore a large-disked sun-hat, with a brim like a wheel whose spokes were radiating folds of muslin lining the brim, a black margin beyond the muslin being the felloe. Beneath this brim her hair was massed low upon her brow, the colour of the thick tresses being probably, from her complexion, repeated in the irises of her large, deep eyes. Her rather nervous lips were thin and closed, so that they only appeared as a delicate red line. A changeable temperament was shown by that mouth—quick transitions from affection to aversion, from a pout to a smile.

It was Avice the Third.

Jocelyn and the second Avice continued to gaze ardently at her.

'Ah! she is not coming in now; she hasn't time,' murmured the mother, with some disappointment. 'Perhaps she means to run across in the evening.'

The tall girl, in fact, went past and on till she was out of sight. Pierston stood as in a dream. It was the very she, in all essential particulars, and with an intensification of general charm, who had kissed him forty years before. When he turned his head from the window his eyes fell again upon the intermediate Avice at his side. Before but the relic of the Well-Beloved, she had now become its empty shrine. Warm friendship, indeed, he felt for her; but whatever that might have done towards the instauration of a former dream was now hopelessly barred by the rivalry of the thing itself in the guise of a lineal successor.

MISGIVINGS ON THE
RE-EMBODIMENT
III.—ii.

PIERSTON had been about to leave, but he sat down again on being asked if he would stay and have a cup of tea. He hardly knew for a moment what he did; a dim thought that Avice—the renewed Avice—might come into the house made his reseating himself an act of spontaneity.

He forgot that twenty years earlier he had called the now Mrs. Pierston an elf, a witch; and that lapse of time had probably not diminished the subtleties implied by those epithets. He did not know that she had noted every impression that her daughter had made upon him.

How he contrived to attenuate and disperse the rather tender personalities he had opened up with the new Avice's mother, Pierston never exactly defined. Perhaps she saw more than he thought she saw—read something in his face—knew that about his nature which he gave her no credit for knowing. Anyhow, the conversation took the form of a friendly gossip from that minute, his remarks being often given while his mind was turned elsewhere.

But a chill passed through Jocelyn when there had been time for reflection. The renewed study of his art in Rome without any counterbalancing practical pursuit had nourished and developed his natural responsiveness to impressions; he now felt that his old trouble, his doom—his curse, indeed, he had sometimes called it—was come back again. His divinity was not yet propitiated for that original sin against her image in the person of Avice the First, and now, at the age of one-and-sixty, he was urged on and on like the Jew Ahasuerus—or, in the phrase of the islanders themselves, like a blind ram.

The Goddess, an abstraction to the general, was a fairly real personage to Pierston. He had watched the marble images of her which stood in his working-room, under all

A silence followed, and nobody came. The voice spoke again; 'John Stoney!'

Neither was this summons attended to. The cry continued, with more entreaty: 'William Scribben!'

The voice was that of a Pierston—there could be no doubt of it—young Avice's, surely? Something or other seemed to be detaining her down there against her will. A sloping path beneath the beetling cliff and the castle walls rising sheer from its summit, led down to the lower level whence the voice proceeded. Pierston followed the pathway, and soon beheld a girl in light clothing—the same he had seen through the window—standing upon one of the rocks, apparently unable to move. Pierston hastened across to her.

'O, thank you for coming!' she murmured with some timidity. 'I have met with an awkward mishap. I live near here, and am not frightened really. My foot has become jammed in a crevice of the rock, and I cannot get it out, try how I will. What *shall* I do?'

Jocelyn stooped and examined the cause of discomfiture. 'I think if you can take your boot off,' he said, 'your foot might slip out, leaving the boot behind.'

She tried to act upon this advice, but could not do so effectually. Pierston then experimented by slipping his hand into the crevice till he could just reach the buttons of her boot, which, however, he could not unfasten any more than she. Taking his penknife from his pocket he tried again, and cut off the buttons one by one. The boot unfastened, and out slipped the foot.

'O, how glad I am!' she cried joyfully. 'I was fearing I should have to stay here all night. How can I thank you enough?'

He was tugging to withdraw the boot, but no skill that he could exercise would move it without tearing. At last she said: 'Don't try any longer. It is not far to the house. I can walk in my stocking.'

'I'll assist you in,' he said.

She said she did not want help, nevertheless allowed him to help her on the unshod side. As they moved on she

explained that she had come out through the garden door;
had been standing on the boulders to look at something
out at sea just discernible in the evening light as assisted by
the moon, and, in jumping down, had wedged her foot as
he had found it.

Whatever Pierston's years might have made him look by
day, in the dusk of evening he was fairly presentable as a
pleasing man of no marked antiquity, his outline differing
but little from what it had been when he was half his years.
He was well preserved, still upright, trimly shaven, agile
in movement; wore a tightly buttoned suit which set off a
naturally slight figure; in brief, he might have been of any
age as he appeared to her at this moment. She talked to
him with the co-equality of one who assumed him to be
not far ahead of her own generation; and, as the growing
darkness obscured him more and more, he adopted her
assumption of his age with increasing boldness of tone.

The flippant, harmless freedom of the watering-place
Miss, which Avice had plainly acquired during her sojourn
at the Sandbourne school, helped Pierston greatly in this
rôle of *jeune premier* which he was not unready to play.
Not a word did he say about being a native of the island;
still more carefully did he conceal the fact of his having
courted her grandmother, and engaged himself to marry
that attractive lady.

He found that she had come out upon the rocks through
the same little private door from the lawn of the modern
castle which had frequently afforded him egress to the
same spot in years long past. Pierston accompanied her
across the grounds almost to the entrance of the
mansion—the place being now far better kept and planted
than when he had rented it as a lonely tenant; almost,
indeed, restored to the order and neatness which had
characterized it when he was a boy.

Like her granny she was too inexperienced to be reserved,
and during this little climb, leaning upon his arm, there
was time for a great deal of confidence. When he had bid-
den her farewell, and she had entered, leaving him in the
dark, a rush of sadness through Pierston's soul swept

down all the temporary pleasure he had found in the charming girl's company. Had Mephistopheles sprung from the ground there and then with an offer to Jocelyn of restoration to youth on the usual terms of his firm, the sculptor might have consented to sell a part of himself which he felt less immediate need of than of a ruddy lip and cheek and of an unploughed brow.

But what could have been treated as a folly by outsiders was almost a sorrow for him. Why was he born with such a temperament? And this concatenated interest could hardly have arisen, even with Pierston, but for a conflux of circumstances only possible here. The three Avices, the second something like the first, the third a glorification of the first, at all events externally, were the outcome of the immemorial island customs of intermarriage and of prenuptial union, under which conditions the type of feature was almost uniform from parent to child through generations: so that, till quite latterly, to have seen one native man and woman was to have seen the whole population of that isolated rock, so nearly cut off from the mainland. His own predisposition and the sense of his early faithlessness did all the rest.

He turned gloomily away, and let himself out of the precincts. Before walking along the couple of miles of road which would conduct him to the little station on the shore, he redescended to the rocks whereon he had found her, and searched about for the fissure which had made a prisoner of this terribly belated edition of the Beloved. Kneeling down beside the spot he inserted his hand, and ultimately, by much wriggling, withdrew the pretty boot. He mused over it for a moment, put it in his pocket, and followed the stony route to the Street of Wells.

THE RENEWED IMAGE
BURNS ITSELF IN

III.—iii.

THERE was nothing to hinder Pierston in calling upon the new Avice's mother as often as he should choose, beyond the five miles of intervening railway and additional mile or two of clambering over the heights of the island. Two days later, therefore, he repeated his journey and knocked about tea-time at the widow's door.

As he had feared, the daughter was not at home. He sat down beside the old sweetheart who, having eclipsed her mother in past days, had now eclipsed herself in her child. Jocelyn produced the girl's boot from his pocket.

'Then, 'tis *you* who helped Avice out of her predicament?' said Mrs. Pierston, with surprise.

'Yes, my dear friend; and perhaps I shall ask you to help me out of mine before I have done. But never mind that now. What did she tell you about the adventure?'

Mrs. Pierston was looking thoughtfully upon him. 'Well, 'tis rather strange it should have been you, sir,' she replied. She seemed to be a good deal interested. 'I thought it might have been a younger man—a much younger man.'

'It might have been as far as feelings were concerned. . . . Now, Avice, I'll to the point at once. Virtually I have known your daughter any number of years. When I talk to her I can anticipate every turn of her thought, every sentiment, every act, so long did I study those things in your mother and in you. Therefore I do not require to learn her; she was learnt by me in her previous existences. Now, don't be shocked: I am willing to marry her—I should be overjoyed to do it, if there would be nothing preposterous about it, or that would seem like a man making himself too much of a fool, and so degrading her in consenting. I can make her comparatively rich, as you know, and I would indulge her every whim. There is the idea, bluntly put. It

would set right something in my mind that has been wrong
for forty years. After my death she would have plenty of
freedom and plenty of means to enjoy it.'

Mrs. Isaac Pierston seemed only a little surprised; certainly not shocked.

'Well, if I didn't think you might be a bit taken with her!'
she said with an arch simplicity which could hardly be
called unaffected. 'Knowing the set of your mind, from my
little time with you years ago, nothing you could do in this
way would astonish me.'

'But you don't think badly of me for it?'

'Not at all. . . . By-the-bye, did you ever guess why I
asked you to come? . . . But never mind it now: the matter
is past. . . . Of course, it would depend upon what Avice
felt. . . . Perhaps she would rather marry a younger man.'

'And suppose a satisfactory younger man should not
appear?'

Mrs. Pierston showed in her face that she fully recognized
the difference between a rich bird in hand and a young bird in
the bush. She looked him curiously up and down.

'I know you would make anybody a very nice husband,'
she said. 'I know that you would be nicer than many men
half your age; and, though there is a great deal of difference
between you and her, there have been more unequal
marriages, that's true. Speaking as her mother, I can say
that I shouldn't object to you, sir, for her, provided she
liked you. That is where the difficulty will lie.'

'I wish you would help me to get over that difficulty,' he
said gently. 'Remember, I brought back a truant husband
to you twenty years ago.'

'Yes, you did,' she assented; 'and, though I may say no
great things as to happiness came of it, I've always seen
that your intentions towards me were none the less noble
on that account. I would do for you what I would do for
no other man, and there is one reason in particular which
inclines me to help you with Avice—that I should feel
absolutely certain I was helping her to a kind husband.'

'Well, that would remain to be seen. I would, at any
rate, try to be worthy of your opinion. Come, Avice, for

old times' sake, you must help me. You never felt anything but friendship in those days, you know, and that makes it easy and proper for you to do me a good turn now.'

After a little more conversation his old friend promised that she really would do everything that lay in her power. She did not say how simple she thought him not to perceive that she had already, by writing to him, been doing everything that lay in her power; had created the feeling which prompted his entreaty. And to show her good faith in this promise she asked him to wait till later in the evening, when Avice might possibly run across to see her.

Pierston, who fancied he had won the younger Avice's interest, at least, by the part he had played upon the rocks the week before, had a dread of encountering her in full light till he should have advanced a little further in her regard. He accordingly was perplexed at this proposal, and, seeing his hesitation, Mrs. Pierston suggested that they should walk together in the direction whence Avice would come, if she came at all.

He welcomed the idea, and in a few minutes they started, strolling along under the now strong moonlight, and when they reached the gates of Sylvania Castle turning back again towards the house. After two or three such walks up and down the gate of the castle grounds clicked, and a form came forth which proved to be the expected one.

As soon as they met the girl recognized in her mother's companion the gentleman who had helped her on the shore; and she seemed really glad to find that her chivalrous assistant was claimed by her parent as an old friend. She remembered hearing at divers times about this worthy London man of talent and position, whose ancestry were people of her own isle, and possibly, from the name, of a common stock with her own.

'And you have actually lived in Sylvania Castle yourself, Mr. Pierston?' asked Avice the daughter, with her innocent young voice. 'Was it long ago?'

'Yes, it was some time ago,' replied the sculptor, with a sinking at his heart lest she should ask how long.

'It must have been when I was away—or when I was very little?'

'I don't think you were away.'

'But I don't think I could have been here?'

'No, perhaps you couldn't have been here.'

'I think she was hiding herself in the parsley-bed,' said Avice's mother blandly.

They talked in this general way till they reached Mrs. Pierston's house; but Jocelyn resisted both the widow's invitation and the desire of his own heart, and went away without entering. To risk, by visibly confronting her, the advantage that he had already gained, or fancied he had gained, with the re-incarnate Avice required more courage than he could claim in his present mood.

Such evening promenades as these were frequent during the waxing of that summer moon. On one occasion, as they were all good walkers, it was arranged that they should meet halfway between the island and the town in which Pierston had lodgings. It was impossible that by this time the pretty young governess should not have guessed the ultimate reason of these rambles to be a matrimonial intention; but she inclined to the belief that the widow rather than herself was the object of Pierston's regard; though why this educated and apparently wealthy man should be attracted by her mother—whose homeliness was apparent enough to the girl's more modern training—she could not comprehend.

They met accordingly in the middle of the Pebble-bank, Pierston coming from the mainland, and the women from the peninsular rock. Crossing the wooden bridge which connected the bank with the shore proper they moved in the direction of Henry the Eighth's Castle, on the verge of the rag-stone cliff. Like the Red King's Castle on the island, the interior was open to the sky, and when they entered and the full moon streamed down upon them over the edge of the enclosing masonry, the whole present reality faded from Jocelyn's mind under the press of memories. Neither of his companions guessed what Pierston was thinking of.

It was in this very spot that he was to have met the grand-mother of the girl at his side, and in which he would have met her had she chosen to keep the appointment, a meeting which might—nay, must—have changed the whole current of his life.

Instead of that, forty years had passed—forty years of severance from Avice, till a secondly renewed copy of his sweetheart had arisen to fill her place. But he, alas, was not renewed. And of all this the pretty young thing at his side knew nothing.

Taking advantage of the younger woman's retreat to view the sea through an opening of the walls, Pierston appealed to her mother in a whisper: 'Have you ever given her a hint of what my meaning is? No? Then I think you might, if you really have no objection.'

Mrs. Pierston, as the widow, was far from being so coldly disposed in her own person towards her friend as in the days when he wanted to marry her. Had she now been the object of his wishes he would not have needed to ask her twice. But like a good mother she stifled all this, and said she would sound Avice there and then.

'Avice, my dear,' she said, advancing to where the girl mused in the window-gap, 'what do you think of Mr. Pierston paying his addresses to you—coming courting, as *I* call it in my old-fashioned way. Supposing he were to, would you encourage him?'

'To *me*, mother?' said Avice, with an inquiring laugh. 'I thought—he meant you!'

'O no, he doesn't mean me,' said her mother hastily. 'He is nothing more than my friend.'

'I don't want any addresses,' said the daughter.

'He is a man in society, and would take you to an elegant house in London suited to your education, instead of leaving you to mope here.'

'I should like that well enough,' replied Avice carelessly.

'Then give him some encouragement.'

'I don't care enough about him to do any encouraging. It is his business, I should think, to do all.'

She spoke in her lightest vein; but the result was that

when Pierston, who had discreetly withdrawn, returned to them, she walked docilely, though perhaps gloomily, beside him, her mother dropping to the rear. They came to a rugged descent, and Pierston took her hand to help her. She allowed him to retain it when they arrived on level ground.

Altogether it was not an unsuccessful evening for the man with the unanchored heart, though possibly initial success meant worse for him in the long run than initial failure. There was nothing marvellous in the fact of her tractability thus far. In his modern dress and style, under the rays of the moon, he looked a very presentable gentleman indeed, while his knowledge of art and his travelled manners were not without their attractions for a girl who with one hand touched the educated middle-class and with the other the rude and simple inhabitants of the isle. Her intensely modern sympathies were quickened by her peculiar outlook.

Pierston would have regarded his interest in her as over-much selfish if there had not existed a redeeming quality in the substratum of old pathetic memory by which such love had been created—which still permeated it, rendering it the tenderest, most anxious, most protective instinct he had ever known. It may have had in its composition too much of the boyish fervour that had characterized such affection when he was cherry-cheeked, and light in the foot as a girl; but, if it was all this feeling of youth, it was more.

Mrs. Pierston, in fearing to be frank, lest she might seem to be angling for his fortune, did not fully divine his cheerful readiness to offer it, if by so doing he could make amends for his infidelity to her family forty years back in the past. Time had not made him mercenary, and it had quenched his ambitions; and though his wish to wed Avice was not entirely a wish to enrich her, the knowledge that she would be enriched beyond anything that she could have anticipated was what allowed him to indulge his love.

He was not exactly old he said to himself the next morning as he beheld his face in the glass. And he looked considerably younger than he was. But there was history in his face—distinct chapters of it; his brow was not that blank page it once had been. He knew the origin of that line in his forehead; it had been traced in the course of a month or two by past troubles. He remembered the coming of this pale wiry hair; it had been brought by the illness in Rome, when he had wished each night that he might never wake again. This wrinkled corner, that drawn bit of skin, they had resulted from those months of despondency when all seemed going against his art, his strength, his happiness. 'You cannot live your life and keep it, Jocelyn,' he said. Time was against him and love, and time would probably win.

'When I went away from the first Avice,' he continued with whimsical misery, 'I had a presentiment that I should ache for it some day. And I am aching—have ached ever since this jade of an Ideal learnt the unconscionable trick of inhabiting one image only.'

Upon the whole he was not without a bodement that it would be folly to press on.

A DASH FOR THE
LAST INCARNATION

III.—iv.

THIS desultory courtship of a young girl which had been brought about by her mother's contrivance was interrupted by the appearance of Somers and his wife and family on the Budmouth Esplanade. Alfred Somers, once the youthful, picturesque as his own paintings, was now a middle-aged family man with spectacles—spectacles worn, too, with the single object of seeing through them—and a row of daughters tailing off to infancy, who at present added appreciably to the income of the bathing-machine women established along the sands.

Mrs. Somers—once the intellectual, emancipated Mrs. Pine-Avon—had now retrograded to the petty and timid mental position of her mother and grandmother, giving sharp, strict regard to the current literature and art that reached the innocent presence of her long perspective of girls, with the view of hiding every skull and skeleton of life from their dear eyes. She was another illustration of the rule that succeeding generations of women are seldom marked by cumulative progress, their advance as girls being lost in their recession as matrons; so that they move up and down the stream of intellectual development like flotsam in a tidal estuary. And this perhaps not by reason of their faults as individuals, but of their misfortune as child-rearers.

The landscape-painter, now an Academician like Pierston himself—rather popular than distinguished—had given up that peculiar and personal taste in subjects which had marked him in times past, executing instead many pleasing aspects of nature addressed to the furnishing householder through the middling critic, and really very good of their kind. In this way he received many large cheques from persons of wealth in England and America, out of which he built himself a sumptuous studio and an awkward house around it, and paid for the education of the growing maidens.

The vision of Somers's humble position as jackal to this lion of a family and house and studio and social reputation—Somers, to whom strange conceits and wild imaginings were departed joys never to return—led Pierston, as the painter's contemporary, to feel that he ought to be one of the bygones likewise, and to put on an air of unromantic bufferism. He refrained from entering Avice's peninsula for the whole fortnight of Somers's stay in the neighbouring town, although its grey poetical outline—'throned along the sea'—greeted his eyes every morn and eve across the roadstead.

When the painter and his family had gone back from their bathing holiday, he thought that he, too, would leave the neighbourhood. To do so, however, without wishing at least the elder Avice good-bye would be unfriendly, considering the extent of their acquaintance. One evening, knowing this time of day to suit her best, he took the few-minutes' journey to the rock along the thin connecting string of junction, and arrived at Mrs. Pierston's door just after dark.

A light shone from an upper chamber. On asking for his widowed acquaintance he was informed that she was ill, seriously, though not dangerously. While learning that her daughter was with her, and further particulars, and doubting if he should go in, a message was sent down to ask him to enter. His voice had been heard, and Mrs. Pierston would like to see him.

He could not with any humanity refuse, but there flashed across his mind the recollection that Avice the youngest had never yet really seen him, had seen nothing more of him than an outline, which might have appertained as easily to a man thirty years his junior as to himself, and a countenance so renovated by faint moonlight as fairly to correspond. It was with misgiving, therefore, that the sculptor ascended the staircase and entered the little upper sitting-room now arranged as a sick-chamber.

Mrs. Pierston reclined on a sofa, her face emaciated to a surprising thinness for the comparatively short interval since her attack. 'Come in, sir,' she said, as soon as she saw him, holding out her hand. 'Don't let me frighten you.'

Avice was seated beside her, reading. The girl jumped up, hardly seeming to recognize him. 'O! it's Mr. Pierston,' she said in a moment, adding quickly, with evident surprise and off her guard: 'I thought Mr. Pierston was——'

What she had thought he was did not pass her lips, and it remained a riddle for Jocelyn until a new departure in her manner towards him showed that the words 'much younger' would have accurately ended the sentence. Had Pierston not now confronted her anew, he might have endured philosophically her changed opinion of him. But he was seeing her again, and a rooted feeling was revived.

Pierston now learnt for the first time that the widow had been visited by sudden attacks of this sort not infrequently of late years. They were said to be due to angina pectoris, the latter paroxysms having been the most severe. She was at the present moment out of pain, though weak, exhausted, and nervous. She would not, however, converse about herself, but took advantage of her daughter's absence from the room to broach the subject most in her thoughts.

No compunctions had stirred her as they had her visitor on the expediency of his suit in view of his years. Her fever of anxiety lest after all he should not come to see Avice again had been not without an effect upon her health; and it made her more candid than she had intended to be.

'Troubles and sickness raise all sorts of fears, Mr. Pierston,' she said. 'What I felt only a wish for, when you first named it, I have hoped for a good deal since; and I have been so anxious that—that it should come to something! I am glad indeed that you are come.'

'My wanting to marry Avice, you mean, dear Mrs. Pierston?'

'Yes—that's it. I wonder if you are still in the same mind? You are? Then I wish something could be done—to make her agree to it—so as to get it settled. I dread otherwise what will become of her. She is not a practical girl as I was—she would hardly like now to settle down as an islander's wife; and to leave her living here alone would trouble me.'

'Nothing will happen to you yet, I hope, my dear old friend.'

'Well, it is a risky complaint; and the attacks, when they come, are so agonizing that to endure them I ought to get rid of all outside anxieties, folk say. Now—do you want her, sir?'

'With all my soul! But she doesn't want me.'

'I don't think she is so against you as you imagine. I fancy if it were put to her plainly, now I am in this state, it might be done.'

They lapsed into conversation on the early days of their acquaintance, until Mrs. Pierston's daughter re-entered the room.

'Avice,' said her mother, when the girl had been with them a few minutes. 'About this matter that I have talked over with you so many times since my attack. Here is Mr. Pierston, and he wishes to be your husband. He is much older than you; but, in spite of it, that you will ever get a better husband I don't believe. Now, will you take him, seeing the state I am in, and how naturally anxious I am to see you settled before I die?'

'But you won't die, mother! You are getting better!'

'Just for the present only. Come, he is a good man and a clever man, and a rich man. I want you, O so much, to be his wife! I can say no more.'

Avice looked appealingly at the sculptor, and then on the floor. 'Does he really wish me to?' she asked almost inaudibly, turning as she spoke to Pierston. 'He has never quite said so to me.'

'My dear one, how can you doubt it?' said Jocelyn quickly. 'But I won't press you to marry me as a favour, against your feelings.'

'I thought Mr. Pierston was younger!' she murmured to her mother.

'That counts for little, when you think how much there

s on the other side. Think of our position, and of his—a sculptor, with a mansion, and a studio full of busts and statues that I have dusted in my time, and of the beautiful studies you would be able to take up. Surely the life would just suit you? Your expensive education is wasted down here!'

Avice did not care to argue. She was outwardly gentle as her grandmother had been, and it seemed just a question with her of whether she must or must not. 'Very well—I feel I ought to agree to marry him, since you tell me to,' she answered quietly, after some thought. 'I see that it would be a wise thing to do, and that you wish it, and that Mr. Pierston really does—like me. So—so that——'

Pierston was not backward at this critical juncture, despite unpleasant sensations. But it was the historic ingredient in this genealogical passion—if its continuity through three generations may be so described—which appealed to his perseverance at the expense of his wisdom. The mother was holding the daughter's hand; she took Pierston's, and laid Avice's in it.

No more was said in argument, and the thing was regarded as determined. Afterwards a noise was heard upon the window-panes, as of fine sand thrown; and, lifting the blind, Pierston saw that the distant lightship winked with a bleared and indistinct eye. A drizzling rain had come on with the dark, and it was striking the window in handfuls. He had intended to walk the two miles back to the station, but it meant a drenching to do it now. He waited and had supper; and, finding the weather no better, accepted Mrs. Pierston's invitation to stay over the night.

Thus it fell out that again he lodged in the house he had been accustomed to live in as a boy, before his father had made his fortune, and before his own name had been heard of outside the boundaries of the isle.

He slept but little, and in the first movement of the dawn sat up in bed. Why should he ever live in London or any other fashionable city if this plan of marriage could be carried out? Surely, with this young wife, the island would be the best place for him. It might be possible to rent Sylvania

Castle as he had formerly done—better still to buy it. If life
could offer him anything worth having it would be a home
with Avice there on his native cliffs to the end of his days.

As he sat thus thinking, and the daylight increased, he
discerned, a short distance before him, a movement of
something ghostly. His position was facing the window,
and he found that by chance the looking-glass had swung
itself vertical, so that what he saw was his own shape. The
recognition startled him. The person he appeared was too
grievously far, chronologically, in advance of the person
he felt himself to be. Pierston did not care to regard the
figure confronting him so mockingly. Its voice seemed to
say 'There's tragedy hanging on to this!' But the question
of age being pertinent he could not give the spectre up, and
ultimately got out of bed under the weird fascination of the
reflection. Whether he had overwalked himself lately, or
what he had done, he knew not; but never had he seemed
so aged by a score of years as he was represented in the
glass in that cold grey morning light. While his soul was
what it was, why should he have been encumbered with
that withering carcase, without the ability to shift it off for
another, as his ideal Beloved had so frequently done?

By reason of her mother's illness Avice was now living
in the house, and, on going downstairs, he found that they
were to breakfast *en tête-à-tête*. She was not then in the
room, but she entered in the course of a few minutes.
Pierston had already heard that the widow felt better this
morning, and elated by the prospect of sitting with Avice
at this meal he went forward to her joyously. As soon as
she saw him in the full stroke of day from the window she
started; and he then remembered that it was their first
meeting under the solar rays.

She was so overcome that she turned and left the room
as if she had forgotten something; when she re-entered she
was visibly pale. She recovered herself, and apologized.
She had been sitting up the night before the last, she said,
and was not quite so well as usual.

There may have been some truth in this; but Pierston
could not get over that first scared look of hers. It was

enough to give daytime stability to his night views of a possible tragedy lurking in this wedding project. He determined that, at any cost to his heart, there should be no misapprehension about him from this moment.

'Miss Pierston,' he said as they sat down, 'since it is well you should know all the truth before we go any further, that there may be no awkward discoveries afterwards, I am going to tell you something about myself—if you are not too distressed to hear it?'

'No—let me hear it.'

'I was once the lover of your mother, and wanted to marry her; only she wouldn't, or rather couldn't, marry me.'

'O how strange!' said the girl, looking from him to the breakfast things, and from the breakfast things to him. 'Mother has never told me that. Yet of course, you might have been. I mean, you are old enough.'

He took the remark as a satire she had not intended. 'O yes—quite old enough,' he said grimly. 'Almost too old.'

'Too old for mother? How's that?'

'Because I belonged to your grandmother.'

'No? How can that be?'

'I was her lover likewise. I should have married her if I had gone straight on instead of round the corner.'

'But you couldn't have been, Mr. Pierston! You are not old enough? Why, how old are you?—you have never told me.'

'I am very old.'

'My mother's, and my grandmother's,' said she, looking at him no longer as at a possible husband, but as a strange fossilized relic in human form. Pierston saw it, but meaning to give up the game he did not care to spare himself.

'Your mother's and your grandmother's young man,' he repeated.

'And were you my great-grandmother's too?' she asked, with an expectant interest in his case as a drama that overcame her personal considerations for a moment.

'No—not your great-grandmother's. Your imagination beats even my confessions! . . . But I am *very* old, as you see.'

'I did not know it!' said she in an appalled murmur. 'You
do not look so; and I thought that what you looked you
were.'

'And you—you are very young,' he continued.

A stillness followed, during which she sat in a troubled
constraint, regarding him now and then with something in
her open eyes and large pupils that might have been sympathy or nervousness. Pierston ate scarce any breakfast,
and rising abruptly from the table said he would take a
walk on the cliffs as the morning was fine.

He did so, proceeding along the north-east heights for
nearly a mile. He had virtually given Avice up, but not for-
mally. His intention had been to go back to the house in
half-an-hour and pay a morning visit to the invalid; but by
not returning the plans of the previous evening might be
allowed to lapse silently, as mere *pourparlers* that had
come to nothing in the face of Avice's want of love for
him. Pierston accordingly went straight along, and in the
course of an hour was at his Budmouth lodgings.

Nothing occurred till the evening to inform him how
his absence had been taken. Then a note arrived from
Mrs. Pierston; it was written in pencil, evidently as she
lay.

'I am alarmed,' she said, 'at your going so suddenly.
Avice seems to think she has offended you. She did not
mean to do that. I am sure. It makes me dreadfully
anxious! Will you send a line? Surely you will not desert
us now—my heart is so set on my child's welfare!'

'Desert you I won't,' said Jocelyn. 'It is too much like the
original case. But I must let her desert me!'

On his return, with no other object than that of wishing
Mrs. Pierston good-bye, he found her painfully agitated.
She clasped his hand and wetted it with her tears.

'O don't be offended with her!' she cried. 'She's young.
We are one people—don't marry a kimberlin! It will break
my heart if you forsake her now! Avice!'

The girl came. 'My manner was hasty and thoughtless
this morning,' she said in a low voice. 'Please pardon me.
I wish to abide by my promise.'

Her mother, still tearful, again joined their hands; and the engagement stood as before.

Pierston went back to Budmouth, but dimly seeing how curiously, through his being a rich suitor, ideas of beneficence and reparation were retaining him in the course arranged by her mother, and urged by his own desire in the face of his understanding.

ON THE VERGE OF POSSESSION

III.—v.

IN anticipation of his marriage Pierston had taken a new red house of the approved Kensington pattern, with a new studio at the back as large as a mediæval barn. Hither, in collusion with the elder Avice—whose health had mended somewhat—he invited mother and daughter to spend a week or two with him, thinking thereby to exercise on the latter's imagination an influence which was not practicable while he was a guest at their house; and by interesting his betrothed in the fitting and furnishing of this residence to create in her an ambition to be its mistress.

It was a pleasant, reposeful time to be in town. There was nobody to interrupt them in their proceedings, and, it being out of the season, the largest tradesmen were as attentive to their wants as if those firms had never before been honoured with a single customer whom they really liked. Pierston and his guests, almost equally inexperienced—for the sculptor had nearly forgotten what knowledge of householding he had acquired earlier in life—could consider and practise thoroughly a species of skeleton-drill in receiving visitors when the pair should announce themselves as married and at home in the coming winter season.

Avice was charming, even if a little cold. He congratulated himself yet again that time should have reserved for him this final chance for one of the line. She was somewhat like her mother, whom he had loved in the flesh, but she had the soul of her grandmother, whom he had loved in the spirit—and, for that matter, loved now. Only one criticism had he to pass upon his choice: though in outward semblance her grandam idealized, she had not the first Avice's candour, but rather her mother's closeness. He never knew exactly what she was thinking and feeling. Yet he seemed to have such prescriptive rights in women of her blood that her occasional want of confidence did not deeply trouble him.

It was one of those ripe and mellow afternoons that sometimes colour London with their golden light at this time of the year, and produce those marvellous sunset effects which, if they were not known to be made up of kitchen coal-smoke and animal exhalations, would be rapturously applauded. Behind the perpendicular, oblique, zigzagged, and curved zinc 'tall-boys,' that formed a grey pattern not unlike early Gothic numerals against the sky, the men and women on the tops of the omnibuses saw an irradiation of topaz hues, darkened here and there into richest russet.

There had been a sharp shower during the afternoon, and Pierston—who had to take care of himself—had worn a pair of goloshes on his short walk in the street. He noiselessly entered the studio, inside which some gleams of the same mellow light had managed to creep, and where he guessed he should find his prospective wife and mother-in-law awaiting him with tea. But only Avice was there, seated beside the teapot of brown delf, which, as artists, they affected, her back being toward him. She was holding her handkerchief to her eyes, and he saw that she was weeping silently.

In another moment he perceived that she was weeping over a book. By this time she had heard him, and came forward. He made it appear that he had not noticed her distress, and they discussed some arrangements of furniture. When he had taken a cup of tea she went away, leaving the book behind her.

Pierston took it up. The volume was an old schoolbook; Stièvenard's 'Lectures Françaises,' with her name in it as a pupil at Sandbourne High School, and date-markings denoting lessons taken at a comparatively recent time, for Avice had been but a novice as governess when he discovered her.

For a school-girl—which she virtually was—to weep over a school-book was strange. Could she have been affected by some subject in the readings? Impossible. Pierston fell to thinking, and zest died for the process of furnishing, which he had undertaken so gaily. Somehow, the bloom was again disappearing from his approaching marriage. Yet he loved Avice more and more tenderly; he feared sometimes that in the solicitousness of his affection he was spoiling her by indulging her every whim.

He looked round the large and ambitious apartment, now becoming clouded with shades, out of which the white and cadaverous countenances of his studies, casts, and other lumber peered meditatively at him, as if they were saying, 'What are you going to do now, old boy?' They had never looked like that while standing in his past homely workshop, where all the real labours of his life had been carried out. What should a man of his age, who had not for years done anything to speak of—certainly not to add to his reputation as an artist—want with a new place like this? It was all because of the elect lady, and she apparently did not want him.

Pierston did not observe anything further in Avice to cause him misgiving till one dinner-time, a week later, towards the end of the visit. Then, as he sat himself between her and her mother at their limited table, he was struck with her nervousness, and was tempted to say, 'Why are you troubled, my little dearest?' in tones which disclosed that he was as troubled as she.

'Am I troubled?' she said with a start, turning her gentle hazel eyes upon him. 'Yes, I suppose I am. It is because I have received a letter—from an old friend.'

'You didn't show it to me,' said her mother.

'No—I tore it up.'

'Why?'

'It was not necessary to keep it, so I destroyed it.'

Mrs. Pierston did not press her further on the subject, and Avice showed no disposition to continue it. They retired rather early, as they always did, but Pierston remained pacing about his studio a long while, musing on many things, not the least being the perception that to wed a woman may be by no means the same thing as to be united with her. The 'old friend' of Avice's remark had sounded very much like 'lover.' Otherwise why should the letter have so greatly disturbed her?

There seemed to be something uncanny, after all, about London, in it relation to his contemplated marriage. When she had first come up she was easier with him than now. And yet his bringing her there had helped his cause; the house had decidedly impressed her—almost overawed her, and though he owned that by no law of nature or reason had her mother or himself any right to urge on Avice partnership with him against her inclination, he resolved to make the most of having her under his influence by getting the wedding details settled before she and her mother left.

The next morning he proceeded to do this. When he encountered Avice there was a trace of apprehension on her face; but he set that down to a fear that she had offended him the night before by her taciturnity. Directly he requested her mother, in Avice's presence, to get her to fix the day quite early, Mrs. Pierston became brighter and brisker. She, too, plainly had doubts about the wisdom of delay, and turning to her daughter said, 'Now, my dear, do you hear?'

It was ultimately agreed that the widow and her daughter should go back in a day or two, to await Pierston's arrival on the wedding-eve, immediately after their return.

In pursuance of the arrangement Pierston found himself on the south shore of England in the gloom of the aforesaid evening, the isle, as he looked across at it with his approach, being just discernible as a moping countenance, a creature sullen with a sense that he was about to withdraw from its keeping the rarest object it had ever owned. He had come alone, not to embarrass them, and had intended to halt a couple of hours in the neighbouring seaport to give some orders relating to the wedding, but the little railway train being in waiting to take him on, he proceeded with a natural impatience, resolving to do his business here by messenger from the isle.

He passed the ruins of the Tudor castle and the long featureless rib of grinding pebbles that screened off the outer sea, which could be heard lifting and dipping rhythmically in the wide vagueness of the Bay. At the under-hill island townlet of the Wells there were no flys, and leaving his things to be brought on, as he often did, he climbed the eminence on foot.

Half-way up the steepest part of the pass he saw in the dusk a figure pausing—the single person on the incline. Though it was too dark to identify faces, Pierston gathered from the way in which the halting stranger was supporting himself by the handrail, which here bordered the road to assist climbers, that the person was exhausted.

'Anything the matter?' he said.

'O no—not much,' was returned by the other. 'But it is steep just here.'

The accent was not quite that of an Englishman, and struck him as hailing from one of the Channel Islands. 'Can't I help you up to the top?' he said, for the voice, though that of a young man, seemed faint and shaken.

'No, thank you. I have been ill; but I thought I was all right again; and as the night was fine I walked into the island by the road. It turned out to be rather too much for me, as there is some weakness left still; and this stiff incline brought it out.'

'Naturally. You'd better take hold of my arm—at any rate to the brow here.'

Thus pressed the stranger did so, and they went on towards the ridge, till, reaching the lime-kiln standing there the stranger abandoned his hold, saying: 'Thank you for your assistance, sir. Good-night.'

'I don't think I recognize your voice as a native's?'

'No, it is not. I am a Jersey man. Good-night, sir.'

'Good-night, if you are sure you can get on. Here, take this stick—it is no use to me.' Saying which, Pierston put his walking-stick into the young man's hand.

'Thank you again. I shall be quite recovered when I have rested a minute or two. Don't let me detain you, please.'

The stranger as he spoke turned his face towards the south, where the Beal light had just come into view, and stood regarding it with an obstinate fixity. As he evidently wished to be left to himself Jocelyn went on, and troubled no more about him, though the desire of the young man to be rid of his company, after accepting his walking-stick and his arm, had come with a suddenness that was almost emotional; and impressionable as Jocelyn was, no less now than in youth, he was saddened for a minute by the sense that there were people in the world who did not like even his sympathy.

However, a pleasure which obliterated all this arose when Pierston drew near to the house that was likely to be his dear home on all future visits to the isle, perhaps even his permanent home as he grew older and the associations of his youth re-asserted themselves. It had been, too, his father's house, the house in which he was born, and he amused his fancy with plans for its enlargement under the supervision of Avice and himself. It was a still greater pleasure to behold a tall and shapely figure standing against the light of the open door and presumably awaiting him.

Avice, who it was, gave a little jump when she recognized him, but dutifully allowed him to kiss her when he reached her side; though her nervousness was only too apparent, and was like a child's towards a parent who may prove stern.

'How dear of you to guess that I might come on at once instead of later!' says Jocelyn. 'Well, if I had stayed in the town to go to the shops and so on, I could not have got here till the last train. How is mother?—our mother, as I shall call her soon.'

Avice said that her mother had not been so well—she feared not nearly so well since her return from London, so that she was obliged to keep her room. The visit had perhaps been too much for her. 'But she will not acknowledge that she is much weaker, because she will not disturb my happiness.'

Jocelyn was in a mood to let trifles of manner pass, and he took no notice of the effort which had accompanied the last word. They went upstairs to Mrs. Pierston, whose obvious relief and thankfulness at sight of him was grateful to her visitor.

'I am so, O so glad you are come!' she said huskily, as she held out her thin hand and stifled a sob. 'I have been so——'

She could get no further for a moment, and Avice turned away weeping, and abruptly left the room.

'I have so set my heart on this,' Mrs. Pierston went on, 'that I have not been able to sleep of late, for I have feared I might drop off suddenly before she is yours, and lose the comfort of seeing you actually united. Your being so kind to me in old times has made me so sure that she will find a good husband in you, that I am over anxious, I know. Indeed, I have not liked to let her know quite how anxious I am.'

Thus they talked till Jocelyn bade her good-night, it being noticeable that Mrs. Pierston, chastened by her illnesses, maintained no longer any reserve on her gladness to acquire him as her son-in-law; and her feelings destroyed any remaining scruples he might have had from perceiving that Avice's consent was rather an obedience than a desire. As he went downstairs, and found Avice awaiting his descent, he wondered if anything had occurred here during his absence to give Mrs. Pierston new uneasiness about the marriage, but it was an inquiry he could not address to a girl whose actions could alone be the cause of such uneasiness.

He looked round for her as he supped, but though she had come into the room with him she was not there now. He remembered her telling him that she had had supper with her mother, and Jocelyn sat on quietly musing and sipping his wine for something near half-an-hour. Wondering then for the first time what had become of her, he rose and went to the door. Avice was quite near him after all—only standing at the front door as she had been doing when he came, looking into the light of the full moon, which had risen since his arrival. His sudden opening of the dining-room door seemed to agitate her.

'What is it, dear?' he asked.

'As mother is much better and doesn't want me, I ought to go and see somebody I promised to take a parcel to—I

feel I ought. And yet, as you have just come to see me—I
suppose you don't approve of my going out while you are
here?'

'Who is the person?'

'Somebody down that way,' she said indefinitely. 'It is
not very far off. I am not afraid—I go out often by myself
at night hereabout.'

He reassured her good-humouredly. 'If you really wish
to go, my dear, of course I don't object. I have no authority
to do that till to-morrow, and you know that if I had it I
shouldn't use it.'

'O but you have! Mother being an invalid, you are in her
place, apart from—to-morrow.'

'Nonsense, darling. Run across to your friend's house by
all means if you want to.'

'And you'll be here when I come in?'

'No, I am going down to the inn to see if my things are
brought up.'

'But hasn't mother asked you to stay here? The spare
room was got ready for you. . . . Dear me, I am afraid I
ought to have told you.'

'She did ask me. But I have some things coming, directed
to the inn, and I had better be there. So I'll wish you good-
night, though it is not late. I will come in quite early to-
morrow, to inquire how your mother is going on, and to
wish you good-morning. You will be back again quickly
this evening?'

'O yes.'

'And I needn't go with you for company?'

'O no, thank you. It is no distance.'

Pierston then departed, thinking how entirely her manner was that of one to whom a question of doing anything
was a question of permission and not of judgment. He had
no sooner gone than Avice took a parcel from a cupboard,
put on her hat and cloak, and following by the way he had
taken till she reached the entrance to Sylvania Castle, there
stood still. She could hear Pierston's footsteps passing
down East Quarriers to the inn; but she went no further in
that direction. Turning into the lane on the right, of which

mention has so often been made, she went quickly past the
last cottage, and having entered the gorge beyond she
clambered into the ruin of the Red King's or Bow-and-
Arrow Castle, standing as a square black mass against the
moonlit, indefinite sea.

THE WELL-BELOVED
IS—WHERE?

III.—vi.

MRS. PIERSTON passed a restless night, but this she let nobody know; nor, what was painfully evident to herself, that her prostration was increased by anxiety and suspense about the wedding on which she had too much set her heart.

During the very brief space in which she dozed Avice came into her room. As it was not infrequent for her daughter to look in upon her thus she took little notice, merely saying to assure the girl: 'I am better, dear. Don't come in again. Get to sleep yourself.'

The mother, however, went thinking anew. She had no apprehensions about this marriage. She felt perfectly sure that it was the best thing she could do for her girl. Not a young woman on the island but was envying Avice at that moment; for Jocelyn was absurdly young for three score, a good-looking man, one whose history was generally know here; as also were the exact figures of the fortune he had inherited from his father, and the social standing he could claim—a standing, however, which that fortune would not have been large enough to procure unassisted by his reputation in his art.

But Avice had been weak enough, as her mother knew, to indulge in fancies for local youths from time to time, and Mrs. Pierston could not help congratulating herself that her daughter had been so docile in the circumstances. Yet to every one except, perhaps, Avice herself, Jocelyn was the most romantic of lovers. Indeed was there ever such a romance as that man embodied in his relations to her house? Rejecting the first Avice, the second had rejected him, and to rally to the third with final achievement was an artistic and tender finish to which it was ungrateful in anybody to be blind.

The widow thought that the second Avice might probably not have rejected Pierston on that occasion in the London studio so many years ago if destiny had not arranged that she should have been secretly united to another when the proposing moment came.

But what had come was best. 'My God,' she said at times that night, 'to think my aim in writing to him should be fulfilling itself like this!'

When all was right and done, what a success upon the whole her life would have been. She who had begun her career as a cottage-girl, a small quarry-owner's daughter, had sunk so low as to the position of laundress, had engaged in various menial occupations, had made an unhappy marriage for love which had, however, in the long run, thanks to Jocelyn's management, much improved her position, was at last to see her daughter secure what she herself had just missed securing, and established in a home of affluence and refinement.

Thus the sick woman excited herself as the hours went on. At last, in her tenseness it seemed to her that the time had already come at which the household was stirring, and she fancied she heard conversation in her daughter's room. But she found that it was only five o'clock, and not yet daylight. Her state was such that she could see the hangings of the bed tremble with her tremors. She had declared overnight that she did not require any one to sit up with her, but she now rang a little hand-bell, and in a few minutes a nurse appeared; Ruth Stockwool, an island woman and neighbour, whom Mrs. Pierston knew well, and who knew all Mrs. Pierston's history.

'I am so nervous that I can't stay by myself,' said the widow. 'And I thought I heard Becky dressing Miss Avice in her wedding things.'

'O no—not yet, ma'am. There's nobody up. But I'll get you something.'

When Mrs. Pierston had taken a little nourishment she went on: 'I can't help frightening myself with thoughts that she won't marry him. You see he is older than Avice.'

'Yes, he is,' said her neighbour. 'But I don't see how anything can hender the wedden now.'

'Avice, you know, had fancies; at least one fancy for another man; a young fellow of five-and-twenty. And she's been very secret and odd about it. I wish she had raved and cried and had it out; but she's been quite the other way. I know she's fond of him still.'

'What—that young Frenchman, Mr. Leverre o' Sandbourne? I've heard a little of it. But I should say there wadden much between 'em.'

'I don't think there was. But I've a sort of conviction that she saw him last night. I believe it was only to bid him good-bye, and return him some books he had given her; but I wish she had never known him; he is rather an excitable, impulsive young man, and he might make mischief. He isn't a Frenchman, though he has lived in France. His father was a Jersey gentleman, and on his becoming a widower he married as his second wife a native of this very island. That's mainly why the young man is so at home in these parts.'

'Ah—now I follow 'ee. She was a Bencomb, his stepmother: I heard something about her years ago.'

'Yes; her father had the biggest stone-trade on the island at one time; but the name is forgotten here now. He retired years before I was born. However, mother used to tell me that she was a handsome young woman, who tried to catch Mr. Pierston when he was a young man, and scandalized herself a bit with him. She went off abroad with her father, who had made a fortune here; but when he got over there he lost it nearly all in some way. Years after she married this Jerseyman, Mr. Leverre, who had been fond of her as a girl, and she brought up his child as her own.'

Mrs. Pierston paused, but as Ruth did not ask any question she presently resumed her self-relieving murmur:

'How Miss Avice got to know the young man was in this way. When Mrs. Leverre's husband died she came from Jersey to live at Sandbourne; and made it her business one day to cross over to this place to make inquiries about Mr. Jocelyn Pierston. As my name was Pierston she called upon me with her son, and so Avice and he got acquainted. When Avice went back to Sandbourne to the finishing school they kept up the acquaintance in secret. He taught French somewhere there, and does still, I believe.'

'Well, I hope she'll forget en. He idden good enough.'

'I hope so—I hope so. . . . Now I'll try to get a little nap.'

Ruth Stockwool went back to her room, where, finding it would not be necessary to get up for another hour, she lay down again and soon slept. Her bed was close to the staircase, from which it was divided by a lath partition only, and her consciousness either was or seemed to be aroused by light brushing touches on the outside of the partition, as of fingers feeling the way downstairs in the dark. The slight noise passed, and in a few seconds she dreamt or fancied she could hear the unfastening of the back door.

She had nearly sunk into another sound sleep when precisely the same phenomena were repeated; fingers brushing along the wall close to her head, down, downward, the soft opening of the door, its close, and silence again.

She now became clearly awake. The repetition of the process had made the whole matter a singular one. Early as it was the first sounds might have been those of the housemaid descending, though why she should have come down so stealthily and in the dark did not make itself clear. But the second performance was inexplicable. Ruth got out of bed and lifted her blind. The dawn was hardly yet pink, and the light from the sandbank was not yet extinguished. But the bushes of euonymus against the white palings of the front garden could be seen, also the light surface of the road winding away like a riband to the north entrance of Sylvania Castle, thence round to the village, the cliffs, and the Cove behind. Upon the road two dark figures could just be discerned, one a little way behind the other, but overtaking and joining the foremost as Ruth looked. After all they might be quarriers or lighthouse-keepers from the south of the island, or fishermen just landed from a night's work. There being nothing to connect them with the noises she had heard indoors she dismissed the whole subject, and went to bed again.

Jocelyn had promised to pay an early visit to ascertain the state of Mrs. Pierston's health after her night's rest, her precarious condition being more obvious to him than to Avice, and making him a little anxious. Subsequent events caused him to remember that while he was dressing he casually observed two or three boatmen standing near the cliff beyond the village, and apparently watching with deep interest what seemed to be a boat far away towards the opposite shore of South Wessex. At half-past eight he came from the door of the inn and went straight to Mrs. Pierston's. On approaching he discovered that a strange expression which seemed to hang about the house-front that morning was more than a fancy, the gate, door, and two windows being open, though the blinds of other windows were not drawn up, the whole lending a vacant, dazed look to the domicile, as of a person gaping in sudden stultification. Nobody answered his knock, and walking into the dining-room he found that no breakfast had been laid. His flashing thought was, 'Mrs. Pierston is dead.'

While standing in the room somebody came downstairs, and Jocelyn encountered Ruth Stockwool, an open letter fluttering in her hand.

'O Mr. Pierston, Mr. Pierston! The Lord-a-Lord!'

'What? Mrs. Pierston——'

'No, no! Miss Avice! She is gone!—yes—gone! Read ye this, sir. It was left in her bedroom, and we be fairly gallied out of our senses!'

He took the letter and confusedly beheld that it was in two handwritings, the first section being in Avice's:

MY DEAR MOTHER,—How ever will you forgive me for what I have done! So deceitful as it seems. And yet till this night I had no idea of deceiving either you or Mr. Pierston.

Last night at ten o'clock I went out, as you may have guessed, to see Mr. Leverre for the last time, and to give him back his books, letters, and little presents to me. I went only a few steps—to Bow-and-Arrow Castle, where we met as we had agreed to do, since he could not call. When I reached the place I found him there waiting, but quite ill. He had been unwell at his mother's house for some days, and had been obliged to stay in bed, but he had got up on purpose to come and bid me good-bye. The over-exertion of the journey upset him, and though we stayed and stayed till twelve o'clock he felt quite unable to go back home—unable, indeed, to move more than a few yards. I had tried so hard not to love him any longer, but I loved him so now that I could not desert him and leave him out there to catch his death. So I helped him—nearly carrying him—on and on to our door, and then round to the back. Here he got a little better, and as he could not stay there, and everybody was now asleep, I helped him upstairs into the room we had prepared for Mr. Pierston if he should have wanted one. I got him into bed, and then fetched some brandy and a little of your tonic. Did you see me come into your room for it, or were you asleep?

I sat by him all night. He improved slowly, and we talked over what we had better do. I felt that, though I had intended to give him up, I could not now becomingly marry any other man, and that I ought to marry him. We decided to do it at once, before anybody could hinder us. So we came down before it was light, and have gone away to get the ceremony solemnized.

Tell Mr. Pierston it was not premeditated, but the result of an accident. I am sincerely sorry to have treated him with what he will think unfairness, but though I did not love him I meant to obey you and marry him. But God sent this necessity of my having to give shelter to my Love, to prevent, I think, my doing what I am now convinced would have been wrong.—Ever your loving daughter,

AVICE.

The second was in a man's hand:

DEAR MOTHER (as you will soon be to me),—Avice has clearly explained above how it happened that I have not been able to give her up to Mr. Pierston. I think I should have died if I had not accepted the hospitality of a room in your house this night, and your daughter's tender nursing through the dark dreary hours. We love each other beyond expression, and it is obvious that, if we are human, we cannot resist marrying now, in spite of friends' wishes. Will you please send the note lying beside this to my mother. It is merely to explain what I have done.—Yours with warmest regard,

HENRI LEVERRE.

Jocelyn turned away and looked out of the window.

'Mrs. Pierston thought she heard some talking in the

night, but of course she put it down to fancy. And she remembers Miss Avice coming into her room at one o'clock in the morning, and going to the table where the medicine was standing. A sly girl—all the time her young man within a yard or two, in the very room, and a using the very clean sheets that you, sir, were to have used! They are our best linen ones, got up beautiful, and a kept wi' rosemary. Really, sir, one would say you stayed out o' your chammer o' purpose to oblige the young man with a bed!'

'Don't blame them, don't blame them!' said Jocelyn in an even and characterless voice. 'Don't blame her, particularly. She didn't make the circumstances. I did. . . . It was how I served her grandmother. . . . Well, she's gone! You needn't make a mystery of it. Tell it to all the island: say that a man came to marry a wife, and didn't find her at home. Tell everybody that she's run away. It must be known sooner or later.'

One of the servants said, after waiting a few moments: 'We shan't do that, sir.'

'O—why won't you?'

'We liked her too well, with all her faults.'

'Ah—did you,' said he; and he sighed. He perceived that the younger maids were secretly on Avice's side.

'How does her mother bear it?' Jocelyn asked. 'Is she awake?'

Mrs. Pierston had hardly slept, and, having learnt the tidings inadvertently, became so distracted and incoherent as to be like a person in a delirium; till, a few moments before he arrived, all her excitement ceased, and she lay in a weak, quiet silence.

'Let me go up,' Pierston said. 'And send for the doctor.'

Passing Avice's chamber he perceived that the little bed had not been slept on. At the door of the spare room he looked in. In one corner stood a walking-stick—his own.

'Where did that come from?'

'We found it there, sir.'

'Ah yes—I gave it to him. 'Tis like me to play another's game!'

It was the last spurt of bitterness that Jocelyn let escape him. He went on towards Mrs. Pierston's room, preceded by the servant.

'Mr. Pierston has come, ma'am,' he heard her say to the invalid. But as the latter took no notice the woman rushed forward to the bed, 'What has happened to her, Mr. Pierston? O what do it mean?'

Avice the Second was lying placidly in the position in which the nurse had left her; but no breath came from her lips, and a rigidity of feature was accompanied by the precise expression which had characterized her face when Pierston had her as a girl in his studio. He saw that it was death, though she appeared to have breathed her last only a few moments before.

Ruth Stockwool's composure deserted her. 'Tis the shock of finding Miss Avice gone that has done it!' she cried. 'She has killed her mother!'

'Don't say such a terrible thing!' exclaimed Jocelyn.

'But she ought to have obeyed her mother—a good mother as she was! How she had set her heart upon the wedding, poor soul; and we couldn't help her knowing what had happened! O how ungrateful young folk be! That girl will rue this morning's work!'

'We must get the doctor,' said Pierston, mechanically, hastening from the room.

When the local practitioner came he merely confirmed their own verdict, and thought her death had undoubtedly been hastened by the shock of the ill news upon a feeble heart, following a long strain of anxiety about the wedding. He did not consider that an inquest would be necessary.

The two shadowy figures seen through the grey gauzes of the morning by Ruth, five hours before this time, had gone on to the open place by the north entrance of Sylvania Castle, where the lane to the ruins of the old castle branched off. A listener would not have gathered that a single word passed between them. The man walked with difficulty, supported by the woman. At this spot they stopped and kissed each other a long while.

'We ought to walk all the way to Budmouth, if we wish not to be discovered,' he said sadly. 'And I can't even get across the island, even by your help, darling. It is two miles to the foot of the hill.'

She, who was trembling, tried to speak consolingly:

'If you could walk we should have to go down the Street of Wells, where perhaps somebody would know me. Now if we get below here to the Cove, can't we push off one of the little boats I saw there last night, and paddle along close to the shore till we get to the north side? Then we can walk across to the station very well. It is quite calm, and as the tide sets in that direction, it will take us along of itself, without much rowing. I've often got round in a boat that way.'

This seemed to be the only plan that offered, and abandoning the straight road they wound down the defile spanned further on by the old castle arch, and forming the original fosse of the fortress.

The stroke of their own footsteps, lightly as these fell, was flapped back to them with impertinent gratuitousness by the vertical faces of the rock, so still was everything around. A little further, and they emerged upon the open ledge of the lower tier of cliffs, to the right being the sloping pathway leading down to the secluded creek at their base—the single practicable spot of exit from or entrance to the isle on this side by a seagoing craft; once an active wharf, whence many a fine public building had sailed—including Saint Paul's Cathedral.

The timorous shadowy shapes descended the foot-way, one at least of them knowing the place so well that she found it scarcely necessary to guide herself down by touching the natural wall of stone on her right hand, as her companion did. Thus, with quick suspensive breathings they arrived at the bottom, and trod the few yards of shingle which, on the forbidding shore hereabout, could be found at this spot alone. It was so solitary as to be unvisited often for four-and-twenty hours by a living soul. Upon the confined beach were drawn up two or three fishing-lerrets, and a couple of smaller ones, beside them being a rough slipway for launching, and a boathouse of tarred boards. The two lovers united their strength to push the smallest of the boats down the slope, and floating it they scrambled in.

The girl broke the silence by asking, 'Where are the oars?'

He felt about the boat, but could find none. 'I forgot to look for the oars!' he said.

'They are locked in the boathouse, I suppose. Now we can only steer and trust to the current!'

The currents here were of a complicated kind. It was true, as the girl had said, that the tide ran round to the north, but at a special moment in every flood there set in along the shore a narrow reflux contrary to the general outer flow, called 'The Southern' by the local sailors. It was produced by the peculiar curves of coast lying east and west of the Beal; these bent southward in two back streams the up-Channel flow on each side of the peninsula, which two streams united outside the Beal, and there met the direct tidal flow, the confluence of the three currents making the surface of the sea at this point to boil like a pot, even in calmest weather. The disturbed area, as is well known, is called the Race.

Thus although the outer sea was now running northward to the roadstead and the mainland of Wessex, 'The Southern' ran in full force towards the Beal and the Race beyond. It caught the lovers' hapless boat in a few moments, and, unable to row across it—mere river's width that it was—they beheld the grey rocks near them, and the grim wrinkled forehead of the isle above, sliding away northwards.

They gazed helplessly at each other, though, in the long-living faith of youth, without distinct fear. The undulations increased in magnitude, and swung them higher and lower. The boat rocked, received a smart slap of the waves now and then, and wheeled round, so that the lightship which stolidly winked at them from the quicksand, the single object which told them of their bearings, was sometimes on their right hand and sometimes on their left.

it in all their natural circumstances, weaknesses, and stains. And then as he came to himself their voices grew fainter; they had all gone off on their different careers, and he was left here alone.

The probable ridicule that would result to him from the events of the day he did not mind in itself at all. But he would fain have removed the misapprehensions on which it would be based. That, however, was impossible. Nobody would ever know the truth about him; *what* it was he had sought that had so eluded, tantalized, and escaped him; what it was that had led him such a dance, and had at last, as he believed just now in the freshness of his loss, been discovered in the girl who had left him. It was not the flesh; he had never knelt low to that. Not a woman in the world had been wrecked by him, though he had been impassioned by so many. Nobody would guess the further sentiment—the cordial loving-kindness—which had lain behind what had seemed to him the enraptured fulfilment of a pleasing destiny postponed for forty years. His attraction to the third Avice would be regarded by the world as the selfish designs of an elderly man on a maid.

His life seemed no longer a professional man's experience, but a ghost story; and he would fain have vanished from his haunts on this critical afternoon, as the rest had done. He desired to sleep away his tendencies, to make something happen which would put an end to his bondage to beauty in the ideal.

So he sat on till it was quite dark, and a light was brought. There was a chilly wind blowing outside, and the lightship on the quicksand afar looked harassed and forlorn. The haggard solitude was broken by a ring at the door.

Pierston heard a voice below, the accents of a woman. They had a ground quality of familiarity, a superficial articulation of strangeness. Only one person in all his experience had ever possessed precisely those tones; rich, as if they had once been powerful. Explanations seemed to be asked for and given, and in a minute he was informed that a lady was downstairs whom perhaps he would like to see.

'Who is the lady?' Jocelyn asked.

The servant hesitated a little. 'Mrs. Leverre—the mother of the—young gentleman Miss Avice has run off with.'

'Yes—I'll see her,' said Pierston.

He covered the face of the dead Avice, and descended. 'Leverre,' he said to himself. His ears had known that name before to-day. It was the name those travelling Americans he had met in Rome gave the woman he supposed might be Marcia Bencomb.

A sudden adjusting light burst upon many familiar things at that moment. He found the visitor in the drawing-room, standing up veiled, the carriage which had brought her being in waiting at the door. By the dim light he could see nothing of her features in such circumstances.

'Mr. Pierston?'

'I am Mr. Pierston.'

'You represent the late Mrs. Pierston?'

'I do—though I am not one of the family.'

'I know it. . . . I am Marcia—after forty years.'

'I was divining as much, Marcia. May the lines have fallen to you in pleasant places since we last met! But, of all moments of my life, why do you choose to hunt me up now?'

'Why—I am the step-mother and only relation of the young man your bride eloped with this morning.'

'I was just guessing that, too, as I came downstairs. But——'

'And I am naturally making inquiries.'

'Yes. Let us take it quietly, and shut the door.'

Marcia sat down. And he learnt that the conjunction of old things and new was no accident. What Mrs. Pierston had discussed with her nurse and neighbour as vague intelligence, was now revealed to Jocelyn at first hand by Marcia herself; how, many years after their separation, and when she was left poor by the death of her impoverished father, she had become the wife of that bygone Jersey lover of hers, who wanted a tender nurse and mother for the infant left him by his first wife recently deceased; how he had died a few years later, leaving her with the boy, whom she had brought up at St. Heliers and in Paris, educating him as well as she could with her limited means, till he became the French master at a school in Sandbourne; and how, a year ago, she and her son had got to know Mrs. Pierston and her daughter on their visit to the island, 'to ascertain,' she added, more deliberately, 'not entirely for sentimental reasons, what had become of the man with whom I eloped in the first flush of my young womanhood, and only missed marrying by my own will.'

Pierston bowed.

'Well, that was how the acquaintance between the children began, and their passionate attachment to each other.' She detailed how Avice had induced her mother to let her take lessons in French of young Leverre, rendering their meetings easy. Marcia had never thought of hindering their intimacy, for in her recent years of affliction she had acquired a new interest in the name she had refused to take in her purse-proud young womanhood; and it was not until she knew how determined Mrs. Pierston was to make her daughter Jocelyn's wife that she had objected to her son's acquaintance with Avice. But it was too late to hinder what had been begun. He had lately been ill, and she had been frightened by his not returning home the night before. The note she had received from him that day had only informed her that Avice and himself had gone to be married immediately—whither she did not know.

'What do you mean to do?' she asked.

'I do nothing: there is nothing to be done. . . . It is how I served her grandmother—one of Time's revenges.'

'Served her so for me.'

'Yes. Now she me for your son.'

Marcia paused a long while thinking that over, till arousing herself she resumed: 'But can't we inquire which way they went out of the island, or gather some particulars about them?'

'Aye—yes. We will.'

And Pierston found himself as in a dream walking beside Marcia along the road in their common quest. He discovered that almost every one of the neighbouring inhabitants knew more about the lovers than he did himself.

At the corner some men were engaged in conversation on the occurrence. It was allusive only, but knowing the dialect, Pierston and Marcia gathered its import easily. As soon as it had got light that morning one of the boats was discovered missing from the creek below, and when the flight of the lovers was made known it was inferred that they were the culprits.

Unconsciously Pierston turned in the direction of the creek, without regarding whether Marcia followed him, and though it was darker than when Avice and Leverre had descended in the morning he pursued his way down the incline till he reached the water-side.

'Is that you, Jocelyn?'

The inquiry came from Marcia. She was behind him, about half-way down.

'Yes,' he said, noticing that it was the first time she had called him by his Christian name.

'I can't see where you are, and I am afraid to follow.'

Afraid to follow. How strangely that altered his conception of her. Till this moment she had stood in his mind as the imperious, invincible Marcia of old. There was a strange pathos in this revelation. He went back and felt for her hand. 'I'll lead you down,' he said. And he did so.

They looked out upon the sea, and the lightship shining as if it had quite forgotten all about the fugitives. 'I am so uneasy,' said Marcia. 'Do you think they got safely to land?'

'Yes,' replied some one other than Jocelyn. It was a boatman smoking in the shadow of the boathouse. He informed her that they were picked up by the lightship men, and afterwards, at their request, taken across to the opposite shore, where they landed, proceeding thence on foot to the nearest railway station and entering the train for London. This intelligence had reached the island about an hour before.

'They'll be married to-morrow morning!' said Marcia.

'So much the better. Don't regret it, Marcia. He shall not

lose by it. I have no relation in the world except some twentieth cousins in this isle, of whom her father was one, and I'll take steps at once to make her a good match for him. As for me . . . I have lived a day too long.'

'ALAS FOR THIS GREY SHADOW,
ONCE A MAN!'

III.—viii.

IN the month of November which followed, Pierston was lying dangerously ill of a fever at his house in London.

The funeral of the second Avice had happened to be on one of those drenching afternoons of the autumn, when the raw rain flies level as the missiles of the ancient inhabitants across the beaked promontory which has formed the scene of this narrative, scarcely alighting except against the upright sides of things sturdy enough to stand erect. One person only followed the corpse into the church as chief mourner, Jocelyn Pierston—fickle lover in the brief, faithful friend in the long run. No means had been found of communicating with Avice before the interment, though the death had been advertised in the local and other papers in the hope that it might catch her eye.

So, when the pathetic procession came out of the church and moved round into the graveyard, a hired vehicle from Budmouth was seen coming at great speed along the open road from Top-o'-Hill. It stopped at the churchyard gate, and a young man and woman alighted and entered, the vehicle waiting. They glided along the path and reached Pierston's side just as the body was deposited by the grave.

He did not turn his head. He knew it was Avice, with Henri Leverre—by this time, he supposed, her husband. Her remorseful grief, though silent, seemed to impregnate the atmosphere with its heaviness. Perceiving that they had not expected him to be there Pierston edged back; and when the service was over he kept still further aloof, an act of considerateness which she seemed to appreciate.

Thus, by his own contrivance, neither Avice nor the young man held communication with Jocelyn by word or by sign. After the burial they returned as they had come.

It was supposed that his exposure that day in the

bleakest churchyard in Wessex, telling upon a distracted mental and bodily condition, had thrown Pierston into the chill and fever which held him swaying for weeks between life and death shortly after his return to town. When he had passed the crisis, and began to know again that there was such a state as mental equilibrium and physical calm, he heard a whispered conversation going on around him, and the touch of footsteps on the carpet. The light in the chamber was so subdued that nothing around him could be seen with any distinctness. Two living figures were present, a nurse moving about softly, and a visitor. He discerned that the latter was feminine, and for the time this was all.

He was recalled to his surroundings by a voice murmuring the inquiry: 'Does the light try your eyes?'

The tones seemed familiar; they were spoken by the woman who was visiting him. He recollected them to be Marcia's, and everything that had happened before he fell ill came back to his mind.

'Are you helping to nurse me, Marcia?' he asked.

'Yes. I have come up to stay here till you are better, as you seem to have no other woman friend who cares whether you are dead or alive. I am living quite near. I am glad you have got round the corner. We have been very anxious.'

'How good you are! . . . And—have you heard of the others?'

'They are married. They have been here to see you, and are very sorry. She sat by you, but you did not know her. She was broken down when she discovered her mother's death, which had never once occurred to her as being imminent. They have gone away again. I thought it best she should leave, now that you are out of danger. Now you must be quiet till I come and talk again.'

Pierston was conscious of a singular change in himself, which had been revealed by this slight discourse. He was no longer the same man that he had hitherto been. The malignant fever, or his experiences, or both, had taken away something from him, and put something else in its place.

During the next days, with further intellectual expansion, he became clearly aware of what this was. The artistic sense had left him, and he could no longer attach a definite sentiment to images of beauty recalled from the past. His appreciativeness was capable of exercising itself only on utilitarian matters, and recollection of Avice's good qualities alone had any effect on his mind; of her appearance none at all.

At first he was appalled; and then he said 'Thank God!'

Marcia, who, with something of her old absolutism, came to his house continually to inquire and give orders, and to his room to see him every afternoon, found out for herself in the course of his convalescence this strange death of the sensuous side of Jocelyn's nature. She had said that Avice was getting extraordinarily handsome, and that she did not wonder her stepson lost his heart to her—an inadvertent remark which she immediately regretted, in fear lest it should agitate him. He merely answered, however, 'Yes; I suppose she is handsome. She's more—a wise girl who will make a good housewife in time. . . . I wish you were not handsome, Marcia.'

'Why?'

'I don't quite know why. Well—it seems a stupid quality to me. I can't understand what it is good for any more.'

'O—I as a woman think there's good in it.'

'Is there? Then I have lost all conception of it. I don't know what has happened to me. I only know I don't regret it. Robinson Crusoe lost a day in his illness; I have lost a faculty, for which loss Heaven be praised!'

There was something pathetic in this announcement, and Marcia sighed as she said, 'Perhaps when you get strong it will come back to you.'

Pierston shook his head. It then occurred to him that never since the reappearance of Marcia had he seen her in full daylight, or without a bonnet and thick veil, which she always retained on these frequent visits, and that he had been unconsciously regarding her as the Marcia of their early time, a fancy which the small change in her voice well sustained. The stately figure, the good colour, the classical profile, the rather large handsome nose and somewhat prominent, regular teeth, the full dark eye, formed still the Marcia of his imagination; the queenly creature who had infatuated him when the first Avice was despised and her successors unknown. It was this old idea which, in his revolt from beauty, had led to his regret at her assumed handsomeness. He began wondering now how much remained of that presentation after forty years.

'Why don't you ever let me see you, Marcia?' he asked.

'O, I don't know. You mean without my bonnet? You have never asked me to, and I am obliged to wrap up my face with this wool veil because I suffer so from aches in these cold winter winds, though a thick veil is awkward for any one whose sight is not so good as it was.'

The impregnable Marcia's sight not so good as it was, and her face in the aching stage of life: these simple things came as sermons to Jocelyn.

'But certainly I will gratify your curiosity,' she resumed good-naturedly. 'It is really a compliment that you should still take that sort of interest in me.'

She had moved round from the dark side of the room to the lamp—for the daylight had gone—and she now suddenly took off the bonnet, veil and all. She stood revealed to his eyes as remarkably good-looking, considering the lapse of years.

'I am—vexed!' he said, turning his head aside impatiently. 'You are fair and five-and-thirty—not a day more. You still suggest beauty. *You* won't do as a chastisement, Marcia!'

'Ah, but I may! To think that you know woman no better after all this time!'

'How?'

'To be so easily deceived. Think: it is lamplight; and your sight is weak at present; and . . . Well, I have no reason for being anything but candid now, God knows! So I will tell you. . . . My husband was younger than myself; and he had an absurd wish to make people think he had married a young and fresh-looking woman. To fall in with

his vanity I tried to look it. We were often in Paris, and
I became as skilled in beautifying artifices as any *passée*
wife of the Faubourg St. Germain. Since his death I have
kept up the practice, partly because the vice is almost
ineradicable, and partly because I found that it helped me
with men in bringing up his boy on small means. At this
moment I am frightfully made up. But I can cure that. I'll
come in to-morrow morning, if it is bright, just as I really
am; you'll find that Time has not disappointed you.
Remember I am as old as yourself; and I look it.'

The morrow came and with it Marcia, quite early, as she
had promised. It happened to be sunny, and shutting the
bedroom door she went round to the window, where she
uncovered immediately, in his full view, and said, 'See if
I am satisfactory now—to you who think beauty vain. The
rest of me—and it is a good deal—lies on my dressing-table
at home. I shall never put it on again—never!'

But she was a woman; and her lips quivered, and there
was a tear in her eye, as she exposed the ruthless treatment
to which she had subjected herself. The cruel morning
rays—as with Jocelyn under Avice's scrutiny—showed in
their full bareness, unenriched by addition, undisguised by
the arts of colour and shade, the thin remains of what had
once been Marcia's majestic bloom. She stood the image
and superscription of Age—an old woman, pale and
shrivelled, her forehead ploughed, her cheek hollow, her
hair white as snow. To this the face he once kissed had
been brought by the raspings, chisellings, scourgings, bakings, freezings of forty invidious years—by the thinkings
of more than half a lifetime.

'I am sorry if I shock you,' she went on huskily but
firmly, as he did not speak. 'But the moth frets the garment
somewhat in such an interval.'

'Yes—yes! . . . Marcia, you are a brave woman. You
have the courage of the great women of history. I can no
longer love; but I admire you from my soul!'

'Don't say I am great. Say I have begun to be passably
honest. It is more than enough.'

'Well—I'll say nothing then, more than how wonderful

it is that a woman should have been able to put back the clock of Time thirty years!'

'It shames me now, Jocelyn. I shall never do it any more!'

As soon as he was strong enough he got her to take him round to his studio in a carriage. The place had been kept aired, but the shutters were shut, and they opened them themselves. He looked round upon the familiar objects— some complete and matured, the main of them seedlings, grafts, and scions of beauty, waiting for a mind to grow to perfection in.

'No—I don't like them!' he said, turning away. 'They are as ugliness to me! I don't feel a single touch of kin with or interest in any one of them whatever.'

'Jocelyn—this is sad.'

'No—not at all.' He went again towards the door. 'Now let me look round.' He looked back, Marcia remaining silent. 'The Aphrodites—how I insulted her fair form by those failures!—the Freyjas, the Nymphs and Fauns, Eves, Avices, and other innumerable Well-Beloveds—I want to see them never any more! . . . "Instead of sweet smell there shall be stink, and there shall be burning instead of beauty," said the prophet.'

And they came away. On another afternoon they went to the National Gallery, to test his taste in paintings, which had formerly been good. As she had expected, it was just the same with him there. He saw no more to move him, he declared, in the time-defying presentations of Perugino, Titian, Sebastiano, and other statuesque creators than in the work of the pavement artist they had passed on their way.

'It is strange!' said she.

'I don't regret it. That fever has killed a faculty which has, after all, brought me my greatest sorrows, if a few little pleasures. Let us be gone.'

He was now so well advanced in convalescence that it was deemed a most desirable thing to take him down into his native air. Marcia agreed to accompany him. 'I don't

see why I shouldn't,' said she. 'An old friendless woman
like me, and and you an old friendless man.'

'Yes. Thank Heaven I am old at last. The curse is
removed.'

It may be shortly stated here that after his departure for
the isle Pierston never again saw his studio or its contents.
He had been down there but a brief while when, finding his
sense of beauty in art and nature absolutely extinct, he
directed his agent in town to disperse the whole collection;
which was done. His lease of the building was sold, and in
the course of time another sculptor won admiration there
from those who knew not Joseph. The next year his name
figured on the retired list of Academicians.

As time went on he grew as well as one of his age could
expect to be after such a blasting illness, but remained on
the isle, in the only house he now possessed, a comparatively small one at the top of the Street of Wells. A
growing sense of friendship which it would be foolish to
interrupt led him to take a somewhat similar house for
Marcia quite near, and remove her furniture thither from
Sandbourne. Whenever the afternoon was fine he would
call for her, and they would take a stroll together towards
the Beal, or the ancient Castle, seldom going the whole
way, his sciatica and her rheumatism effectually preven-
ting them, except in the driest atmospheres. He had now
changed his style of dress entirely, appearing always in a
homely suit of local make, and of the fashion of thirty
years before, the achievement of a tailoress at East Quarriers. He also let his iron-grey beard grow as it would, and
what little hair he had left from the baldness which had
followed the fever. And thus, numbering in years but two-
and-sixty, he might have passed for seventy-five.

Though their early adventure as lovers had happened so
long ago, its history had become known in the isle with
mysterious rapidity and fulness of detail. The gossip to
which its bearings on their present friendship gave rise was
the subject of their conversation on one of these walks
along the cliffs.

'It is extraordinary what an interest our neighbours take in our affairs,' he observed. 'They say "Those old folk ought to marry; better late than never." That's how people are—wanting to round off other people's histories in the best machine-made conventional manner.'

'Yes. They keep on about it to me, too, indirectly.'

'Do they! I believe a deputation will wait upon us some morning, requesting in the interests of match-making that we will please to get married as soon as possible. . . . How near we were to doing it forty years ago, only you were so independent! I thought you would have come back, and was much surprised that you didn't.'

'My independent ideas were not blameworthy in me, as an islander, though as a kimberlin young lady perhaps they would have been. There was simply no reason from an islander's point of view why I should come back, since no result threatened from our union; and I didn't. My father kept that view before me, and I bowed to his judgment.'

'And so the island ruled our destinies, though we were not on it. Yes—we are in hands not our own. . . . Did you ever tell your husband?'

'No.'

'Did he ever hear anything?'

'Not that I am aware.'

Calling upon her one day, he found her in a state of great discomfort. In certain gusty winds the chimneys of the little house she had taken here smoked intolerably, and one of these winds was blowing then. Her drawing-room fire could not be kept burning, and rather than let a woman who suffered from rheumatism shiver fireless he asked her to come round and lunch with him as she had often done before. As they went he thought, not for the first time, how needless it was that she should be put to this inconvenience by their occupying two houses, when one would better suit their now constant companionship, and disembarrass her of the objectionable chimneys. Moreover, by marrying Marcia, and establishing a parental relation with the young people, the rather delicate business of his making them a regular allowance would become a natural proceeding.

And so the zealous wishes of the neighbours to give a geometrical shape to their story were fulfilled almost in spite of the chief parties themselves. When he put the question to her distinctly, Marcia admitted that she had always regretted the imperious decision of her youth; and she made no ado about accepting him.

'I have no love to give, you know, Marcia,' he said. 'But such friendship as I am capable of is yours till the end.'

'It is nearly the same with me—perhaps not quite. But, like the other people, I have somehow felt, and you will understand why, that I ought to be your wife before I die.'

It chanced that a day or two before the ceremony, which was fixed to take place very shortly after the foregoing conversation, Marcia's rheumatism suddenly became acute. The attack promised, however, to be only temporary, owing to some accidental exposure of herself in making preparations for removal, and as they thought it undesirable to postpone their union for such a reason, Marcia, after being well wrapped up, was wheeled into the church in a chair.

A month thereafter, when they were sitting at breakfast one morning, Marcia exclaimed 'Well—good heavens!' while reading a letter she had just received from Avice, who was living with her husband in a house Pierston had bought for them at Sandbourne.

Jocelyn looked up.

'Why—Avice says she wants to be separated from Henri! Did you ever hear of such a thing! 'She's coming here about it to-day.'

'Separated? What does the child mean!' Pierston read the letter. 'Ridiculous nonsense!' he continued. 'She doesn't know what she wants. I say she shan't be separated! Tell her so, and there's an end of it. Why—how long have they been married? Not twelve months. What will she say when they have been married twenty years!'

Marcia remained reflecting. 'I think that remorseful feeling she unluckily has at times, of having disobeyed her mother, and caused her death, makes her irritable,' she murmured. 'Poor child!'

Lunch-time had hardly come when Avice arrived, looking very tearful and excited. Marcia took her into an inner room, had a conversation with her, and they came out together.

'O it's nothing,' said Marcia. 'I tell her she must go back directly she has had some luncheon.'

'Ah, that's all very well!' sobbed Avice. 'B-b-but if you had been m-married so long as I have, y-you wouldn't say go back like that.'

'What is it all about?' inquired Pierston.

'He said that if he were to die I—I—should be looking out for somebody with fair hair and grey eyes, just—just to spite him in his grave, because he's dark, and he's quite sure I don't like dark people! And then he said——But I won't be so treacherous as to tell any more about him! I wish——'

'Avice, your mother did this very thing. And she went back to her husband. Now you are to do the same. Let me see; there is a train——'

'She must have something to eat first. Sit down, dear.'

The question was settled by the arrival of Henri himself at the end of luncheon, with a very anxious and pale face. Pierston went off to a business meeting, and left the young couple to adjust their differences in their own way.

His business was, among kindred undertakings which followed the extinction of the Well-Beloved and other ideals, to advance a scheme for the closing of the old natural fountains in the Street of Wells, because of their possible contamination, and supplying the townlet with water from pipes, a scheme that was carried out at his expense, as is well known. He was also engaged in acquiring some old moss-grown, mullioned Elizabethan cottages, for the purpose of pulling them down because they were damp; which he afterwards did, and built new ones with hollow walls, and full of ventilators.

At present he is sometimes mentioned as 'the late Mr.

Pierston' by gourd-like young art-critics and journalists; and his productions are alluded to as those of a man not without genius, whose powers were insufficiently recognized in his lifetime.

THE END

APPENDIX

A COMPARISON OF THE BOOK VERSION WITH THE ORIGINAL SERIAL VERSION OF THE STORY

(Section A makes possible a comparison between the story we read now and what the readers of the *Illustrated London News* serialization saw in 1892 by collating brief summaries of the passages containing the major differences; Section B prints in full the passages from 1892 summarized in Section A.)

SECTION A

1897 and Subsequent Editions	1892 Serial Version
Before I.i *(First chapter of 1892 was deleted from 1897.)*	(1) CHAPTER I Jocelyn Pearston, a young sculptor, was preparing to leave London to visit his father in Portland. He tried but failed to burn packages of old love-letters, so he wrapped them in his coat.
I.ii (p. 14) Pierston was stopping to look at garden flowers when he heard Avice's voice.	(2) From CHAPTER III Mrs Caro's servant returned his coat to him and he removed the letters. When he was burning them in a garden fire he heard Avice's voice.
(p. 15) *(After Pierston kissed Avice 1 and asked her forgiveness, reference to the love-letters has been removed.)*	(3) Avice was sad to find him burning the love-letters. On impulse, Pearston proposed to her.

(p. 16)

Never much considering that
the Well-Beloved was a subjective phenomenon, Pierston
dreamt of her as Aphrodite
herself.

(Not in 1892)

(p. 18)

The evening and night winds
over Deadman's Bay seemed to
Pierston to be charged with the
spirits of the drowned. He and
Avice wandered a long way
that night. In the old Hope
Churchyard he kissed her.

(Not in 1892)

(p. 19)

Pierston wondered if Avice
regretted the discontinuance of
the old custom of ratifying a
betrothal.

(4)

Pearston wondered if Avice
expected ratification of their
betrothal. To find out he asked
her to meet him in the old
Hope Churchyard.

I.iii (p. 20)

Pierston said he must return to
London the next day but defer-
red his departure till night. He
proposed a farewell walk along
Chesil Beach (with no specific
reference to its purpose).

(5) From CHAPTER IV

In the churchyard Pearston
asked Avice her view of the
ancient custom of a pre-marital
relationship. She was reluctant
to meet him the following
evening for that purpose.

I.iv (pp. 22–3)

Jocelyn was surprised to
receive Avice's letter, which he
considered naive, and was
disappointed to be deprived of
her company. Hardy reminds
the reader that the action of the
story took place forty years
earlier.

(Not in 1892)

I.v (p. 31)
As Pierston dried Marcia's clothes he realized that the Well-Beloved was 'moving house'. Avice's refusal to meet him had brought this about. *(He made no reference to marrying her.)*

(6) From CHAPTER V
As he sat drying Marcia's clothes before the fire he realized his Well-Beloved had transferred to Marcia; but he felt he must still marry Avice.

I.vi (p. 35)
Pierston told Somers he was under a curse; under the influence of Aphrodite.

(Not in 1892)

I.vii (p. 40)
Pierston told Somers that Marcia would be compromised if he did not marry her. Knowing himself accursed, he had seldom ventured on a close acquaintance with any woman.

(Not in 1892)

(p. 41)
Pierston told Miss Bencomb they could not marry yet as he had admitted to the authorities that they did not have the residential qualification required by law. She was displeased.

(Not in 1892)

I.viii (pp. 42–3)
Pierston and Marcia continued to live together at a London hotel unmarried. She was still vexed that he had bungled the wedding arrangements. She tried but failed to persuade him to write to her parents. She wrote herself, but annoyed Pierston by criticizing his father.

(7) From CHAPTER VIII
Pearston and Marcia, married two months, returned from a Continental trip to his Kensington house. Marcia's parents did not communicate with them. She learned that they were in Italy and expressed regret that she was not with them.

(p. 44)

Marcia was amazed by a letter from her father ignoring her circumstances, refusing his consent to her marriage, and telling her to return home if she wanted his help.

(pp. 44–8)

After a quarrel over their parents, Pierston refused to apologize and Marcia left him to go to her aunt's and later to her parents' home. Eventually Pierston learned that Avice had married her cousin and the Bencombs had started their world tour. He concluded that Marcia was with them and had not become pregnant.

I.ix (p. 49)

Pierston returned to his customary routine. He only once had news of the Bencombs, which confirmed that Marcia was abroad with her parents and had not become pregnant. For the first year of their separation he felt bound to keep faith with her but sometimes feared that the Well-Beloved would seduce him in another incarnation. He avoided potential contacts by walking the other way.

II.i (p. 55)

He often wondered what had become of Marcia. He had not troubled her for twenty years though he had missed her as a friend.

(8)

Pearston returned to his customary routine; Marcia became bored. Her parents returned from abroad but would not call on them.

(9)

After quarrelling, Pearston and Marcia both found the life-long tie of matrimony irksome. Jocelyn saw that this had hastened the departure of the Well-Beloved. Marcia regretted she could not accompany her parents abroad. A more violent quarrel developed.

(10) From CHAPTER IX

After four years of quarrelling, Marcia and Pearston parted by common consent. The separation was informal but each promised never to intrude on the other's life and Marcia suggested by letter that they consider themselves free to marry again.

(11) From CHAPTER X

He had not troubled Marcia for a dozen years. Now that he had inherited his father's fortune he made enquiries to see if she needed help but could not trace her.

(p. 63)
Pierston was aware that it was the Well-Beloved who influenced his interest in Mrs Pine-Avon. He had become a sculptor of the Dea's form only but he thought this new interest might prove to be a punishment for his artistic failures.

(Not in 1892)

II.ii (p. 65)
He wondered whether Mrs Pine-Avon knew his history and was aware that his obsession with the pursuit of the Well-Beloved, his 'restlessly ideal . . . fancies', rendered him useless as a potential husband.

(Not in 1892)

II.iii (pp. 73–4)
Pierston 'began to divine the truth': that only a woman like Avice I, with the same family and racial background, could provide the 'groundwork of character' for him to love. It was his artist's superstition that only 'one of the old island breed', formerly worshippers of Venus, could provide 'the true star of his soul'.

(Not in 1892)

II.vii (pp. 99–100)
As he had once thought, only the Caro family possessed the 'clay' from which to produce the ideal supplement to his own imperfect nature and 'round it with a perfect whole' — though this might never happen.

(Not in 1892)

II.viii (p. 104)
The 'startling parallel in the idiosyncrasies' of Avice II and himself probably derived from a common ancestry.

(Not in 1892)

II.xii (p. 131)
Pierston dismissed the thought of asking Avice II to live with him unmarried.

(Not in 1892)

III.i (pp. 141–3)
Pierston received a letter from Avice II telling him that her husband had been killed; and that she herself had been ill. As a result, he returned to the 'Isle' from Rome, but delayed visiting her for several days. He was surprised to receive another letter from her expressing anxiety that he had not called.

(12) From CHAPTER XXIII
Pearston felt it his duty to return to the 'Isle' to check if his wife Marcia was there, but he failed to find her. He heard of a recent accident at a quarry and learned that Isaac Pearston, Avice II's husband, had been killed.

III.iii (p. 159)
Mrs Pierston, 'in fearing to be frank', did not fully realize how willing Pierston was to make amends for his infidelity forty years earlier and to enrich her daughter, Avice III, by marrying her.

(Not in 1892)

III.iv (pp. 67–8)
Pierston told Avice III his past history: that he had been the lover of both her mother and her grandmother. She said she had not realized he was so old. In her eyes was a look 'that might have been sympathy or nervousness'.

(Not in 1892 at this point. See [14].)

III.iv (p. 170)

In anticipation of marriage, Pierston had taken a new house. He invited Avice III and her mother to spend a few weeks there. He and Avice III were able to practise receiving visitors in preparation for their married life.

(p. 173)

Pierston felt there was 'something uncanny . . . about London, in its relation to his contemplated marriage'. He decided to make the most of having Avice III under his roof to advance the wedding arrangements. He and her mother persuaded Avice III that the wedding-day should be soon; mother and daughter were to go back to the 'Isle' and await Pierston's early arrival for the wedding.

(13) From CHAPTER XXVII

Mrs Pearston, reclining in her invalid's room, examined approvingly her daughter dressed for her wedding. She waited contentedly while the wedding took place. After the celebrations Pearston and Avice III caught the train for London. They travelled in the north of England for their honeymoon and returned to London to superintend the furnishing of Pearston's new house.

(14) From CHAPTER XXVIII

Pearston went up to their bedroom but the look of dread in Avice III's eyes when she awoke made him pause. Sitting in his dressing-gown he told her he had been the lover of her mother and grandmother. When he had finished she did not go to sleep again and her state of tension was distressing to him. He 'knew that his cause was lost with her' and went to an adjoining bedroom. He hoped that a visit to the 'Isle' would improve their relationship, but at Budmouth sent Avice on ahead. When he arrived next day she informed him that her mother was very ill. As there was no room for a married couple at Avice II's house, Pearston slept at a lodging nearby.

(pp. 173–8)

Pierston returned to the south coast in accordance with their arrangement, crossed over to the 'Isle' by the local train and began to climb the hill on foot. He lent his stick and his assistance to a young Jersey man still suffering from illness. Avice III gave a little jump of surprise when he arrived at her door. He was pleased because he thought (mistakenly) that she was waiting for him. She told him that her mother was much weaker. Avice II expressed great relief and thankfulness at his arrival. Jocelyn wondered whether she had some new cause for uneasiness about the marriage and about her daughter. He left Avice III to return to the inn. As soon as he had gone, she took a parcel from a cupboard and went to the ruin of the Red King's Castle.

III.vi (pp. 179–89)

Mrs Pierston passed a restless night on the eve of the wedding. She was pleased at her success in arranging the marriage but worried about her daughter's attitude. She expressed her fears to Ruth Stockwool, especially about Avice III's friendship with Henri Leverre. Pierston arrived in the morning to find Avice III and Henri had eloped. Mrs Pierston died shortly after the

(15) CHAPTER XXIX

Pearston felt he had tried to be good to his wife. After Avice II's death he returned to London leaving Avice III in her mother's cottage. A month later he returned to the south-coast seaport. As he had missed the last local train he decided to walk the whole way. Halfway across the pebble bank he met a young foreigner who had been coughing up blood. He assisted him across to the foot of the 'Isle', where he disappeared. When Pearston reached Avice III's house, he noticed her nervousness. She soon left him to visit someone who was ill. After a while he went out to look for her. Unobserved, he discovered his wife talking in anguished tones at Red King's Castle to the young invalid he had helped. When they parted Pearston thought they might have kissed.

(16) CHAPTERS XXX–XXXII

Pearston took a short cut home and, when Avice arrived, asked her where she had been. She told him about Henri and was distressed because he had returned to her too late and was ill. Pearston obtained medical help for him. He decided to find a remedy for the two young people's plight by sacrificing his own married happiness and 'resuscitating' his first wife, Marcia. He wrote discovery. Avice and Henri got into difficulties in a boat but were seen by the lightship crew and rescued.

to Somers explaining his plan, but shortly after changed his mind and attempted suicide in a small boat in the dangerous currents off Portland Bill. Instead of drowning he was injured in a sudden crash and rescued by the lightship men.

III.vii (pp. 190–5)
Jocelyn sat beside the body of Mrs Pierston. Marcia arrived and explained that she was the step-mother of Henri Leverre. She went with Pierston to enquire which way the young couple had gone. They found that Avice and Henri had caught the London train. Jocelyn said he would support them financially.

(Not in 1892)

III.viii (p. 196)
In November Pierston was dangerously ill from a fever resulting from attending Avice II's funeral in drenching rain. He had seen Avice III and Henri arrive at the grave-side but they had not spoken.

(Not in 1892)

(pp. 197–206)
When Pierston had passed the crisis, he found that Marcia was attending him in his illness. She told him Avice and Henri were married. He discovered that he had lost his artistic and aesthetic sense. He persuaded her to let him see her without make-up and she was revealed as an aged

(17) CHAPTER XXXIII
When Pearston recovered consciousness he found that Marcia was attending him. In the darkened room he imagined her still to be the 'queenly creature' he had known in his youth. When she later let light into the room he found her to be a 'wrinkled crone'. A telegram arrived to declare his

woman. He proposed to her again and they were married. A month later they helped to resolve a quarrel between the young people. Pierston became involved in various philanthropic undertakings to improve the town. He was remembered as a man 'not without genius'.

marriage to Avice III annulled. He put up his hand to tear open his wound but changed his mind and laughed hysterically at the contrast between Avice and Marcia.

SECTION B

CHAPTER I

(1) Once—and that not long ago—there was a young sculptor who had not quite made a great name; and pending that event he lived on a small income allowed him by his father, an inartistic man of trade and commerce merely.

The sculptor was not engaged in his art on one particular midnight in the summer season, when, having packed up such luggage as he might require for a sojourn in the country, he sat down in his temporary rooms in a London square to destroy a mass of papers that he did not wish to carry with him and objected to leave behind.

Among them were several packets of love-letters, in sundry hands.

He took the first bundle, laid it in the grate, lit a match under it, and waited. The bundle of hard, close-lying note sheets would not burn.

He cut the string, loosened the letters, and kindled another match. The flames illuminated the handwriting, which sufficiently recalled to his knowledge her from whom that batch had come, and enabled him to read tender words and fragments of sentences addressed to him in his teens by the writer. Many of the sentiments, he was ashamed to think, he had availed himself of in some attempts at lyric verse, as having in them that living fire which no lucubration can reach. The edges of some of the sheets began to be browned by the flame; but they would not in this cold grate light up and consume as he had expected.

By this time he had begun to experience a sentimental feeling for the letters, though, till the present evening, he had not once thought of them for a twelvemonth. He had no longer heart to burn them. That packet, at least, he would preserve for the writer's sake, notwithstanding that the person of the writer, wherever she might be, was now but as an empty shell which had once contained his ideal for a transient time. He drew the letters from the grate, shook them clean, and laid them aside.

The next package was in a contrasting hand—thick and rotund, generated by a scratching quill. A school-girl she: he had never much cared for her; and her effusions were unceremoniously tumbled in.

The young man repeated the match-lighting process, stirring the letters with the poker. Some flamed, but the majority remained clean and legible as when written. Her handwriting had been so large and inky that she had spread over a multitude of sheets a very small quantity of thought and affection; and the bundle, made up of only a short correspondence, was enormous. There was no destroying it in a hurry, unless a fiery furnace into which to thrust it could have been improvised.

Suddenly there arose a little fizzle in the dull flicker: something other than paper was burning. It was hair—*her* hair.

"Good heavens!" said the budding sculptor to himself. "How can I be such a brute? I am burning *her*—part of her form—many of whose curves as remembered by me I have worked into statuettes and tried to sell. I cannot do it—at any rate, to-night."

All that remained of the bundle—by far the greater part—he hastily withdrew from the grate, shook the feathery black scales of paper-ash from the pages, refastened them, and put them back for preservation also.

He looked at the other packages. One signed in round-hand, one in long-hand, one in square-hand, one in pointed-hand, crippled and pinched. She had been much older than he. They all showed affection which once had lived, though now it was past and gone. . . No, he could not burn them here and alone.

What could he do with them? He would take them with him, and reconsider their existence. But all his luggage was packed; in his portmanteaus and hand baggage not a square inch of room remained. At last he took his summer overcoat, which he would certainly not require to use till wet weather recommenced, rolled it hastily round the lumps of undying affection, strapped the whole compactly together, and, flinging it down beside his portmanteaus, went to bed.

FROM CHAPTER III

(2) He had hardly left the door when Mrs. Caro's servant ran out to ask him if he had left his coat behind him when he called on the day of his arrival. They had found it in the house, and had not been sure whose it was.

"O, yes, it is mine," said Jocelyn hastily. "I forgot it."

The great coat was strapped up round the letters just as he had arranged it; but he wondered as he walked on whether Mrs. Caro or Avice had looked inside as a means of identification. Determining to run no further risks, he set about destroying the letters there and then. To burn them in a grate was an endless task. He went into the garden, threw them down, made a loose heap of a portion, and put a match to the windy side.

By the help of a pitchfork to stir them about he was fairly successful, though as soon as he ceased to stir they ceased to burn. He was deeply occupied in the business of feeding the fire from the adjoining heap when he heard a voice behind him.

(3) She blushed, looked rather than spoke her forgiveness, and shrank away, sitting down upon a squared stone, around which the unburnt sheets of paper were strewn. With some embarrassment at her presence he withdrew another handful from the collection and threw it on the flames.

"What are you burning?" she asked.

"O, only some papers I hadn't time to destroy before I left town, and which I forgot till to-day that I had brought with me."

"Ah, that was the parcel you left at our house, perhaps?"

"Yes."

She scanned more closely the packets scattered round her. "They are letters, in different handwritings."

"Yes."

"O, Joce—Mr. Pearston—they are in women's hands; they are love-letters?"

He did not answer for a moment, during which interval a sudden sadness overspread her face, which had just before blushed so significantly under his caress. She bent her head and covered her eyes with her hands. "I see—I see now!" she whispered, "I am—only one—in a long, long row!"

From the white sheets of paper about her seemed to rise the ghosts of Isabella, Florence, Winifred, Lucy, Jane, and Evangeline—each writer from her own bundle respectively—and Maud and Dorothea from the flames. He hardly knew what to say to the new personality in the presence of the old. Then a sudden sense of what a good and sincere girl Avice was overpowered the spectres, and, rushing up to her and kneeling down upon the letters, he exclaimed, "Avice, dear Avice!—I say to you what I have never said to one of them, or to any other woman, living or dead, 'Will you have me as your husband?' "

"Ah!—I am only one of many!"

"You are not, dear. You knew me when I was young, and they didn't—at least, not many of them. Still, what does it matter? We must gain experience."

. . . he wondered if, in her natural melancholy at his leaving, she (4) expected any such ceremony as a formal ratification of their betrothal, according to the precedent of their sires and grandsires.

To scent her views on the point he asked her to meet him in the old Hope churchyard one evening at seven o'clock.

FROM CHAPTER IV

The Hope churchyard lay in a dell formed by a landslip ages ago, (5) and the church had long been a ruin. At the hour appointed she descended the rocks and found him waiting at the foot of them.

They wandered hither and thither in the shades, and the solemnity of the spot and the absence of daylight assisted him in sounding her mind on a subject which could not be approached with levity.

He found that, in common with all the islanders born, she knew of the observance. But it was obvious that, in view of herself as a modern young woman, she had never expected it to arise as a practical question between him and her. Some of the working quarriers kept it up, but nobody else, she said. Jocelyn hastened to inform her that he only wished to consult her desires as to the terms of their engagement, and not knowing how far she respected the island's history, felt bound to mention it; though urge it he did not.

"Well," said he; "here we are, arrived at the fag-end of my holiday. What a pleasant surprise my old home, which I have thought not worth coming to see for more than two years, had in store for me!"

"You must go to-morrow?" she said uneasily.

"Yes." He reflected, and decided that instead of leaving in the daytime he would defer his departure till the night mail-train from Budmouth. He had hardly looked into his father's quarries, and this would give him time to do so, and enable her, if she chose, to accompany him a little way. If she would agree, he purposed to send on his luggage to the aforesaid watering-place, and ask her to walk with him along the beach as far as to Henry the Eighth's Castle above the sands, where they could stay and see the moon rise over the sea. He would see her nearly all the way back, and there would be ample time after that for him to catch the last train.

"You can reserve your answer till to-morrow," he added.

She hesitated. "I understand you to mean, dear Jocelyn," she said, "that my accompanying you to the castle would signify that I conform to the custom of working the spell?"

"Well, yes," he answered.

"I will think it over to-morrow, and ask mother if I ought to, and decide," said she. "I fear it is heathen and ungodly."

FROM CHAPTER V

(6) As the steam went up he fell into a delicious reverie, and regarded the fair white linen that screened his face from the fire with a curious interest. His eyes traced the pattern of the wondrous flowers and leaves in the delicate lace-work, the wheels, rockets, quatrefoils, and spirals of the embroidery, all the while that their owner above was little thinking of the care he was taking that she should not get cold. The fabrics seemed almost part and parcel of her queenly person. He again became conscious of the germ with which he had been impregnated. The Well-Beloved was moving house—had gone over to the wearer of this attire.

He kissed each of the articles of apparel, and in the course of ten minutes adored her.

And how about little Avice Caro? He did not think of her as before.

He was not sure that he had ever seen the Well-Beloved in that friend of his youth, solicitous as he was for her welfare. But, loving her or not, he perceived that the spirit, emanation, idealism, which called itself his Love was flitting stealthily from some remoter figure to the near one in the chamber overhead.

But he must carry out his engagement to marry Avice. True, she had not kept her engagement to meet him this evening, and the irrevocable ratification of their betrothal had not been reached. Still, he was bound to marry her.

FROM CHAPTER VIII

The pair had been married two months, and had just returned (7) from a Continental trip to Pearston's house in Hintock Road, Kensington. They were getting through the heavy task of opening a heap of letters and papers which had accumulated since the last batch had been forwarded.

Pearston was filled with zest for availing himself to the utmost of the artistic stimulus afforded by London—that great and enlightened city, which dedicates its squares, streets, and parks to figure-heads and *fainéants*, and a lane at the East-End to Shakspere; and, with a view to showing its sympathy with a more rapid form of mental elevation than results from the tedious process of picture-gazing, makes its taverns the Sunday resort by closing its museums. Nevertheless, for them it was London or nowhere, and here they were going to make the best of their recent matrimonial plunge.

Marcia's parents, finding from the newspapers what had happened, put as hopeful a face as they could on the matter, but did not communicate with the truants. In birth the pair were about equal, but Marcia's family had gained a start in the accumulation of wealth and in the initiation of social distinction, which lent a colour to the feeling that the advantages of the match had been mainly on one side. Nevertheless, Pearston was a sculptor rising to fame by fairly rapid strides; and potentially the marriage was not a bad one for a woman who, beyond being the probable successor to a stone-merchant's considerable fortune, had no exceptional opportunities.

Among their letters was one for her, in which she was informed that her father and mother had gone to spend the winter in the Riviera and Italy. On this particular morning, as on most mornings, the London atmosphere was of a neat drab with the twenty-ninth fog of the season, and Marcia looked out of the window as far as she could see, which was two feet, and sighed. She had been eight weeks Pearston's wife.

"I should have been in the City of Flowers by this time if"——

"You hadn't been so foolish as to marry me," laughed Jocelyn.

By degrees Pearston fell into his customary round of existence; (8) his profession occupied him to the exclusion of domestic affairs; but with Marcia life began to be rather dull. Her parents were not resentful or bitter, but they were not very warm. They had returned to London, and, while willing to receive Marcia at their house, refrained from calling on the young couple.

(9)   "It is untrue! There was no such proceeding!"

Pearston, without replying for a moment, gazed at the fine picture of scorn that his Juno-wife's face and dark eyes presented.

"I ought to have known it," he murmured.

"What?"

"That such a face as that meant temper."

She left the room. Some days after the subject was renewed by their seeing in a local paper an announcement of the marriage of Avice Caro with her cousin. Jocelyn remembered him, though but indistinctly. He had been the manager of her mother's quarries since her father's death, and had recently been thrown much in her company.

Jocelyn sat in a reverie.

"You spoke of my temper the other day," said she. "Do you think temper had nothing to do with your dear Avice's quick marriage?"

"She was not 'dear,' not dear enough, at any rate, to me."

"Unfortunately for me."

"Well, yes, I ought to have married her, because she was the only woman I never loved. But instead of wedding Rosaline, Romeo must needs go marrying Juliet; and that's where he made the mistake. A fortunate thing for the affections of those two that they died. In a month or two the enmity of their families would have proved a fruitful source of dissension; Juliet would have lived with her people, he with his; the subject would have split them as much as it has split us."

Thus it began and continued in the home of these hastily wedded ones. Sometimes it was worse, far worse, than a hot quarrel. There was a calm, cold reasoning in their discussions, and they talked in complete accord of the curse of matrimony. In their ill-matched junction on the strength of a two or three days' passion they felt the full irksomeness of a formal tie which, as so many have discovered, did not become necessary till it was a cruelty to them.

A legal marriage it was, but not a true marriage. In the night they heard sardonic voices and laughter in the wind at the ludicrous facility afforded them by events for taking a step in two days which they could not retrace in a lifetime, despite their mutual desire as the two persons solely concerned.

Marcia's haughty temper unfolded in the direction of irascibility when she beheld clearly in what a trap she had been ensnared. She was her husband's property, like one of his statues that he could not sell. "Was there ever anything more absurd in history," she said bitterly to him one day, "than that grey-headed legislators from time immemorial should have gravely based inflexible laws upon the ridiculous dream of young people that a transient mutual desire for each other was going to last for ever!"

Jocelyn saw that the slow and mournful departure of the Well-Beloved from the form at his side was hastened, to one of his unfortunate temperament, by the tie that was supposed to hinder it. He thought sometimes that if the law had ordained separate residences, with periodical visitations strictly limited to Sundays and holidays as the rigorous matrimonial condition, he might have got on with Marcia, despite her *Quos ego* and high-handed rulings; indeed, in such circumstances those traits would not have been unattractive to him. But love's dewy freshness could not live under a vertical sun, and that gradual substitution of friendship, which is indispensable and, perhaps, usual in marriage, was not possible with natures so jarring as these.

There followed a long period of dreary calm, and then the storm which had been gathering under its silence burst forth with unmitigated fury.

The Well-Beloved had quite vanished away. What had become of her Pearston knew not, but not a line of her was any longer discoverable in Marcia's contours, not a sound of her in Marcia's accents. Having entered into a signed and sealed contract to do no such thing, he would not in honour look about to discover the other's lurking-place; but he sometimes trembled at the thought of what would become of that solemn covenant if she were suddenly to disclose herself and confront him before he was aware. Once or twice he fancied that he saw her in the distance—at the end of a street, on the far sands of a shore, in a window, or at the opposite side of a railway station; but he always religiously turned on his heel and walked the other way (especially if Marcia was with him).

There came a day when she returned from visiting her mother at Kensington, bringing the news that, travel having benefited her father's health so markedly on the last occasion, her parents had decided on a tour round the world, and a possible stay with her uncle, who was a banker in San Francisco. Since retiring from his large business old Mr. Bencomb had not known what to do with his leisure. They were going to let their house on a lease or sell it outright, rating London life as dreary by comparison with cosmopolitan freedom and an absence of responsibility in the conduct of the world's affairs.

"And here am I chained to London!" Marcia added. "You said you were going to revisit Rome and Athens, but you don't. I wish I could go with them."

"Go, in Heaven's name! I don't hinder you," said he. "You are always, it seems to me, dwelling upon the inconveniences I have caused you by marrying you, and thereby interfering with your natural life. Why doesn't your father come and talk over his project like a man, and perhaps I could arrange to go with them."

"That would be treachery to your own dear parent, so cruelly robbed by my wicked one."

"Now, no more of that, Marcia! . . . Though it is true enough."

"It is not!"

"It is. I have the papers to prove it."

"I tell you it is not so, Sir!" she cried. "It was an honest trade rivalry. Don't you be so fond of your insinuations! A miserly, grasping skin-flint"——

"Upon my soul, Marcia, I won't hear you, or anybody else, call my father names! Why, you mean woman, we are partly living, aren't we, at this very moment, upon what he allows me; and you can put your tongue to such an expression as that!"

"And you can put your tongue to call me a mean hussy!"

"I didn't."

"You did!"

Jocelyn sprang up to leave the room, and her anger being culminative, she caught up the first thing she could seize, which happened to be one of his statuettes, and flung it at his head. The figure missed him, but struck the wall, and fell broken to atoms. The sight of his darling little work irretrievably ruined so exasperated Pearston that he rushed back, took her by the shoulders, and shook her: after which he went out of the room, put on his hat, and departed for his club.

FROM CHAPTER IX

(10) After four years of common residence, diversified by drawing-room incidents of this lively character, these two irreconcilables parted by common consent. The voyage of Marcia's parents had implanted in them a zest for the New World, already the home of some relatives; Marcia's father, a man still in full vigour of life except at intervals, found occupation for the leisure which the

sale of his business afforded him in investing capital in undertakings commensurate with the scale of the country wherein they were to be carried out; and when in the development of these schemes he again rejoined his brother in the Western States Marcia accompanied him.

The separation was quite of an informal kind, each merely promising the other never to intrude into that other's life again, by written word or personal presence: its object being to undo, as far as lay in their power, the mischief that misapprehension of each other's characters had effected during the past few years.

Marcia declared she would never return to England, but would make her home with her uncle on the Pacific shore. "And for my part," she added in this her last letter to him, "I fail to see why, in making each our own home, we should not make our own matrimonial laws if we choose. This may seem an advanced view, but I am not ashamed of advanced views. If I strictly confine myself to one hemisphere, and you, as I expect you to do, confine yourself to the other, any new tie we may form can affect nobody but ourselves. As I shall feel myself at liberty to form such, I accord the same liberty to you."

Whether the advanced idea were a Parthian fling of defiance, which she had no intention whatever of acting on, or whether it were written coolly, as a possible contingency, with an eye on the jilted Indian captain, Pearston had no means of knowing.

A long period of outward stagnation followed the break-up of his house and home.

FROM CHAPTER X

He had promised his wife never to trouble her again; nor for a (11) whole dozen years had he done so; but in this access of means he considered that it behoved him to make inquiries, so as to ascertain if she wished for an allowance.

Neither letters nor advertisements brought any tidings. Nothing more could be done without personal search; and that he resolved to make the year following, if he heard nothing of her earlier.

FROM CHAPTER XXIII

Nevertheless, he felt it to be his duty to ascertain what truth (12) might lie in this chance fancy; and about a week later he stood once more at the foot of the familiar steep whereon the houses of Slopeway Well were perched like pigeons on a roof-side.

He pursued his inquiries as privately as possible, for his intention was to make himself known here no more. As he had ceased since his last residence here to wear his beard in the island fashion, nobody recognised him, though he had aged but little under the inactivity of twenty years. Nothing had been heard of any such lady, the nearest approach to a visit of the kind being that made by a woman whom a flyman had driven over the island in search of a family now dead. As this lady did not answer to the description, and the persons she sought were bearers of another name, Pearston concluded he had got to the bottom of the matter in considering it a casual correspondence only.

In returning to the town and station at eventide his attention was attracted by the busy doings around a quarry which lay at a distance on his left; he observed several men on the spot whom he might recognise. He was inclined to cross thither, feeling sure that the quarry was Ike Pearston's, and stood looking in that direction, where the numerous black hoisting-cranes scattered over the central plateau of the island had the appearance of a swarm of daddy-longlegs resting there. The way across was rugged, and nothing would be gained by making himself known. He proceeded on his way, having no real wish at present to encounter Avice's husband or friends.

At the station he found he had to wait a little while. Presently other people who had come from Top o' Hill (the summit of the rock was thus called) also entered the booking-office, and they were talking reflectively about an accident which had happened a week or two before. The name that caught his ear caused him to turn quickly to one of the quarrymen.

"Who do you say was killed?" Pearston asked.

"Mr. Isaac Pearston—Castleway Pearston as we did call 'n—'cause there's so many Isaac Pearstons—was killed in his own quarry."

While Jocelyn stood silent at this intelligence the men went on conversing among themselves.

"I said to 'en that morning, 'Don't th' stand there, for Heaven's sake!' Born in a quarry a'most, you'd ha' thought he'd ha' known, if anybody would. But he was a man who'd never listen to argument—that one must say, though 'a's squatted. He went away shortly after, and we didn't expect to see 'en again that day. But 'a did come back, worse luck for 'n; and that was how it ended."

More details of the catastrophe and circumstances of the victim's life were given, from which Pearston gathered that though the Avice who had once been his Avice was now a widow, she had friends and sympathisers about her which would render any attention on his part at this juncture unnecessary. He therefore mechanically took his seat in the train and remained musing during the run along the Pebble Bank and round to the watering-place five miles off, at which he had taken up his quarters for a few days.

Here, as he stayed on, he heard further rumours of the accident; till Avice, who had been little in his mind of late, began to take up a somewhat distinct position there. He was fully aware that since his earlier manhood a change had come over his regard of woman. Once the individual had been nothing more to him than the temporary abiding-place of the typical or ideal; now his heart showed an extraordinary fidelity to the specimen, with all her pathetic flaws of detail; which, indeed, so far from sending him further, increased his tenderness. This maturer feeling, though more noble and generous, was less convenient, for the warmth of passion remained as in youth without the recuperative intervals which had accompanied evanescence.

The revived emotion detained him long and yet longer at this spot, where he could see the island that was Avice's home lying like a great snail upon the sea across the bay. It was the spring of the year; local steamers had begun to run, and he was never tired of standing on the thinly occupied deck of one of these as it skirted the island and revealed to him on the cliffs far up its height the ruins of Red King Castle, behind which the little village of East Wake lay.

Thus matters went on, if they did not rather stand still, for at least a month before Pearston had the courage of his romanticism, and ventured to seek out Avice. Even when he did go he was so afraid that he had intruded upon her too soon as to approach with unwonted diffidence. He need have shown no such concern.

FROM CHAPTER XXVII

It was the little upper room at Mrs. Pearston's, now fitted up as (13) an invalid's chamber, wherein the widow was still reclining. Though she did not sit up, she was well enough to be left alone, and had been occupying herself in sewing pieces of silk together, to form some fantastic article, suggestive of a bazaar bargain or wedding present. This needlework, however, lay neglected beside her now, while, lost in thought, she gazed out of the window at the long up-Channel view which the situation of the house afforded—not intentionally, but because such a prospect was unavoidable.

A rustling and bustling about, audibly proceeding in a neighbouring chamber, together with the invalid's desertion, denoted that something unusual was afoot, absorbing the whole strength of the domicile. Presently the accents of feminine voices, light and excited, mixed in with the rustling movements; and then the door of Mrs. Pearston's room, which had stood ajar, was pushed open, and Avice appeared before her mother's eyes. She smiled as the matron regarded her, and, placing herself at the foot of the couch, stood passively under scrutiny in a charmingly statuesque pose.

"Yes—it does very well," said the mother. "Not too young— not too old."

Avice was dressed for immediate marriage, and well she looked in the habiliments chosen, which had been of a kind to suit the simple style proposed for the ceremony and the bridegroom's maturity. A walking-dress of dove-coloured silk and a bonnet of somewhat similar shade formed the costume, which, despite its prettiness was, for a bridal adornment, a cruel toning down of youthful charms that would have done justice to the airiest tissues ever woven by art.

Avice's mother inquired if Mr. Pearston had arrived.

"No. . . . Yes—it is he," murmured Avice, as the noise of a vehicle coming round by the wall of Dell-i'-th'-rock increased till it stopped at the door below. In a few minutes footsteps briskly ascended the stairs, and Pearston, wearing a white waistcoat and flower, was shown into the sick-chamber.

He pressed the fingers of the invalid the hand she gave being light and diaphanous as a falling leaf, as thin as if cut out in paper. Avice, with a curious access of modesty, had stood somewhat behind the door, and she vented a constrained little laugh when he kissed her on the cheek. There was now only time to speak in business-like tones of the formal matters in hand. Mrs. Pearston declared that she wished to be left by herself, since she was unable to go and give her daughter away; gloves were then put on, and the couple descended the stairs. Below they were joined by a few local friends, and soon Mrs. Pearston heard the bridal party go off to the church on the western cliff.

The house sank into sunny silence, disturbed only by the faint noises of the two servants in the kitchen and the chipping and sawing of the quarrymen afar. Mrs. Pearston timed the party's

absence by the clock on the mantel—five minutes to get along the
crooked road through East Wake, ten minutes longer going
across to the west side of the isle to Forne, where the church
stood; the service, with entering, signing, and coming out, half
an hour, a quarter returning; about one hour altogether.

She had no compunctions about this marriage. She felt perfectly
sure that it was the best thing she could do for her girl. Not a
young woman in the island but was envying Avice at that
moment, for Pearston was still less than three-score—though, to
be sure, not much less—a good-looking man as yet, one whose
history was generally known here; also the exact figures of the
fortune he had inherited from his father, and the social standing
he could claim—a standing which that fortune would not have
been large enough to procure unassisted by his reputation in his
art.

But Avice had been weak enough, as her mother knew, to
indulge in fancies for local youths from time to time; and Mrs.
Pearston could not help terrifying herself by the picture of a
possible return of the wedding party in consternation, declaring
Avice recalcitrant at the last moment, and still no wife. Yet to
everyone, except, perhaps, Avice herself, Pearston was the most
romantic of lovers. Indeed, was there ever such a romance as that
man embodied in his relations to her house? Rejecting the first
Avice, the second had rejected him, and to decline upon the third
with final achievement was an artistic and tender finish to which
it was ungrateful in anybody to be blind.

The widow thought that, after all, the second Avice might not
have rejected Pearston if destiny had not arranged that she should
be secretly united to another when the proposing moment came.

The sunny pattern of the window-panes on the carpet had
moved some way onward; fifty-five minutes had passed; the
vehicles could be heard returning, and a little colour came into
Mrs. Pearston's pale cheek. If it were all right and done, what a
success, upon the whole, her life would have been! She who had
begun that life as a homely girl, a small quarry-owner's daughter,
had sunk to the position of laundress; had engaged in various
menial occupations; had made an unhappy marriage for love,
which had, however, in the long run much improved her position; was at last to see her daughter established on a good level
of affluence and refinement; and yet not as the wife of a
"kimberlin," but of one of their own race and sympathies.

There was a flutter downstairs denoting the entry of the returned
personages, and she heard them approaching to ascend. Two

people were ascending. In a moment or two they entered the room—Pearston and Avice together. Each came forward and kissed her.

"All was got through easily and satisfactorily, without a single hitch!" cried Pearston. "And here we are, a married couple, hastening up to see you!"

"Have you been no worse all the time, mother?" asked Avice, with an anxious waiving of the chief subject.

Mrs. Pearston said she had been quite easy, and as Avice persisted in keeping away from the event just concluded to talk of her mother's ailments, Jocelyn left them together. When he had gone from the room the widow said, "Now I am contented and thankful, my dear. And I hope you are the same."

"O, I have nothing to say against it!" the girl replied. "I suppose it was necessary, and there's an end of it."

"What—don't you like your husband?"

"Yes—I like him well enough."

"Then have a contented mind."

"I have, mother."

The entry of friends put an end to further conversation of this kind, and there followed the usual accompaniments of a simple country wedding. The present tenants of Dell-i'-th'-rock Castle were among the guests, out of respect for Pearston and liking for their gentle governess. In the afternoon the newly married couple drove over the crest of the island, down the long, steep street of Slopeway Well (where they were recognised by nearly everyone), and onward to the railway station at the foot of the hill, whence they started for London.

Pearston had taken a new red Queen Anne house, of the most approved Kensington pattern, with a studio at the back, in which the only noteworthy feature at present was a rope-ladder for ascending to the upper part. After a brief sojourn in the cathedral cities of the north of England they returned to London in early September, to superintend the fitting and furnishing of this residence.

FROM CHAPTER XXVIII

(14) At eleven o'clock he ascended also, and softly opened the chamber door. Within he paused a moment. Avice was asleep, and his intent ear caught a sound of a little gasping sigh every now and then between her breathings. When he moved forward his light awoke her; she started up as if from a troublous dream,

and regarded him with something in her open eye and large pupils that was not unlike dread. It was so unmistakable that Pearston felt half paralysed, coming, as it did, after thoughts not too assuring; and, placing his candle on the table, he sat down on the couch at the foot of the bed. All of a sudden he felt that he had no moral right to go further. He had no business there.

He stayed and stayed, sitting there in his dressing-gown till the candle had burnt low; she became conscious of his silence, and said, "You rather startled me when you came in."

"I am sorry," said Pierston, "you looked as if you didn't like my coming."

"Did I? I didn't know that."

"Avice, I am going to tell you something, if you are not too sleepy."

"O, no, I am not sleepy."

"I was once your mother's lover, and wanted to marry her— only she wouldn't, or couldn't, marry me."

"How very strange!" said Avice, now thoroughly awake. "Mother has never told me that. Yet, of course you might have been—you are quite old enough."

"O, yes, quite old enough!" he said grimly. "Almost too old."

"Too old for poor mother?" she said musingly. "How's that?"

"Because I rightly belonged to your grandmother."

"No! How can that be?"

"I was her lover likewise. I should have married her if I had gone straight on instead of round the corner."

"But you couldn't, Jocelyn? You are not old enough? Why, how old are you?—you have never told me."

"I am very old."

"My mother's, and my grandmother's," said she, looking at him no longer as at a husband, or even a friend; but as at a strange fossilised relic in human form. Pearston saw this; but he did not mean to spare himself. In a sudden access of remorse he was determined to pursue this to the bitter end—carried on by a wave of revolt against the curse of never being allowed to grow old.

"Your mother's and your grandmother's lover," he repeated.

"And were you my great-grandmother's too?" she asked, with an expectant interest that had overcome her personal feeling as his wife.

"No; not your great-grandmother's." He winced at that question, unreflectingly as it had been put, perceiving that his information, superadded to her previous sentiments, had already operated damagingly. He went on, however, to repeat with a dogged calm: "But I am very old."

"I did not know it was so much!" she said, in an appalled murmur. "You do not look so, and I thought that what you looked you were."

"No, I am *very* old," he unnecessarily reiterated. "And you—you are very young."

A silence followed, his candle burnt still lower; he was waiting for her to sleep, but she did not. Amid so much difference in their accidents there was much resemblance in their essentials; he was as sympathetically nervous as she, and the mere air itself seemed to bring him the knowledge that she lay in a state of tension which was indescribably more distressing than pain.

He knew that his cause was lost with her by his exaggerating their contrasts. The verge of division, on which they long had trembled, she had at last crossed. Pearston noiselessly arose, took up his candle, and went out of the room. He had an impression that he might never again enter that chamber.

He lay down in an adjoining room, and instead of sleeping tried again to conjecture what had disturbed Avice, and, through her, himself, so much as to drive him to court disaster. There seemed to be something uncanny about London in its effect upon his marriage. He began to hate the grimy city and his new house and his new studio, and to wish he had not re-established himself so elaborately there. The momentary defiance of his matrimonial fate which had led him to speak as he had done in his wife's room now passed away, and he hoped again.

To take her back to his and her own native spot for a few weeks seemed the most promising course for shaking off this nightmare which sat upon them here. Her mother's persuasive powers might reconcile Avice to her new position when nothing else would, notwithstanding the unfortunate indiscretion of which in his despair he had been guilty, that of revealing his past attachments. A good practical reason for their return thither existed in the incomplete condition of their house-furnishing here, and in the still unmending state of his mother-in-law. Dell-i'-th'-rock Castle was now, unfortunately, occupied by a permanent tenant, but there were some lodgings near which he thought he might easily obtain.

When he encountered Avice the next morning there was a trace of surprise in her face, but the distant, apprehensive look had not altogether departed. Yet he would have sacrificed everything—his artistic reputation itself—to give her pleasure. He feared that the conversation of the previous night had established her to regard him as a fearful curiosity; but regrets were too late now. He disclosed his proposition to run down to their old place.

"When?" she asked.

"Soon. Say to-day. I don't like being here among these packing-cases, and the quicker we get away the better."

"I shall be glad to go," she said. "Perhaps mother is not so well, and I should like to be near her."

Whatever had upset her, then, it had nothing to do with locality. Pearston thereupon gave sufficient directions for the further garnishing of his town house, and in the afternoon they set out for the south-west by the familiar railway. Pearston stopped at Budmouth for that night, sending on his wife to her mother's home in the isle, where he promised to join her the next day.

It was the first time they had slept under different roofs since their marriage; and when she was gone, and the charm of her personality was idealised by lack of the substance, he felt himself far less able to bear the thought of an estrangement than when her corporeal presence afforded trifling marks for criticism. And yet, concurrently, the conviction grew that, whatever the rights with which the civil law had empowered him, by no law of nature, of reason, had he any right to partnership with Avice against her evident will.

The next day he set out for the island, longing, yet dreading, to see her again. No sooner had he reached the top of the hill and passed the forking of the ways than he discerned in the distance, on the way he had not taken, a form which was unmistakably that of his wife, apparently out on some trifling errand. To go back, take the other road, and join her lest she should miss him, was the obvious thing to do; yet he stood like one enervated, will-bereft, and ashamed. As he stood a man came up, and, noticing his fixity, regarded him with attention.

"A tidy little figure-of-fun that, Sir," said the man.

"Yes. A dainty little creature, like a fairy. . . . Now, would you assert, my friend, that a man has a right to force himself into her presence at all times and seasons, to sit down at her table, to take her hither and thither—all against her liking?"

"No, sure."

"I thought so. And yet a man does it; for he has married her."

"Oh! She's his wife! That's a hoss of another colour. Ha, ha, ha!"

"I don't think it is," said Pearston.

The pedestrian disappeared, and Pearston, still glancing across the quarries at the diverging road, saw that Avice had perceived him, and was standing still, expecting his approach. He climbed over the low side-wall and traversed the open ground to her side. Her young face showed anxiety, and he knew that something had happened.

"I have been looking for you," she said. "I didn't exactly know the time you were coming, or I should have sent somebody to meet the train. Mother has suddenly got so much worse: it seems almost as though my coming had caused it, but it cannot be that, of course, because she is so glad. I am afraid—I am so much afraid she may not live! The change in her has quite shocked me. You would hardly know her. And she has kept it from us that she was not so well, because she would not disturb our happiness. Happiness!"

The last word might have been construed in its relation to her mother or to herself. Pearston was in a mood to suffer anything now, and he did not mind which way she had intended it. They hastened onward together—that is, side by side—with a lineal yard between them, for she was never too ready to take his arm; and soon reached the house at East Wake.

Mrs. Pearston the elder was evidently sinking. The hand she gave him, which had formerly been as thin as a leaf, was now but a cobweb. She was mentally quite at ease, and murmured to him that it was her great comfort and thankfulness to feel that her child was well provided for in the possession of such a good and kind husband.

Avice, her daughter, could not leave the house at night in such circumstances, and, no room being ready for the reception of them as a couple, Pearston left his wife by her mother's side and went out to a lodging near at hand; accident thus making easy of continuance the constraint in their relations which had begun in London.

CHAPTER XXIX

(15) Pearston felt that he certainly had tried to be good and kind to the little sylphlike thing he called his wife. He had been uniformly attentive and courteous, had presented her with every pretty trifle and fancy in the shape of art-works, jewellery, clothing, furniture, that money could buy; had anticipated her every wish and whim in other ways. But whether the primal act of marrying her had been goodness and kindness was open to question.

The mother's life was prolonged but a very few days after this;

and they buried her not far from the spot where Avice the First had been laid, in that old churchyard over the western cliffs, which was like a miniature forest of oolite, the plethora of freestone in the locality placing a carved memorial within the reach of all. It seemed to Pearston but a season or two earlier that he had stood there in the dusk after the first interment, when the vision of the then daughter appeared, to pull him back to youth anew.

This sad office being performed he hastened up to town, leaving Avice in her mother's late residence, which they now adopted as their own country cottage. She liked remaining there, she said, and, having taken care that she should have every attention, he did not hurry back to her side. A feeling which many people might have called Quixotic was acquiring such strength in him as to make future relations with his charming prize a perplexing problem to a man whose pursuits had taught him to regard impressions and sentiments as more cogent than legal rights, and humours as more cogent than reasons.

It was, therefore, not until nearly a month had passed—during which he had endeavoured to stifle his disappointment at being only the nominal protector of Avice by attending to many long-neglected things—that he found himself one evening at the seaport whence the run into the peninsula was by a short line of railway. Nine o'clock, however, had struck, and the last train had left twenty minutes earlier. He felt stiff and chilly with sitting in the London train so long, and, telegraphing to Avice to expect him late, resolved to walk to her home by the old road, which he had not pursued for many, many years, and which now lay bleached by the moonlight.

His course was over the bridge and through the old town, afterwards skirting the cliffs, till there arose on his left hand, gaunt and bare against the sea, the Tudor castle ruins where he had met his own particular third Avice some time ago, the second Avice earlier; where he would have met the first, and, but for chance, have shaped for himself and the two others a different history. He duly crossed the long framed and braced wooden bridge, its whiteness intensified now by the rays, after which there lay before him the long, featureless road within the pebble barrier that screened it from the outer sea. The bay within lifted and dropped placidly under the moon; the pebble bank ran straight ahead, diminishing in a haze, above which swelled the vast rock that the line of pebbles seemed to tether. It was the place, unchanged almost, that he had traversed in the rain beside the woman whom he had rashly married in his first youth and inexperience.

He had reached about halfway between the island and the main shore when a black spot appeared by the road in front of him, hitherto absolutely deserted. Drawing forward, he found the object to be only the figure of a man sitting upon the bank, his face towards the moonlight. This was strong enough to show Pearston as he passed by that his fellow-pedestrian was a young man of apparently five-and-twenty, with a curly dark moustache. Pearston said "Goodnight!" and a reply was returned to him in an accent which was not that of an Englishman. Moreover, the voice was faint and shaken. Pearston halted.

"I hope you are not ill," he said.

"I am unwell," said the foreigner.

"Going my way?"

"Yes."

"Then let me help you onward."

He approached and assisted the stranger, who rose with some difficulty. He was a well-dressed, gentlemanly young fellow, and beside where he had been sitting a white handkerchief lay upon the dry pale pebbles, the handkerchief being stained with what appeared to be blood.

"Have you been coughing?" said Pearston.

"No. I crossed this morning from Havre, and the seasickness brought on a slight hæmorrhage. It is not serious."

"I am not so sure about that," said Pearston.

He took the young man's arm, and together they pursued the remainder of the level way to the foot of the isle, where began the little town of Slopeway Well.

"How do you feel now?" Pearston asked. "Can I take you to any house or person?"

"No, no; I thank you," the stranger replied. "I have lodgings here, which I secured by letter; but I missed the train, or I should have been in them by this time. I am much better now, and require no more attention. For that you have given me receive my deepest thanks and courtesies."

'Well, accept my stick, at any rate—you will get along better, if it is only a few steps."

This the young man did, and they parted. There was not a fly left at the station, and, seeing that he would have to walk the remainder of the distance, Pearston entered an inn a few yards up the street to get some simple refreshment by which he might fortify himself for the ascent. When he came out the young man had disappeared.

It was a pleasure indeed to Pearston when, drawing near to the house which was now again his own dear home, he beheld a little figure standing against the door, and presumably awaiting him. Avice, for it was she, dutifully allowed him to kiss her when he reached her side, though her nervousness, only too apparent, was that of a child towards a parent who may prove stern.

While seated indoors at a supper of a more appetising character than the inn had supplied, he became aware that Avice had left the room. Thinking that she had gone upstairs to supervise preparations for his accommodation, he sat on quietly musing and sipping his glass for something like half an hour. Wondering then, for the first time, what had become of her, he rose suddenly and began looking around. She was quite near him, after all; only standing at the front door as she had been doing when he arrived, gazing into the moonlight. But she was agitated now, unmistakably.

"What is it?" he asked.

"I must go and see somebody who is ill—I feel I ought to go! And yet—as you have just come—I suppose you don't approve of my going out."

"Who is the person?"

She did not give any name. "Somebody down that way," she said indefinitely. "I only heard of it just now. It is not very far to the house."

"If you really wish to go, my dear, of course I don't object. I will sit and await your coming back, if you prefer to go alone."

Avice replied by instantly taking advantage of the offer—putting on a hat and cloak and starting forthwith. In leaving him she glanced at him for a moment, as if expecting him to ask a further question. But Pearston refrained.

He continued alone, thinking how entirely her manner was that of one to whom a question of doing anything was merely a question of permission and not of judgment. When she had been gone some little while, he observed that it was getting rather late. How absurd of her, he thought, not to let him accompany her at such an hour! At length, in a state bordering on irritation, he rose, and went out to look for her.

There was no sign for her returning along the road, though he strolled on so far as to the bend round by the north entrance of Dell-i'-th'-rock Castle. Reaching that entrance he stood still under the trees and wall, being unsure by which way to expect her, and the spot commanding the length of the village street or highway.

He was not aware how entirely invisible he had been standing till he perceived two figures—one a man, walking by the aid of a stick, the other a woman, from whom the man also derived some assistance. The place was deserted, and their voices could be heard, though not the words they were saying. The man spoke in a French accent, and he was obviously the young invalid whom Pearston had assisted along the shore.

The woman was weeping. Her accents were so low and the fact was so far from his expectation that Pearston did not at first dream of her being his wife. Then he had a suspicion, and, as they had turned the corner, he felt justified in following them.

They passed at the same slow pace down the lane or gorge leading to the old castle ruins. A heart-sickness had well-nigh prostrated the unhappy Pearston by this time: he was no nearer to the third Avice than he had been to the second and the first.

They reached the corner of the Red King's Castle, where there were some large blocks of loose rock, carved with the initials of natives of past generations. "Do you think it well to go farther?" asked the woman, as if she were anxious that he should return.

"I fear I cannot," he said.

Pearston was now sure that Avice was the young man's companion, and standing under the sheer face of the rock he found that it reflected their words.

"Why did you come, after being away so long? How could I help thinking you had given up all wish to—do what we planned, and had decided to stay in your own country?"

The wind interfered for a moment; then he heard her repeat, like a wounded bird, "Why did you come, Henri, after being absent so long, and bring me and yourself into such trouble as this?"

Her notes of anguish so moved Pearston that he sank his jealousy in pity of her. Whatever had happened, it had been against her will and expectation.

She soon remarked anxiously that she could not stay longer, and begged her companion to seek the rest he needed. Pearston was obliged to remain where he was till they had gone past.

"I am sorry I have no right to offer you shelter in my house," she said. "But it is not because my husband is come that I may not do this. I feel I must not—ought not—even though you are so ill as to make it almost inhuman! O, it is hard for you, Henri: but what can I do!"

"It is not necessary. I have a lodging quite near, where I can stay till to-morrow, and then I can get back to the station; and then—I will see you no more—if it is your command."

"It is—it must be," said she.

They crept slowly back as far as to the north entrance of Dell-i'-th'-rock, where their ways parted.

"Then I sha'n't see you again?" he said, facing her, and leaning on Pearston's stick.

"How can you!"

"I see your reason well enough, but it is no consolation to me. What a blow! Who could expect it? To come so far, and to be so disappointed! You broke an implicit promise, Avice, even if not a verbal one!"

"Don't reproach me, Henri! My poor mother—— There, don't let us talk of it. I couldn't have married you, dear. It would have grieved my mother so. There, I am going! Can you really walk back?" •

Perhaps he kissed her—more than once; perhaps he did not. There were sniffings and sighings at least, and the young man went along the north road. Avice stood awhile watching his feeble gait; then, as if she could bear it no longer, walked wildly towards her own house.

CHAPTER XXX

Meanwhile, Pearston had entered the gate of the new castle (16) precincts, and, knowing the grounds well, hastened across them inside the wall to the gate opening near their dwelling. He had just time to slip over the way and reach the porch before she arrived round by the regular road.

"Where have you been so long, Avice?" sternly asked the man of nine-and-fifty.

"I will tell you," said Sweet-and-Twenty, with breathless humility. "I have kept you up, haven't I? And you so tired! I could not help it, as you will say when I explain."

She accompanied him indoors, sat down without removing her hat or cloak, and went on to him, as he seated himself opposite. "I have been crying; you can see that, I dare say." While he regarded, she could not repress renewed tears. "It has happened in this way. Just before you arrived, a young man, whom I had not seen for two years, wrote to me saying he was coming to the island to claim me. He—he had been my lover" (here Avice's delicate lip and chin quivered) "when he lived here in England. But I thought—he had deserted me. . . . However, he came, not knowing that I—that I—was m-married; not wishing to be seen by anybody till he had found out if I was faithful, he sent a boy with a message; and my name being still Pearston, he did not discover I could not be his, and I had to go out to him and tell him. He had been taken very unwell in crossing, and has not yet recovered, because the sea-sickness caused him some internal bleeding." She continued, sobbing outright: "I wish—he could see a doctor!"

"He shall see a doctor. I'll send one to him at his lodging, if you'll tell me where that is."

"It is at the Green Mermaid."

"How did you get to know this young man originally?" asked Nine-and-Fifty.

"He was the French master at B—B—Budmouth two or three years ago," Twenty replied; "and I learnt of him, and"——

"Fell in love with him."

"I suppose I did. But he did with me—first!"

"And why, in the name of common-sense, didn't you marry him before ever you saw me?"

"We would have married! Only mother thought—she was quite wrong—she thought that as he was penniless and I should have a little money he wanted me on that account. And she didn't like the idea of my marrying a foreigner. Then he went away to his own country to see his friends and get them to help him, so that he might be no poorer than I. They, too, objected to his marrying. He then wrote to say he would not bind me, but if he did get rich and independent he would let me know. As he didn't get richer, he was too honourable to write to me."

"Why did he come back, then?"

"He said he couldn't help it, because he kept thinking of me!" she murmured. "I wish he hadn't come! But I am rightly punished for thinking he could ever forget me! . . . There was not time for me to hinder his coming, and he didn't know how matters were till we stood face to face."

Pearston could not help picturing the scene of the meeting of the two young things and the moment of her sad announcement, under the light of the moon.

"He'll go away to-morrow," she pleaded, "and I shall never see him any more! I hope you'll forgive me, Sir. I am sure not to see him again, because—because, if he reaches home alive, he'll soon die!"

Avice had spoken with great self-command up to this moment, but her firmness gave way, and she burst into a violent fit of weeping.

"I can't—help crying—I know I ought not to—but I loved him

very much, and he loved me! And I didn't know he would come again!"

Pearston himself was affected to tears by her utter misery. The results of this marriage were beginning to be bad enough for him; but his was, at worst, a negative grief. To her it was direct and terrible. He took her hand. She had been so frank in her speech, and honourable in her conduct, that he was on her side as against himself.

"I do not blame you at all, dear one," he said. "You would be justified in eloping with him, after such a trial. . . . I wish I could mend all this misery I have caused so unintentionally by my persistence in a cruel blunder."

"I'll try—not to mind, Sir; and I'll do everything I can to forget him—as I ought to do, I know. I could have done it better if he had not been taken ill. O! do you think he'll die?"

"No, no. You must not trouble about that, my child. We'll get the best advice for him if a doctor becomes necessary. I'll go and see him this very night or to-morrow morning. What is he like? Have you a photograph? You have, for certain!"

"I had one; but I destroyed it the day before I married you, because I thought it was not well to keep it."

"Suppose you had never seen me, do you think you would have married him now, since he has come back?"

"O, you can guess well enough—if he had not been too ill! And if he had been too ill I should have nursed him—seeing how he is alone here, without a friend; all because of me!"

"You shall nurse him now. Your having married me need not make any difference at all."

Pearston's sense of his cruelty grew so strong that he could not help kissing her forehead in pure sympathy, as if she were a child under his care. Then he hastily went out—to smoke and think, he told her.

In the open space before the house he walked up and down, the prospect eastward being bounded by the distance-line of the sea; so faintly and delicately drawn, yet the most permanent of features in the prospect. On the other side of him rose the front of his wife's home. There was now a light in her chamber-window, showing that she had retired for the night. The longer he looked the less was he able to escape the conviction that he was the kill-joy of that young life. To any man it would have been an uneasy consideration; to him it was a double and treble gloom of responsibility; for this life was the quintessence of his own past life, the crowning evolution of the idea expressed by the word "Avice," typifying the purest affection it had ever been his lot to experience.

It was certainly an age of barbarism in which he lived; since, whatever were his honest wish to right this ill matter, he could not do it. More, a formal legal ceremony gave him the power at this moment, or at any other, to force his presence upon that suffering girl.

Instead of re-entering Pearston walked along the few hundred yards to the Green Mermaid. A light, too, was in an upper room of the small inn. He wondered if it were Henri's bed-room, and entered the house, though it was on the point of being closed.

To his inquiry of the landlord, a home-come sailor, if a gentleman had taken a room there, an affirmative was returned. "A French gent—Mr. Mons Leverre—him as used to teach in Budmouth. He's badish wi' his stomach, and had to go to bed. We be going to take 'en up a cup of cocoa."

"Will you ask him if he can see me? Tell him I am a friend—that's all."

The sailor went upstairs, and on returning said that Mr. Mons Leverre would be glad to see him. Pearston found his way to the chamber where poor young "Mons" (as he had used to be called in Budmouth, from the appearance of his name on the doorplate) welcomed him feebly from his pillow. A handsome young man with a silken moustache and black curly hair, he seemed little more than Avice's age, though he was probably older, his large anxious eyes and nervous temperament subtracting somewhat from his years. Having resided in this country with few interruptions since he was fifteen, his English was nearly as good as Pearston's.

"I come as a friend," said the latter. "We met an hour or two ago, if you remember. I am the husband of Avice Pearston. Don't start or disturb yourself. I bear you no ill-will, my lad, on that account. I have only come to inquire how you feel."

The young man confusedly replied that he had felt better since lying down, and his visitor said that he would send a doctor on the morrow, if only for his own satisfaction.

"But, Sir; why should you be anxious about me?"

"Never mind that. Now tell me frankly—Did you come from your own country on purpose to see Avice?"

"Yes; but, Heaven! I didn't know my Avice was a wife! I came to marry her!" He turned his face away to the wall, and murmured to himself his regrets.

"Well, don't think too much of that just at present. If you would like to see her again she shall come with me to-morrow."

"You are very kind!" cried the young man, turning back to Pearston and seizing his hand. "Let me see her once—once only! I would not wish to see her but once! I shall be well in a day or two. I shall leave. I will never inconvenience you or her, Sir, any more afterwards."

Pearston bade him compose himself, ensured that he should be well attended to, and paced back sadly to his own house, where he glanced up at the window-blind that had been illuminated when he left. It was in darkness now. He strained his eyes back towards the inn: that, too, was dark. How wrong it was that there should stand a barrier, hard as the stone isle itself, between a heart in that house and a heart in this!

Having entered he wrote a note to the local surgeon, asking him to call at the Green Mermaid in the morning, and left it on the hall table with a direction that it should be delivered early. Then he went softly upstairs, and listened at the door of her room. She was not asleep, and he heard her gasp and start when he accidentally brushed against the handle. Pearston moved onward to the adjoining chamber, and what he sighed to himself might have been aptly paraphrased by two lines from "Troilus and Cressida"—

> I had good argument for kissing once,
> But that's no argument for kissing now.

Why should he not play the benign giant to these two dwarfs, as they were in their emotional history, with its one little year of love-tempest to his forty years of the same? Because by that act of charity he would break the laws and ordinances.

CHAPTER XXXI

It was in the full sunshine of next morning that the mock-married couple walked towards the inn. Avice looked up fearfully at her husband from time to time. She could not understand her lord and master in any other character than that of lording and mastering her. Her father's bearing towards her mother had been only too often of that quality.

When they were reaching the inn-door the surgeon appeared on the threshold, coming out. Pearston said to his wife: "Henri-Leverre is to be spoken of as a friend of ours, mind. Nobody will suspect your former relations."

On inquiry the doctor informed them that his patient was restless. The hæmorrhage was from the stomach—the direct result of sea-sickness on predisposing conditions. He would have to be taken care of, and with such care there was no reason why the malady should recur. He could bear removal, and ought to be removed to a quieter place.

The young man was sitting up in bed gazing dreamily through the window at the stretch of quarries and cranes it commanded. At sight of Avice behind Pearston he blushed painfully. Avice blushed with equal distress; and her husband went and looked out of the window.

When he turned his head the sorely tried pair had recovered some apparent equanimity. She had, in fact, whispered to her lover: "My husband knows everything. I told him—I felt bound to do so! He trusts us, assuming that we have no other intention but to part for ever; and we must act up to his expectations."

The conversation of the three was impersonal and flat enough: on the state of France, on the profession of teachers of languages. Yet Pearston could not resist an interest in the young man, which deepened every moment. He was a transparency, a soul so slightly veiled that the outer shaped itself to the inner like a tissue. At one moment he was like the poet Keats, at another like Andrea del Sarto. The latter, indeed, seemed to have returned to earth in him, the same poetry of mien being set amid the same weaknesses.

In a solicitude for Henri Leverre which was almost paternal Jocelyn could well-nigh sink his grief at being denied the affection of Avice. That afternoon he obtained quiet lodgings for the young man in a house across the way, and had him removed thither.

Every day Pearston visited the patient here, sometimes taking Avice with him, though she always shrank from the ordeal. To all outward seeming, Pearston was making a mistake by acting thus; but his conduct, begun in waywardness as a possible remedy by surfeit for the malady of the two unhappy ones, had been continued on other grounds, arising from sympathy with them during the process.

"You think his recovery may now be reckoned on?" he said to the doctor one day.

"Yes—from the hæmorrhage. But mentally he is not at rest. He is unhappy, and that keeps him back. Something worries or grieves him. These foreigners are much given to that. I gather that he has quarrelled with his parents, and the thought of it may depress him."

It suddenly struck Pearston that Avice had begun to look wan and leaden-eyed. He met her only at meals and during walks, on which occasions she always looked up at him with misgiving, as if his plan of never obtruding himself upon her were the illusive beginning of some terrible scheme of vengeance upon her for loving illegally.

He was, in fact, pondering a scheme.

But the scheme which Pearston pondered was of a very different nature from any sultanic determination to bring punishment upon the head of his unhappy bride.

After casting about desperately for relief to his lately awakened natural or moral sense, which began to be oppressed by the present most improper situation ruling between himself and Avice—licensed as it might be by engrossings, fees, stamps, and ceremonies—he had come to a conclusion. He could not wean her by surfeit of the sick man; that was obvious. And with the loss of this woman, his third Avice, he had not much left in his life to care for. Pleasant illusions had one by one been dissipated; he could see the black framework where the flaring jets of the illumination had once dazzled his eyes; and the chief satisfaction remaining to him now was that a man finds in setting his house in order before departure.

Pearston was an artist, not a moralist, and his plan was characteristic of his nature. It was based on the idea of resuscitating his first wife, Marcia, in spirit and seeming, since he had never received definite tidings of her decease. Thirty years of silence had left him and others no moral doubt of her death, but he had never received legal testimony of the event. It was by the channel of escape this offered him that he proposed to restore his Avice, whom he loved better than himself, to approximate happiness. Since his marriage with her was a farce, why not treat it as a farce by playing another to match it?

Coming down to breakfast one morning as usual he found Avice awaiting him with that forlorn and hopeless smile of greeting upon her face which cut his heart like a lash; and he was stimulated to take the first step in her deliverance.

"As our relations are not what—I hoped they might have been," he said as he sat down, "the news I have to tell you will not disturb your mind so much as may be expected by other people. You will remember, of course, how before our marriage we went into the question of my first wife Marcia's existence, and decided that it was quite impossible she should be living, though she was never proved to be dead."

"Yes," murmured Avice. And thereupon a strange light seemed to rise and colour her face, such as sometimes comes over a landscape when there are no direct rays to cause it. O, the quickness of thought! It was the hope of release.

"I have reason to think the probability insufficient. That I ought to ascertain her death beyond shadow of doubt. I am going to send telegrams to the Western States of America and elsewhere, directing search for her by advertisement. I shall probably start thither myself soon—journeying first to Salt Lake City. If I find her I shall never come back—never!"

A pause succeeded, in which the noises of their breakfasting seemed obtrusive.

"If you—don't find her?" said Avice then.

"I shall never come back in that case either."

She gazed up at him.

"In any case I will send you directions what to do. You will go on living here on your own freehold, of course, till you hear from me. Not living alone: I will find some suitable companion for you. . . . And, when you find you are no wife of mine, you must promise me one thing: to marry that lover of yours. He will soon recover, and I will make it worth his while to wed you, in every sense."

"But I may not find I am no"——

"I am certain—from premonitions and other perceptions, which I will not enter into now—I am morally certain that you will find yourself free. What I more precisely wish you to promise is to marry Henri promptly, without delay, immediately that you find yourself free."

"I do promise," she said humbly.

Notwithstanding the wilfully conjectural basis of the proposition Pearston seemed to take it as a definite scheme which would work itself out in fact, and work out well. He seemed to possess, concealed in his mind, certain means of effectuation beyond mere chances.

"Now go and tell the sick man what has been the subject of our talk," he added kindly.

"You will go with me, Sir?"

"No, not this time. You may go alone now."

In about an hour she returned, looking flushed with a startling, dreadful sense of ecstasy. She seemed trying to hide from herself the reason why. What ground had her husband for this sudden conviction? He must have had letters.

He met her at the door, where a fly was standing. "I am going up to town again for a few days," he said. "On my way through Budmouth I will get a quiet young person I know of there to come and stay with you. Good-bye!"

Pearston entered the fly. Opposite the door of Henri's lodgings he stopped and inquired how Mr. Leverre was.

"He's wonderful improved since Mrs. Pearston called. I went up just after, and his face had quite a colour—quite healthy like."

Whether the woman thought it odd that Mrs. Pearston should have been able to come and produce this mental effect, Jocelyn did not care to ascertain, and, re-entering the vehicle, drove on.

CHAPTER XXXII

His return was delayed till eighteen or twenty days had passed, and on his way back over the isle to Avice's house he drew up at Leverre's lodgings as he had done on his departing journey. The young man was in the parlour reading. He appeared bright, and advanced in convalescence. After Pearston's preliminary inquiries the young man with almost childish ingenuousness of motive said, "Have you heard, Sir, of"——

"I have still further evidence that Avice will soon be free."

"A formal decree of nullity will be necessary to complete her freedom?"

"No, no. I think not—in this particular case. I don't go back to her home to live any more. I stay in these lodgings for a day or two, and will have my things sent here. Your landlady has probably told you that I wrote to her, and that she has let to me the parlour opposite to this for the few days I shall be here in the isle before starting for good."

"You have had more specific information, Sir?"

"I have almost indubitable proof that—Avice will be free before long. I shall rejoin my wife as soon as I reach my journey's end. I know, beyond any moral doubt, where she is."

"You do, Sir! Where?"

"I won't say, for certain reasons. But I am going there."

"Salt Lake City?"

"No—not Salt Lake City. . . . You know, Henri," he continued after a pause, and his lower lip quivered as he spoke, "if Avice had loved me, as I foolishly thought she might get to do, I should have—turned up no old stones to hide under. But she loved you, I found; and to me healthy natural instinct is true law, and not an Act of Parliament. So I sheer off."

Leverre looked anxious for clearer explanations, but he did not question further. Pearston—whose worn and dried-up face now fully indexed his age, and indeed more than his age, continued calmly—

"Henri—as I may call you—I wish, as you will believe, above all things that Avice may be happy in spite of this unfortunate marriage with me. She is the outcome of my own emotional life, as I may say. There is not doubt that it is within her power to be so. In addition to her own little competency, a large sum of money—a fortune, in short—has been settled upon her within the last few days, and upon any possible children of hers. With that, and her beauty, she'll soon be snapped up by some worthy man who pities her abnormal position."

"Sir, I love her—I love her dearly. Has she said anything to lead you to think her husband will be other than myself?"

"It depends upon you."

"She will not desert me?"

"If she has promised not to. Haven't you asked her?"

"Not as yet. She would not have listened if I had. She is nominally your wife as yet: and it seems premature—too venturesome, daring, to hope, to think, that this idea you have suggested to us will be borne out by fact. I have never known anything like it—can hardly believe it!"

"You will see," said the now aged man. "Are you afraid to give an undertaking on the contingency? If she becomes free, you will be her husband if she consents?"

"I have said so," he replied fervently.

"You may set about your preparations at once," said Pearston, with forced gaiety. "I go to join my truant wife of thirty years ago."

"O that you may find her!"

"That's right. Express your feelings honestly. I like young men who do so."

That night Pearston sat down and wrote a long letter to the only old friend he had in the world, among so many acquaintances—Alfred Somers, the landscape-painter—

"My dear Somers—

"You in your evenly flowing life will be surprised to hear of what has been taking place in my rugged one—inwardly rugged, I mean, which is the true ruggedness."

He thereupon proceeded to give a succinct account of what had happened since his marriage with Avice, of which event Somers was aware, having, in fact, been invited to the ceremony, though he had not found it possible to come. First, the coldness of his young wife, which he had supposed it to be a mere question of time to displace; his lack of any suspicion that in such a remote and quiet existence she had learnt the trick of having a lover before she was eighteen years old; his discovery of his mistake through the return of the young man to claim her, and the whole incidents which followed.

"Now," proceeded Pearston, "some husbands, I suppose, would have sent the young man about this business, and put the young woman under lock-and-key till she came to her senses. This was what I could not do. At first I felt it to be a state of things for which there was no remedy. But I considered that to allow everything to remain *in statu quo* was inanimate, unhuman conduct, worthy only of a vegetable. It was not only being indifferent to my own poor scrap of future happiness, which mattered little, but to hers. And I soon entered with interest, and even with zest, into an apparently, though not really, wild scheme, which has recommended itself to me. This is no less than assuming the existence of my wife Marcia, of whose death, as you know, there has never been absolute proof, unless you consider that not having heard her voice for more than thirty years to be absolute proof of the death of a termagant spouse. Cases of this kind, if you analyse them, turn on very curious points. My marriage with Avice is valid if I have a reasonable belief in my first wife's death. Now, what man's belief is fixed, and who shall enter in my mind and say what my belief is at any particular time? The moment I have a reasonable belief that Marcia lives Avice is not my wife, it seems to me. I have only therefore to assume that belief and disappear, and she is free. That is what I have decided to do.

"Don't attack me for casuistry, artifice, for contumelious treatment of the laws of my country. A law which, in a particular instance, results in a physical cruelty to the innocent deserves to be evaded in that instance if it can be done without injury to anyone. I want the last of the three women, the last embodiment of Avice, to be happy at any cost, and this is the only way of making her so, that I can see. The only detail in my plan that I feel sorry for having been compelled to adopt is the sending of bogus telegrams and advertisements, to prevent my darling's suspicion of unreality. Poor child! but it is for her good.

"During the last three weeks I have been arranging my affairs, and shall now disappear for ever from England. My life probably will not be long anywhere, it cannot be very long in the nature of things, and it matters very little where I say my *Nunc Dimittis*.

"I shall probably find some kind and simple old nurse body or housekeeper on the other side of the Atlantic, whom I can ask to share my home, and call her Marcia, so as to make it all seem right if any intelligence of my state of existence should be wafted across to this side. To clinch the pious fraud I may think it worth while to send the child Avice a cabinet photograph of this old soul and myself in one picture, in which I appear standing behind her chair with my hand on her shoulder, in the orthodox fashion of the irrevocably united.

"Destroy this document, for Avice's sake.

"My sincere regard and affection to you and all your household.   "J. P."

This was duly posted by himself that evening in the little letter-box in the village square.

He went home to bed. Everything was done, even to the packing of his portmanteau. Nothing remained for him but to depart—to an exile on one of the four quarters of the globe, telegraph that he had found the lost one, and be heard of in this isle no more.

But as he lay he asked himself, did he care for the additional score of years which might, at the outside, be yet owing to him from Nature on such conditions as these? The *tædium vitæ*—formerly such a stranger to him, latterly grown familiar—seemed to intensify to violent disgust. Such an ending to his little drama as he had ostensibly sketched on Avice's behalf—was there not to distinct an attempt in it to save his useless self as well as to save her?

His heaviness endured far into the night, and there was no sign of "joy coming in the morning." At two o'clock he arose and dressed himself. Then, sitting down, he penned a second letter to the same friend.

"My dear Somers—

"When I posted to you the letter I wrote a few hours ago, I assumed that I had the spirit and strength and desire to carry through an ingenious device for human happiness, which I would have entered on with the lightest of hearts forty years ago, or even twenty. But my assumption turns out to be, after all, erroneous. I am no longer spirited: I am weak. My youth, so faithful to me, so enduring, so long regarded as my curse, has incontinently departed within the last few weeks. I do not care for

my scheme, which, in my distaste for it, now appears as foolishly
artificial as before it seemed simple and effective.

"I abandon it for a better and a grander one—one more worthy
of my age, my outlook, and my opportunities. What that is you
will know in a few hours.   "J. P."

It was now half-past two. Pearston's next action was to search
his pocket and open his card-case; but finding no card therein he
wrote his name and address on the first piece of paper that came
to hand, and put it in the case. Next, taking out his purse, he
emptied some portion of its contents into another piece of paper,
which he folded round the money, and placed on the table, directing it to his landlady, with the words, "For rent and small bills."
The remainder he rolled up in yet another piece of paper, and
directed that to a local charitable institution.

He referred to an almanac, examining the tide-table. From this
he gathered that the tide was now at about the half-flow, and it
suited him fairly well.

Then he went out of the room, listening at his neighbour's door
as he passed. The young man was sleeping peacefully. Pearston
descended the stairs and went out, closing the door softly behind
him.

The night was not so dark as he had expected it to be, and the
unresting and troubled being went along the road without hesitation till he reached a well-known lonely house on the right hand
beyond the new castle—the farthest that way. This house contained the form which was the last, most permanent, and sweetest
incarnation of the Well-Beloved.

There was no light or sound to be recognised. Pearston paused
before the railing with his head bent upon his hand. Time was
having his turn of revenge now. Of all the shapes into which the
Beloved one had entered she had chosen to remain in this, whose
owner was utterly averse to him.

The place and these thoughts quicked his determination; he
paused no longer, but turned back by the way he had come, till
he reached the point near the north gate of the new castle, where
the lane to the ruin of the old castle branched off. This he followed
as it wound down the narrow defile spanned by the castle arch,
a portion of which defile was, doubtless, the original fosse of the
fortress.

The sound of his own footsteps flapped back to him from the
vertical faces of the rock. A little farther and he emerged upon
the open summit of the lower cliffs, to his right being the sloping

pathway leading down to the little creek at their base.

Pearston descended, knowing the place so well that he found it scarcely necessary to guide himself down by touching the vertical face of stone on his right hand. Thus proceeding he arrived at the bottom, and trod the few yards of shingle which here alone could be found on this side of the island. Upon this confined beach there were drawn up two or three fishing-boats and a few skiffs, beside them being a rough slipway for launching. One of the latter he pushed down the slope, floated it, and jumped into it without an oar.

The currents hereabout were strong and complicated. At a specific moment in every flood tide there set in along the shore a reflux contrary to the outer flow, called "the Southern" by the local sailors. It was produced by the peculiar curves of the coast lying east and west of the Beal; these bent southward in two back streams the up-Channel flow on each side of the isle, which two streams united outside the Beal and there met the direct tidal flow, the confluence of the three currents making the surface of the sea at this point to boil like a pot, even in calmest weather. It is called the Race.

Although the outer tide, therefore, was running towards the mainland, the "Southern" ran in full force towards the Beal and the Race beyond. Pearston's boat was caught by it in a few moments, as he had known it would be; and thereupon the grey rocks rising near him, and the grim stone forehead of the isle above, just discernible against the sky, slid away from Pearston northwards.

He lay down in the bottom of the frail craft, gazing at the sky above. The undulations increased in magnitude, and swung him higher and lower. The boat rocked, received a smart slap of the waves now and then, gyrated; so that the lightship, which stolidly winked at him from the quicksand—the single object which told him his bearings—was sometimes on his right hand and sometimes on his left. Nevertheless, he could always discern from it that his course, whether stemwards or sternwards, was steadily south, towards the Race.

The waves seemed to toss him roughly about, though there was really but little lop on the sea. Presently he heard, or fancied he heard, a new murmur from the distance, above the babble of waters immediately about his cockleshell. It was the nearing voice of the Race. "Thank God, I am near my journey's end," he said.

Yet he was not quite sure about its being the Race. But it did not matter: the Race was sure to come, sooner or later; everything tended thither. He now began to close his eyes. The boat soon shipped larger and larger volumes of spray, and often a pailful came flat upon his face. But he did not mind.

How long this state of jeopardy lasted Pearston hardly knew. It was ended by a sudden crash, which threw him against some hard body, striking his head. He was fully prepared for a liquid death, but a death by concussion was so entirely unanticipated that the shock made him cry out in a fierce resentment at the interruption to his design.

A bright light thereupon shone over him, and some voices shouted out in the island dialect. He knew that the speakers were the lightship men, and felt warm blood running down his head where it had been struck. Then he found himself in the water grasping something; then he was seized in turn, and hauled up. Then he saw faces, and bird-cages, and rabbit-hutches, on a deck—a sort of floating menagerie; and then he remembered no more.

CHAPTER XXXIII

When next Pearston knew that there was such a state as life, and (17) such an attribute of it as perceptiveness, that night of turbulence, spiritual and physical, had a long time passed away. He was lethargically conscious of lying in some soft bed, surrounded by darkness and silence, a warm atmosphere hanging about him, his only trouble being a sense of hugeness as regarded his head, which seemed to be almost the whole of his person, absorbing the rest of his frame into its circumference. Growing more and more conscious of himself, he realised that this enormous head throbbed with a dull pain.

He again lost sense of himself. When he next was cognisant of externals Pearston seemed to hear a whispered conversation going on around him, and the touch of footsteps on a carpet. A dreamy state followed, and a bandage about his head was loosened, and he opened his eyes.

The light in the apartment was so subdued that nothing around him could be seen with any distinctness. A living figure was present, moving about softly. He discerned that it was feminine, and this was all for the time.

He was recalled to his surroundings by a voice murmuring the inquiry: "Does the light try your eyes?"

The tones seemed familiar; they were rich in quality, as if they had once been powerful. Yet he could not attach a personality to them, though he knew they had been spoken by the woman who was nursing him.

Pearston murmured an answer, and tried to understand more of what had happened. Then he felt uneasy, distressed, and stupid again.

Next day he was conscious of a sudden intellectual expansion. For the first time since lying there he seemed to approximate to himself as he had formerly been. Upon the whole, he felt glad that he had not been annihilated by his own act. When he tried to speak he found that he could do so without difficulty, and he said: "Where am I?"

"At your lodgings," the voice of the nurse replied. "At East Wake."

"Was I picked up and brought here?"

"Yes."

That voice—it was known to him absurdly well. Certainly it was. Avice's it was not. As well as his pain would let him, he mentally overhauled the years of his life. Only one woman in all his experience had ever possessed precisely those tones, and he had assumed her to be dead these thirty years, notwithstanding the sending out of bogus advertisements for her to delude Avice into happiness.

Still, that was whose voice it was; and every minute added weight to the conviction that his wife Marcia stood there.

She spoke again about the visit of the surgeon. Yes—it was his wife Marcia.

Pearston was stupefied. Conjecture he could not, would not. It sickened him to enter upon any kind of conjecture whatever. Enough that she was there. As for more, it had always been possible that she should have remained alive, and it was therefore not impossible that she should be here.

She evidently did not know that he had recognised her, and spoke on as the nurse merely. To reveal to her his discovery would have begotten explanations, and he could not endure the thought of explanations. Thus the two remained. Occasionally others came in—a surgeon, an assistant. A conversation in whispers would follow outside the door. But Marcia seemed always to remain at hand.

His mind had nothing else more prominent to fasten upon, and, the room being still kept almost in darkness, he could not avoid adding her fancied figure to the movements he heard. This process carried him considerably backward in his own history. He thought of how he had met this woman on the Pebble Bank, how they had travelled to London together, had hastily married, had repented at leisure; and how thereafter a curtain had dropped between them which had been virtually death, despite a little lifting now. Yes, that very woman was in the room with him, he felt sure.

Since he could not see her, he still continued to imaginatively picture her. The stately, upright figure, the rather high colour, the classical profile, the rather large handsome nose and somewhat prominent though regular teeth, the full dark eye. In short, the queenly—far too queenly—creature who had infatuated him when the first Avice was despised and her successors unknown.

With her comings and goings in the gloom his fancy associated this image so continually that it became not unpleasing to him as an artist in form. The human essence was added when she rendered him the attentions made necessary by his helplessness. But she always kept herself in the remote distance of the room, obviously unaware as yet that he knew her.

"When may I have the daylight let in upon me?" he asked of the doctor.

"Very soon," replied that gentleman. "But the wound is such that you may lose your sight if you are allowed to strain it prematurely."

So he waited, Marcia being always in the background, watchful to tenderness. He hoped she would never attempt to tell him how she came there. He could not endure the thought of having to enter into such details. At present he felt as if he were living in those early days of his marriage with her.

His eyes, having been tested, were deemed able to bear the stress of seeing clearly. Soft daylight was allowed to illuminate the room.

"Nurse," he said. "Let me see you. Why do you always keep behind my head?"

She went to the window, through which the light had only been allowed even now to enter between the blinds. Reaching it she pulled the blind up a little way, till the outer brightness fell full upon her. An unexpected shock was the result. The face which had been stamped upon his mind-sight by the voice, the face of Marcia forty years ago, vanished utterly. In its place was a wrinkled crone, with a pointed chin, her figure bowed, her hair as white as snow. To this the once handsome face had been brought by the raspings, chisellings, stewings, bakings, and freezings of forty years. The Juno of that day was the Witch of Endor of this.

He must have shuddered at the discovery of what time had done, possibly have uttered a slight gasp; at all events, she knew in some way of the shock to his sensitiveness that her skeleton-figure caused him.

"I am sorry to shock you," she said. "But the moth eats the garment somewhat in five-and-thirty years."

"Yes-yes! . . . I am glad I am become an old man during the last month. For now you have a right to be old also. . . . Don't tell me why you came to me. Still, I wonder why?"

"My life's little measure is nearly danced out. So is yours, apparently. Therefore, when I saw your advertisements for me—proving that you were still living—I thought we might as well make our final bows and exits together. . . . Ah!—who is that?" Somebody had tapped at the door, and she crossed the room and opened it.

"Who was it?" he asked, when the door had closed again.

"Somebody with a telegram for me. Dear me! Curious that it should come just now!"

"What?"

"A telegram to inform me that the declaration of nullity as to the marriage between you and Avice Pearston was pronounced this morning."

"At whose instigation was the petition made?"

"At mine. She asked me what she ought to do."

He put up his hand to tear open his wound, and bring eternal night upon this lurid awakening. "But she is happy," he said. "And, as for me"—

His wife passed by the mantelpiece, over which hung an enlarged photograph of Avice, that he had brought thither when he left the other house, as the single object which he cared to bring. The contrast of the ancient Marcia's aspect, both with this portrait and with her own fine former self, brought into his brain a sudden sense of the grotesqueness of things. His wife was—not Avice but that parchment-covered skull moving about his room. An irresistible fit of laughter, so violent as to be an agony, seized upon him, and started in him with such momentum that he could not stop it. He laughed and laughed, till he was almost too weak to draw breath.

Marcia hobbled up, frightened. "What's the matter?" she asked; and, turning to a second nurse, "He is weak—hysterical."

"O—no, no! I—I—it is too, too droll—this ending to my would-be romantic history!" Ho-ho-ho!

EXPLANATORY NOTES

(Where fictional place-names have been identified, the real name is given. References to The Life of Thomas Hardy *are to the single volume edition. References to novels and poems are to Hardy's unless otherwise stated.)*

1 (Title-page) *'One shape of many names.'*: Shelley: 'The Revolt of Islam', I.xxvii.363 and VIII.ix.3276. In both references Shelley is applying an allegory of 'the Spirit of evil' as a powerful oppressor taking many forms (kings, priests, etc.) and holding suffering, deluded mankind in thrall. This is a far cry from Hardy's 'Well-Beloved', and the wording of the phrase is more apt than the context; but there is some relevance in Jocelyn Pierston's fear of 'the implacable Aphrodite' (I.ii) and his 'Sapphic terror of love' (II.vi).

3 *The peninsula . . . are laid*: Portland, called 'the Isle of Slingers' by Hardy. In an interview recorded in *Cassell's Saturday Journal*, 25 June 1892, just before serialization of *The Pursuit of the Well-Beloved* began, Hardy said: 'I always like to have a real place in mind for every scene in a novel. Before writing about it I generally go and see each place.' A letter to Edmund Gosse recalling a visit to Portland, and dated 17 March 1897, refers to 'that pilgrimage of ours. I fancy it was when I was writing, or planning, the tale.'

fantast: a person given to fanciful or whimsical conceits.

one that . . . philosophers: in this context, a reference to the lover's search for the Platonic Idea in the form of ideal beauty; which is a somewhat pretentious expression of a fairly simple (in this case) concept of a man's subjective response to a 'Beloved' in terms of her ability to match his pre-conceived notions of a flawless woman. In Shelley's work there is a more subtle and varied interpretation of the Platonic concept than in Hardy's novel.

coign: projection. (cf. 107: 'coigns of vantage'.)

one nook: Portland prison.

mullions, copings, and corbels: vertical bars, top courses of stones or bricks, and supporting projections in architecture.

PART FIRST

8 —'*Now, if . . . it is She.*': Crashaw: 'Wishes To his (supposed) Mistresse', ll. 107–9 and 112–14. The following lines (115–17) are quoted in *Desperate Remedies*, Ch. X, with reference to Edward Springrove's love for Cytherea: ''Tis She, and here/ Lo! I unclothe and clear/ My wishes' cloudy character'. Earlier lines in the same poem would have provided a more fitting epigraph for Hardy's concept of an ideal Well-Beloved who may choose to inhabit a female form temporarily; 'Where ere shee lye,/ Lock't up from mortall Eye,/ In shady leaves of Destiny:/ . . . / Till that Divine/ *Idaea*, take a shrine/ Of chrystall flesh, through which to shine' (ll. 4–6, 10–12). Nevertheless the lines chosen are very apt for expressing the subjectivity of man's choice of his 'Well-Beloved': the woman who 'dares be' what man wishes her to be.

9 '*cast up by rages of the se*': from *The Itinerary of John Leland in or about the Years 1535–1543* (ed. L. T. Smith), Vol. I, Part III, p. 251. Leland is describing his visit to Portland and the effect of wind and sea on Chesil Beach, Hardy's 'long thin neck of pebbles'.

Vindilia: the Roman name for the 'Island'. (Hardy's source was John Hutchins's *History of Dorset*, 3rd edition, Vol. II, p. 808.)

the Slingers: 'the people [of Portland] be good ther in slyngging of stonys, and use it for defence of the isle' (Leland, op. cit., p. 252).

one man's doorstep rising behind his neighbour's chimney: cf. the same scene in *The Trumpet-Major*, Ch. XXXIV: 'one man's doorstep being behind his neighbour's chimney'.

the whole island as a solid and single block of limestone: cf. *The Trumpet-Major*, Ch. XXXIV: 'the huge lump of freestone which forms the peninsula'.

oolite: limestone.

The melancholy . . . cycles: Shelley: *Prometheus Unbound*, Act IV, ll. 288–9. In this passage Panthea has been referring to 'the secrets of the earth's deep heart' and now describes 'anchors, beaks of ships;/ Planks turned to marble' etc., which, like the oolite, are the physical remains of the long-dead past.

10 *eastern village*: Easton, on Portland, later called 'East Quarriers' by Hardy.

Avice: The Talbothays farm [owned by Hardy's father] was
a small outlying property . . ., its possessors in the reign of
Henry VIII, having been Talbots, from a seventeenth-century
daughter of whom Hardy borrowed the name of Avis or
Avice in *The Well-Beloved*' (*The Life of Thomas Hardy*, p.
6). In a letter to *The Academy* dated 3 April 1897, Hardy
states that ' "Avice" is an old name common in the country,
and "Caro" (like all the other surnames) is an imitation of a
local name . . . this particular modification having been
adopted because of its resemblance to the Italian for "dear" '
(Quoted in *The Life*, p. 286). In Hardy's own copy of this letter in the Dorset County Museum, he has added in pencil
beside 'dear' the words: 'i.e. "Well-Beloved" '. The name
'Avice' also antedated 'Eustacia' in *The Return of the Native*.
(See J. Peterson: *The Making of 'The Return of the Native'*,
pp. 8, 38, 39.)

11 *Mr. Pierston*: spelt 'Pearston' in the original serial version of
1892. Possibly a pun on 'pierre-stone' as his father was a
stone-merchant: or to indicate a degree of kinship with
another idealistic lover, Fitzpiers, who 'seemed likely to err
rather in the possession of too many ideas than too few; to
be a dreamy 'ist of some sort, or too deeply steeped in some
false kind of 'ism' (*The Woodlanders*, Ch. XIV). A possible
motive for the original choice of name is the existence in St
George Reforne churchyard (scene of the burial of the first
Avice) of headstones bearing the names Pearce and Stone.

'ee: retained from the 1897 edition, whereas elsewhere (e.g.
p. 103, l. 32) Hardy amends Avice II's 'ee' to 'you', possibly
as a more up-to-date form of speech for her than for her
mother.

Meanwhile . . . to come: an example of Hardy's economical
garnering of material discarded elsewhere: this is a revised
version of the original opening paragraph of Chapter I in the
1892 serial version.

12 *condescended to accept*: altered in 1912 from 'accepted'.

spawls: also spelt 'spalls'. Splinters or chips, in this case of
stone.

15 *Street of Wells*: Fortuneswell, Portland.

16 *a subjective phenomenon*: cf. the poem 'The Well-Beloved':

'Thou lovest what thou dreamest her'; and also 'Rome, The Vatican: Sala delle Muse': ' "Nay, wooer, thou sway'st not. These are but phases of one;// "And that one is I; and I am projected from thee,/ One that out of thy brain and heart thou causest to be—/ Extern to thee nothing." '

16 *He never knew . . . lead him*: cf. 'He Wonders about Himself', dated 1893: 'Tugged by a force above or under/ Like some fantocine, much I wonder/ What I shall find me doing next!// Shall I be rushing where bright eyes be?'; and also 'After a Journey': 'Where you will next be there's no knowing,/ Facing round about me everywhere', written in 1913 after the death of his first wife.

Daughter of high Zeus: it would be natural for a sculptor to associate the Grecian Aphrodite or Roman Venus, the goddess of love and beauty, with the Idea he was pursuing, and to imagine she was punishing him for the imperfections in his sculptural attempts to reproduce her.

17 *whether presenting herself as tall, fragile, or plump*: cf. Shelley's 'Epipsychidion': 'In many mortal forms I rashly sought/ The shadow of that idol of my thought' (ll. 267–8).

fleshly tabernacle: the human body as a temporary abode, here of the ideal Well-Beloved, usually and formerly of the soul. Cf. Milton: 'In fleshly Tabernacle, and human form' (*Paradise Regain'd*, IV.599), here referring to Christ.

the Old Road: Old Hill. There is still a hand-rail there.

18 *Deadman's Bay*: West Bay, partly bounded by Chesil Beach.

their huge composite ghost . . . the isle: the 'composite ghost' imagery recurs in the same geographical location in 'The Souls of the Slain', where 'A dim-discerned train/ Of sprites without mould' returns to Portland Bill.

Hope Churchyard: Ope Churchyard.

19 *Budmouth*: Weymouth.

the native custom on such occasions: pre-marital sex to ensure that the union would be fruitful. It was a custom in country areas other than Portland, and apparently practised by Hardy's father, as Hardy's mother was already three months' pregnant with Thomas before marriage.

20 *Henry the Eighth's Castle*: Sandsfoot Castle, on the coast at the southern end of Weymouth.

    pebble bank: Chesil Beach. 'Chesil' or 'Chisle' (as in Chislehurst) derives from Old English *ceosol* or *cisel*, meaning 'gravel'.

21 *East Quarriers*: Easton, Portland.

24 *Junonian*: having a regal, stately bearing like Juno, worshipped by the Romans as queen of heaven.

25 *lerrets*: well-built boats particularly designed for use in the heavy seas in the coastal areas of the Isle of Portland.

27 *Sylvania Castle*: Pennsylvania Castle. A castellated mansion built in the nineteenth century and now a hotel.

28 *to play the son of the Montagues*: i.e., to play Romeo to Miss Bencomb's Juliet. In both *Romeo and Juliet* and *The Well-Beloved* there is bitter enmity between the lovers' parents.

    traversing its bottom like the Children of Israel: cf. Exodus 14: 21–31, where it is told that God parted the waters of the Red Sea for the Israelites to walk across and escape from the Egyptians.

29 *'The ethereal . . . divisible.'*: *Paradise Lost*, VI. 330–1: '. . . th'Ethereal substance clos'd/ Not long divisible'.

    the ruined castle: Sandsfoot Castle, where Pierston had arranged to meet Avice I.

32 *flash-telegraph*: a light used for signalling in code.

33 *Juliet*: a continuation of the theme introduced at 28 above. Cf. *The Life of Thomas Hardy*, p. 164: ' "March [1884]. Write a novel entitled *Time against Two*, in which the antagonism of the parents of a Romeo and Juliet *does* succeed in separating the couple and stamping out their love, — alas, a more probable development than the other!" (The idea is briefly used in *The Well-Beloved*.)'

    Doctors' Commons: formerly the college of doctors of law situated in St Paul's Churchyard. The members practised in several courts including the Probate and Divorce Divisions of the High Court of Justice. The corporation was dissolved in 1858. As the story is supposed to be set 'more than forty years ago' (p. 23), in the 1850s, Pierston visited the institution in its last years.

34 *a hansom*: a two-passenger carriage used for public hire.

35 *a sort of Apologia pro vitâ meâ*: Latin: 'A defence of my life'.

An echo of John Henry (later Cardinal) Newman's *Apologia pro Vita sua*, which he was moved to write in defence of his conversion from the Anglican to the Roman Catholic faith in a controversy with the Revd. Charles Kingsley. But Newman published in 1864 so Pierston in the 1850s should not have heard of it; hence anachronistic. Hardy himself had certainly heard of it: he refers to it in the *Life*, p. 48.

36 *chimney-crooks*: hooks for suspending cooking-pots over an open fire; hence only partly 'curled'.

37 *the unpractised . . . sunset*: the same analogy appears in *Desperate Remedies*, Ch.II.

a middle-aged gentlemen . . . also mounted: cf. *Life*, p. 25: 'One day at this time Hardy, then a boy of fourteen, fell madly in love with a pretty girl who passed him on horseback . . .' The account which follows has several similarities to the fictional account.

38 *crabs . . . had fallen in*: cf. 'The Newcomer's Wife': '. . . at the deepest place/ Found him with crabs upon his face.'

40 *like the nest . . . to fill with snow*: Wordsworth's sonnet, 'Why art thou silent!', has the same image of 'a forsaken bird's-nest filled with snow'.

her I used to see there . . . no more: cf. 'The Protean Maiden': 'One noon eclipsed by few girls,/ The next no beauty she.' (F. B. Pinion compares *The Well-Beloved* with 'The Protean Maiden' in *A Commentary on the Poems of Thomas Hardy*, p. 226.)

I have seldom ventured . . . the dear one in her: there are many references in Hardy to love thriving on distance and dying in propinquity.

42 (Chapter title) '*Too like the Lightning*': Shakespeare: *Romeo and Juliet*, II.ii.119. Quoted more fully on p. 46.

50 *A.R.A.*: Associate of the Royal Academy [of Arts], founded in 1768. The number of artists considered sufficiently gifted to become Associates was (and is) very limited. See Marcia's query on p. 33.

51 *when he was green in judgment*: cf. Cleopatra in Shakespeare's *Antony and Cleopatra*, I.v.73–4: 'My salad days,/ When I was green in judgment'.

Royal Moorish Palace of Varieties: music-halls were sometimes referred to as 'palaces' but this title is probably an oblique reference by Hardy to The Alhambra, which bore the name of the palace of the Moorish kings at Granada. The Alhambra was at the height of its success as a music-hall when Hardy was writing *The Well-Beloved*.

52 *Börne's phrase*: Ludwig Börne (1786–1837) was a German author. Hardy quoted Börne's statement again in one of his very few public speeches, on receiving the freedom of Dorchester in 1910. On that occasion he was commenting on the many changes in Dorchester during his lifetime. (Quoted in the *Life*, p. 352.)

As flesh she dies daily, like the Apostle's corporeal self: cf. Paul the Apostle in 1 Corinthians 15: 31: 'I protest . . . I die daily.'

PART SECOND

53 (Part title) *A Young Man of Forty*: cf. Hardy's entry in the *Life* for 13 November 1917: 'I was a child till I was 16; a youth till I was 25; a young man till I was 40 or 50' (op. cit., p. 378).

54 (Epigraph) *'Since Love . . . patiently.'*: from 'The lover determineth to serve faithfully' by Sir Thomas Wyatt (1503–42). The remaining sestets of the poem affirm that the poet is so committed to love that he will continue to 'serve and suffer patiently' however cruelly fate or his love treats him: a fitting epigraph to the account of Pierston's lack of success with Avice II.

56 *linkman*: a 'link' was a torch, so a linkman or linkboy was a person employed to light the way.

the customary 'small and early' . . . a political crisis: cf. *Life*: 'At one of these crushes in the early part of 1885 they [Hardy and his wife] found themselves on a particular evening amid a simmer of political excitement. It was supposed to be a non-political "small-and-early", but on their arrival the house was already full to overflowing' (op. cit., p. 172).

great and late: Hardy has preferred this rhyming phrase to the alliterative 'large and late' of the earlier 1892 version.

60 *beneath this or that . . . above-ground*: cf. a similar view of the potentiality for death beneath a young feminine exterior in a note written by Hardy in May 1870: 'A sweet face is a page of sadness to a man over 30 — the raw material of a corpse'.

60 *trouvaille*: a fortunate discovery. Hardy also uses the word in *The Woodlanders*, Ch. XXVI.

Jill-o'-the-Wisp: a feminine Will-o'-the-Wisp, a shadowy, elusive person. Perhaps some association with the archaic 'Jill-flirt', a wanton, flighty girl.

61 *the Lady Mabella Buttermead . . . a ball*: cf. the typescript of the *Early Life*, p. 270, entry for 16 May 1887: 'Lady Marge W— looked pretty in gauzy muslin—going to a ball, she told me [Hardy].' (Noted by Millgate in *Thomas Hardy: His Career as a Novelist*, p. 301, and by R. H. Taylor in *The Personal Notebooks of Thomas Hardy*, p. 228, Note 733.)

whose gestures beam with mind: slightly misquoted from Shelley's 'The Revolt of Islam', I. liv. 608. The poet and his guide are visiting 'a vast hall' where sat 'The Great, who had departed from mankind,/ A mighty Senate', including 'Some, female forms, whose gestures beamed with mind'. The phrase was also used by Hardy to describe Elizabeth-Jane Farfrae in her newly-married state (*The Mayor of Casterbridge*, Ch. XLV).

pearl-powder: a cosmetic made of a bismuth compound to whiten the skin. The derogatory view of a 'crush' implied by Hardy in this paragraph and in the chapter as a whole is stated more explicitly in the *Life* entry for April 1891: ' ". . . How far nobler in its aspirations is the life here [at Whitelands Training College, which Hardy was visiting] than the life of those I met at the crush two nights back!" ' (op. cit., p. 235).

62 *stays*: a corset or bodice stiffened with vertical strips of whalebone.

63 *the nation of every country dwells in the cottage*: quoted from a speech by John Bright to his constituents at Birmingham on 29 October 1858. He advocated the need for 'a fair share of comfort, contentment, and happiness among the great body of the people'. Together with Hardy's criticism of higher circles of society implied elsewhere in this chapter, it indicates Hardy's preference for the cottage-dwellers.

In this . . . deplorably: the addition of this paragraph after 1892 throws increased emphasis on the relationship between Pierston's pursuit of the ideal in living woman and in his work as a sculptor.

Jumping Jill: a feminine version of a Jumping Jack, a toy which was made to jump by pulling strings.

64 *He could not forget Mrs. Pine-Avon's eyes . . . They were round, inquiring, luminous*: cf. the *Life* transcript passage omitted from the printed version, 14 June 1887: 'Introduced to . . . Lady Kath: Milnes-Gaskell. . . . Round luminous enquiring eyes' (*Personal Notebooks*, pp. 228–9). This passage may also owe something to an entry in Hardy's diary written two years before 1892: '*March 15* [1890]. With E. to a crush at the Jeunes'. Met Mrs. T. and her great eyes in a corner of the rooms' (*Life*, p. 224).

65 *the Wandering Jew*: (see also 'the Jew Ahasuerus' on p. 148). He was a legendary figure who was supposed to be condemned to wander the earth for insulting Christ on his way to Calvary, whom he 'urged on and on'.

66 *The Jilt's Hornpipe*: in 1892 the title was 'Calder Fair'. The change adds a hint of the ironical to Pierston's address to Nichola.

68 *a leading actress . . . translucent, like a balsam or sea-anemone, without shadows, and in movement as responsive as some highly lubricated, many-wired machine, which, if one presses a particular spring, flies open and reveals its works*: cf. Hardy's entry for January 1891, *Life*, p. 232: 'Presently Ellen Terry arrived — diaphanous — a sort of balsam or sea-anemone, without shadow . . . Ellen Terry was like a machine in which, if you press a spring, all the works fly open.' (This similarity is noted by Michael Millgate in *Thomas Hardy: His Career as a Novelist*, p. 300, and by Evelyn Hardy in *Thomas Hardy: A Critical Biography*, p. 145.) 'Balsam' in this context is the aromatic resin.

70 *Nichola Pine-Avon . . . a person of lines and surfaces*: cf. 'At Waking': 'I seemed to behold/ My love in bare/ Hard lines unfold.// . . . An insight . . ./ Killed her old endowment/ Of charm . . ./ . . ./ And showed her but one/ Of the common crowd.'

a language in living cipher no more: the 1892 version had a dash after 'cipher'; its omission has altered the meaning of 'no more'. As it gives more significance to the phrase (i.e. to indicate that Mrs Pine-Avon is no longer of any importance for Pierston), it is probably an authorial emendation rather than a compositor's error. If so, it is one of many examples of Hardy's economy in emendation.

71 *escritoire*: (from earlier French) writing-desk.

73 *to convey it in words would have been as hard as to cage a perfume*: cf. 'he would as soon have thought of carrying an odour in a net as of attempting to convey the intangibilities of his feeling in the coarse meshes of language' (*Far From the Madding Crowd*, Ch. III).

the never-pacified Race: the treacherous stretch of sea south of 'the Beal' (Portland Bill), described more fully by Hardy in Part III, Ch. vi.

Balearic-British: invaders from the Mediterranean region in pre-Roman millenniums.

75 *Praxiteles . . . Lysippus*: both are Greek sculptors of the fourth century BC, Praxiteles from Athens and Lysippus from Sicyon. It was Praxiteles who was noted for his several sculptures of Aphrodite but Somers may have recalled that Lysippus was an innovator in the shapes of his figures and much concerned with precise and realistic detail, which seems to have occupied Pierston's attention. This was an afterthought on Hardy's part: he only added the reference to Lysippus after 1892.

the Beal: see note to p. 73 above.

'Visiting the bottom of the monstrous world': from Milton's 'Lycidas', l. 158, where Milton conjectures whether his drowned friend Edward King 'Visit'st the bottom of the monstrous world'.

78 (Chapter heading): in 1892 Part Second did not begin until this point, where Pearston was about to meet Avice II, but this is three chapters after he was reported as reaching the age of forty; from 1897 onwards the division into three parts was related more precisely to Pierston's age.

She seemed not a year older . . . than when he had parted from her twenty years earlier: see Tennyson's 'The Brook', ll. 204–26, where Lawrence Aylmer, after a gap of twenty years, meets Katie Willows's daughter looking exactly like her mother: 'Too happy, fresh and fair, / Too fresh and fair in our sad world's best bloom, / To be the ghost of one who bore your name / About these meadows, twenty years ago.' Here also the daughter bears the same surname as her mother's maiden name because her mother married her cousin. (For the influence of Tennyson on Hardy, see F. B. Pinion: *A Hardy Companion,* pp. 208–9; and L. A. Björk: *The Literary Notes of Thomas Hardy,* Vol. I/ Notes, 350n.)

81 *euonymus and tamarisk*: usually hardy deciduous shrubs but in the south and west can be cultivated as evergreens providing hedging and windbreaks, as here.

83 *genius loci*: the guardian spirit of a place (Latin); here, thoughts associated with Portland.

88 *Minerva*: Roman goddess of wisdom.

Protean: derived from Proteus, the Greek and Roman sea-god who was able to assume various shapes.

90 *metempsychosis*: transmigration of a soul, here of Avice I into Avice II's body.

91 *the Red King's castle*: Rufus or Bow-and-Arrow Castle.

92 *Sapphic terror of love*: Sappho was a greek poetess writing in the sixth century BC. Hardy may have been referring to the candid expression of personal feeling in many of her poems or to the now discredited story that unrequited love caused her to commit suicide by throwing herself over a cliff.

'*the Weaver of Wiles*': Aphrodite. (See p. 16.) This phrase has been substituted for a direct reference in 1892 to 'the white, implacable Aphrodite'.

Nubian Almeh: or Alma or Almah. An Egyptian or Sudanese dancing-girl.

94 *one of the three goddesses*: Aphrodite, Hera and Athena; Paris awarded the golden apple to Aphrodite.

95 *the World's Desire*: a further reference to Aphrodite.

Ultima Thule: 'most distant Thule'; the farthest point from civilization. In classical times Thule was referred to as a land far north from Britain.

96 *The remark struck his ear unpleasantly*: in 1892 the clause read: 'The remark reminded him unpleasantly of his own experiences'. The meaning has been changed to conform with the plot change after 1892: that Pierston is not married to Marcia. The alteration of 'already' to 'a'ready' and the deletion of 'of his own experiences' implies that Pierston's displeasure is at the rough manner of speech of the man he is listening to, not at the reminder of his (Pearston's) own unfortunate marriage.

 99 *Liliths*: a Lilith was believed to be a female demon, a night-
    hag, a deceiver of Adam before the arrival of Eve.

    she was colder in nature . . . Avice the First: cf. 'Lorna the
    Second': 'Lorna! Yes, you are sweet,/ But you are not your
    mother,/ Lorna the First'.

102 *You passed and brushed my frock*: one of Hardy's frequent
    references to touching or brushing against a woman's
    clothes.

106 *propylæa*: gateways; the houses on each side of the road
    seemed like gateways to the higher ground behind. Derived
    from the propylæum which was the entrance to the
    Acropolis at Athens.

107 '*. . . robed in such exceeding glory . . . not*': Shelley: 'Epip-
    sychidion', ll. 199–200. In the passage from which this
    quotation is taken and which begins: 'There was a Being
    whom my spirit oft/ Met on its visioned wanderings, far
    aloft . . .', the poet is speaking of ideal beauty, a 'Being'
    whose presence he is aware of but who cannot be seen. 'Epip-
    sychidion' was addressed to Emilia Viviani, a lady confined
    to a convent by her father until he had found a suitable hus-
    band for her. Shelley would seem to have believed that in her
    he had found his ideal and in that sense she became his Well-
    Beloved, but, although he and his wife were able to visit her
    freely, her circumstances and his married state conspired to
    keep the relationship on a Platonic level in both the classical
    and looser modern sense: though he speaks with fervour in
    the poem of a future life together, she will 'remain a vestal
    sister still' (l. 390). Nevertheless, Shelley's enthusiasm for her
    at times sounds distinctly lover-like: 'Our breath shall inter-
    mix, our bosoms bound,/ And our veins beat together: and
    our lips/ With other eloquence than words, eclipse/ The soul
    that burns between them' (ll. 565–8).

    coigns of vantage: *Macbeth*, I.vi.7, where projections from
    castle walls are said to be used by birds for nesting purposes;
    here, for observation points by the sentries. (See note to
    p. 3.)

110 *flys*: fast, light, one-horse carriages for hire.

112 *landau*: a four-wheeled carriage which could have the top
    partly or entirely opened.

    Demetrius of Ephesus: a silversmith who made silver statues
    of Diana, goddess of fertility. He created a riot, according to

Acts 19: 23–41, when he feared that Paul's preaching was damaging his trade in Ephesus, one of the most important cities in the Roman province of Asia.

113 *Psyche*: in Greek mythology her beauty brought upon her the hatred of Aphrodite, but the love of Cupid helped her eventually to overcome Aphrodite's antipathy and achieve immortality.

115 *Glengarry cap*: a Highland cap with ribbons at the rear.

121 *collier*: a ship which carries coal.

122 *Rossini's*: Gioacchino Antonio Rossini (1792–1868), Italian composer, popular for the exuberance and tunefulness of his work.

124 *Martinmas*: the feast of St Martin on 11 November.

126 *jerry-built*: of poor construction and built with cheap materials for a quick profit. First recorded in 1881, so still a recently coined word in 1892.

127 *the Empress Faustina's head*: either Faustina the Elder or Faustina the Younger. Both achieved notoriety for their questionable morals, possibly unjustly, but both were apparently held in affection by their emperor husbands, who consecrated them after death.

128 *Isaac Pierston*: Hardy has changed the spelling of this character's surname also from the 'Pearston' of the 1892 version.

131 *Ashtaroth*: or Ashtoreth, Ashtart or Astarte. The goddess, or goddesses, of fertility in Old Testament times and writings, e.g. Judges 2: 13. There is archaeological evidence of religious syncretism between the worship of Astarte and of Aphrodite.

Freyja: the Norse 'love-queen'.

When was it to end . . . moved naturally onward?: cf. 'I look into my glass,/ And view my wasting skin,/ And say, "Would God it came to pass/ My heart had shrunk as thin!" ' ('I Look Into My Glass').

133 *Shambles*: a shambles is a slaughter-house, a shamble an awkward gait or movement; so the name probably arises from the nature of the quicksand as a dangerous place of death to sailors or a place of awkward movement of sea and sand (which would lead to the same outcome). The lightship has been replaced by a buoy.

133 *an infant's wail*: cf. 'Her Death and After' for several points of correspondence with this episode: 'I thought of the man who had left her lone—/ Him who made her his own/ When I loved her, long before.// . . . / From the stairway floated the rise and fall/ Of an infant's call,/ Whose birth had brought her to this.// . . . / [I] bent my tread/ To the bedchamber above.// She took my hand in her thin white own,/ And smiled her thanks—though nigh too weak'.

136 *Hymen*: or Hymenaeus. The god of marriage, represented in art as a young man carrying a torch and veil. His name was invoked at Greek weddings.

Harlequin: a mischievous comic character in light comedy and pantomime. He was the rival of the clown in the courting of Columbine; which suggests that Pierston identifies himself with the unfortunate clown at this point.

PART THIRD

138 *'In me thou seest . . . was nourished by.'*: from Shakespeare's Sonnet LXXIII: 'That time of year thou mayst in me behold'. The poem describes the autumn or 'twilight' of a man's life and is a fitting epigraph to the account of the final episode in Jocelyn's career as a romantic idealist.

143 *Avice, who . . . evanescence.*: a slightly revised version of that which in 1892 had been positioned two paragraphs earlier. There these thoughts of Avice II had been aroused by Pearston's discovery of the recent death of her husband before he had had any contact with her; here by a second letter from Avice requesting an early visit from Pierston.

146 *a still more modernized . . . of that blood*: cf. 'Heredity': 'I am the family face;/ Flesh perishes, I live on,/ Projecting trait and trace/ Through time to times anon . . .'

147 *felloe*: the exterior rim of a wheel which holds the spokes in position.

instauration: restoration, renewal.

148 *the Jew Ahasuerus*: see note above to p. 65, *the Wandering Jew*. Shelley had written about Ahasuerus, the Wandering Jew, in 'Queen Mab' and elsewhere.

the general: archaic. Cf. *Hamlet*, II.ii.465–6: 'the play . . . was caviare to the general' (*Oxford Shakespeare*, p. 884); i.e. to the general populace, to ordinary folk.

152 *jeune premier*: actor playing a young lover's part. (French.)

153 *Mephistopheles*: the evil spirit with whom Faust made a pact to sell his soul in return for favours to be granted him during his lifetime.

154 *She seemed to be a good deal interested.*: in 1892 this formed part of Mrs Pearston's speech; it has therefore changed from referring to Avice III's interest in Pearston (according to her mother) to Avice II's interest in Pierston's encounter with Avice III. This may simply have been a compositor's error in placing quotation marks, but equally it could have been a deliberate alteration by Hardy to change the meaning of the passage. It was characteristic of him to use such economical means to achieve an emendation.

159 *he beheld his face in the glass . . . there was history in his face*: cf. 'I look into my glass,/ And view my wasting skin' ('I Look Into My Glass'). For further reference to this theme, see note below to p. 166, *While his soul was what it was . . .* Cf. also the comment by T. P. O'Connor: '[Hardy's] face was so deeply lined that it looked like the back of a leaf; there wasn't a spot on cheek or forehead that didn't seem to be scarred by wrinkles' ('Personal Traits of Thomas Hardy', Monograph No. 54, The Toucan Press, 1969, p. 236).

160 *He knew the origin of that line in his forehead*: a theme to which Hardy returns in this book and elsewhere, e.g. in his description of Yeobright's face: 'His countenance was overlaid with legible meanings. Without being thought-worn he yet had certain marks' (*Return of the Native*, Book Third, Ch. VI); or Mr Melbury, who 'knew the origin of every one of these cramps' (*The Woodlanders*, Ch. IV).

162 *'throned along the sea'*: from Robert S. Hawker's 'The Quest of the Sangraal' (1863), l. 6: '. . . grim Dundagel, thron'd along the sea!'

163 *angina pectoris*: chest pain associated with heart disease. (Derived from Latin forms.)

166 *something ghostly . . . what he saw was his own shape*: Hardy uses the device of an unusual or startling aspect elsewhere. Cf. Henchard's seeing his effigy in the water: 'a human body, lying stiff and stark . . . he perceived with a sense of horror that it was *himself*' (*The Mayor of Casterbridge*, Ch. XLI).

While his soul was what it was . . . withering carcase: see the reference above in the note to p. 159 to the poem 'I Look Into My Glass'; there the poet expresses the complementary form of Pierston's query: he wishes that his 'heart had shrunk as thin' as his 'wasting skin'.

163 *pourparlers*: informal preliminary discussions before negotiations. (French.)

170 *In anticipation of his marriage . . .*: not in the 1892 version. This and other associated changes following in this passage are in accordance with the plot changes carried out by Hardy after 1892: in the first version Pearston had married Avice III; thereafter Pierston has not done so and Avice II accompanies her daughter.

171 *'tall-boys'*: tall chimney-pots. A new usage of the word, first noted in 1884.

delf: or delft. Glazed earthenware from the town of Delft in Holland.

Stièvenard's 'Lectures Francaises': cf. 'During his residence in London [Hardy] had entered himself at King's College for the French classes, where he studied the tongue through a term or two under Professor Stièvenard . . . He used to say that Stièvenard was the most charming Frenchman he had ever met, as well as being a fine teacher.' (*Life*, p. 49.)

Sandbourne: Bournemouth.

173 *the isle . . . a creature sullen*: cf. Hardy's personification of Egdon Heath: 'It had a lonely face, suggesting tragical possibilities' (*The Return of the Native*, Book First, Ch. I).

183 *So deceitful as it seems*: cf. Avice I's comment on *her* own action: 'So bold as it was' (I.i). Consciously or unconsciously, Hardy has given Avice III a phrase which echoes that of her grandmother.

188 *The two lovers . . . the smallest of the boats*: the account of this episode differs only slightly from the 1892 version, but there it was Pearston who took the boat out, and with suicidal intent; another example of Hardy's economical use of older material, even when the protagonists have changed. There is some similarity to Edward Springrove's rowing Cytherea in Budmouth Bay and on a lake (*Desperate Remedies*, Ch. III and Sequel).

190 (Chapter title) *Tabernacle*: see note above to p. 17.

the pictured Trojan women beheld by Aeneas: Aeneas was

the son of Aphrodite and Anchises and was renowned for his *pietas*, i.e. devotion to his parents as well as the gods. On the walls of a temple of Juno he saw the following scene depicted: 'Next, to the shrine of the unfavourably disposed Pallas Athena were walking the Trojan women with dishevelled hair and bearing a fine robe in supplication, sad and beating their breasts with their palms; but the aloof goddess kept her gaze fixed on the ground.' (From Virgil: *Aeneid*, I.479–82: '*interea ad templum non aequae Palladis ibant/ crinibus Iliades passis peplumque ferebant/ suppliciter, tristes et tunsae pectora palmis;/ diua solo fixos oculos auersa tenebat.*' O.U.P. edition, 1971.) Hardy also refers to Aeneas at Carthage in *A Pair of Blue Eyes*, Ch. XIV.

192 *I am Marcia — after forty years*: cf. 'The Man Who Forgot': 'Forty years' frost and flower/ Had fleeted since I'd used to come/ To meet her'.

May the lines . . . pleasant places: from Psalm 16: 6: 'The lines are fallen unto me in pleasant places', i.e. 'I have had good fortune'. Cf. the phrase 'hard lines', meaning 'bad luck'. As the biblical context is inheritance, the reference is probably to 'inheriting' good or bad fortune.

196 (Chapter title) *'Alas for this Grey Shadow, once a Man!'*: this (mispunctuated) quotation from Tennyson's 'Tithonus' is apt as a phrase to describe the 'strange death of the sensuous side of Jocelyn's nature' (III.viii), but less apt as an analogy between the fates of Tithonus and Jocelyn: Tithonus's problem was that he had been granted immortality but not everlasting youth; Jocelyn, on the other hand, is without immortality but suffers from at least one aspect of everlasting youthfulness until he escapes his 'doom' in this final chapter.

200 *Faubourg St. Germain*: the St Germain suburb of Paris, 'le noble faubourg', was associated with the old French aristocracy.

The cruel morning rays: cf. 'The Revisitation': 'Ah, yes: I am *thus* by day! . . .' There are several points of correspondence between this episode and the poem: the renewed acquaintance after a lapse of many years; the aged appearance of the woman; and the shock of this appearance when it is first revealed by daylight to the former lover.

201 *"Instead of . . . beauty,"*: from Isaiah 3: 24: 'And it shall

come to pass, that instead of sweet smell there shall be stink; and instead of a girdle a rent; and instead of well set hair baldness; and instead of a stomacher a girding of sackcloth; and burning instead of beauty.' As this is a fate prophesied to befall the proud ladies of Jerusalem, it could have an oblique reference to Marcia's changed condition as well as applying more directly to Pierston's Well-Beloveds.

201 *Perugino, Titian, Sebastiano*: three Italian painters of the Renaissance period: Pietro Perugino (1446–1524); Tiziano Vercelli (*c*.1478–1576); and Sebastiano Luciani (*c.* 1485–1547), called Sebastiano del Piombo from 1531 when Pope Clement VII made him keeper of the leaden seals. His largest work, *The Raising of Lazarus*, is in the National Gallery.

202 *those who knew not Joseph*: those who were too young to have known and appreciated Pierston. From Exodus, 1: 8: 'Now there arose up a new king over Egypt, which knew not Joseph.' Hardy uses the same quotation in *Two on a Tower*, Ch. XLI.

205 *supplying the townlet with water from pipes*: thirty years after Hardy wrote this in 1897 there is an echo in his personal notebook entry for 3 January 1927: 'Men putting in pipes for town water.'

DIALECT GLOSSARY

avore before (134)

bo-fet buffet: a cupboard for china or glasses (88)

chammer bedroom (185)

daps likeness; copy (79)

en him (21)

fairly gallied completely frightened (183)

faltered failed in health (69)

git get (134)

good-now you may be sure (79). (See Hardy's comment in *Collected Letters*, I. pp. 277–8.)

hender hinder (180)

huddied hid (102)

idden isn't (84)

if you do mind if you remember (69)

kimberlins mainlanders; foreigners (19)

mid might (80)

nowhen never (84)

opened upon it raised the subject (21)

pitched his nitch put down his burden (79) (variant of 'knitch')

popple pebble (97)

saur sir (119) (Irish)

spakin'-tube speaking-tube for communicating between rooms (119) (Irish)

stwone, stwonen stone (21)

The Lord-a-Lord! exclamation possibly derived from 'Lord, Oh Lord' or 'The Lord of Lords' (183)

tine close (84)

wadden wasn't (181)

wi'en with him (84)

wold old (21)

A SELECTION OF   OXFORD WORLD'S CLASSICS

GEORGE ELIOT	**Adam Bede**
	Daniel Deronda
	Middlemarch
	The Mill on the Floss
	Silas Marner
ELIZABETH GASKELL	**Cranford**
	The Life of Charlotte Brontë
	Mary Barton
	North and South
	Wives and Daughters
THOMAS HARDY	**Far from the Madding Crowd**
	Jude the Obscure
	The Mayor of Casterbridge
	A Pair of Blue Eyes
	The Return of the Native
	Tess of the d'Urbervilles
	The Woodlanders
WALTER SCOTT	**Ivanhoe**
	Rob Roy
	Waverley
MARY SHELLEY	**Frankenstein**
	The Last Man
ROBERT LOUIS STEVENSON	**Kidnapped and Catriona**
	The Strange Case of Dr Jekyll and Mr Hyde and Weir of Hermiston
	Treasure Island
BRAM STOKER	**Dracula**
WILLIAM MAKEPEACE THACKERAY	**Barry Lyndon**
	Vanity Fair
OSCAR WILDE	**Complete Shorter Fiction**
	The Picture of Dorian Gray

THE OXFORD SHERLOCK HOLMES

MORE ABOUT **OXFORD WORLD'S CLASSICS**

The Oxford World's Classics Website

www.worldsclassics.co.uk

- Information about new titles
- Explore the full range of Oxford World's Classics
- Links to other literary sites and the main OUP webpage
- Imaginative competitions, with bookish prizes
- Peruse *Compass*, the Oxford World's Classics magazine
- Articles by editors
- Extracts from Introductions
- A forum for discussion and feedback on the series
- Special information for teachers and lecturers

www.worldsclassics.co.uk

American Literature

British and Irish Literature

Children's Literature

Classics and Ancient Literature

Colonial Literature

Eastern Literature

European Literature

History

Medieval Literature

Oxford English Drama

Poetry

Philosophy

Politics

Religion

The Oxford Shakespeare

A complete list of Oxford Paperbacks, including Oxford World's Classics, OPUS, Past Masters, Oxford Authors, Oxford Shakespeare, Oxford Drama, and Oxford Paperback Reference, is available in the UK from the Academic Division Publicity Department, Oxford University Press, Great Clarendon Street, Oxford OX2 6DP.

In the USA, complete lists are available from the Paperbacks Marketing Manager, Oxford University Press, 198 Madison Avenue, New York, NY 10016.

Oxford Paperbacks are available from all good bookshops. In case of difficulty, customers in the UK can order direct from Oxford University Press Bookshop, Freepost, 116 High Street, Oxford OX1 4BR, enclosing full payment. Please add 10 per cent of published price for postage and packing.